ALL ABOUT ME

of related interest

I Am Special
A Workbook to Help Children, Teens and Adults with Autism Spectrum Disorders to Understand Their Diagnosis, Gain Confidence and Thrive
Peter Vermeulen
ISBN 978 1 84905 266 5
eISBN 978 1 85700 545 8

My Autism Book
A Child's Guide to their Autism Spectrum Diagnosis
Glòria Durà-Vilà and Tamar Levi
ISBN 978 1 84905 438 6
eISBN 978 0 85700 868 8

Can I Tell You about Autism?
A Guide for Friends, Family and Professionals
Jude Welton
Illustrated by Jane Telford
ISBN 978 1 84905 453 9
eISBN 978 1 85700 829 9

A Special Book About Me
A Book for Children Diagnosed with Asperger Syndrome
Josie Santomauro
Illustrated by Carla Marino
ISBN 978 1 84310 655 5
eISBN 978 1 84642 930 9

The ASD Workbook
Understanding Your Autism Spectrum Disorder
Penny Kershaw
ISBN 978 1 84905 195 8
eISBN 978 0 85700 427 7

ALL ABOUT ME

A Step-by-Step Guide to Telling
Children and **Young People** on the
Autism Spectrum about their Diagnosis

ANDREW MILLER

Jessica Kingsley *Publishers*
London and Philadelphia

First published in 2018
by Jessica Kingsley Publishers
73 Collier Street
London N1 9BE, UK
and
400 Market Street, Suite 400
Philadelphia, PA 19106, USA

www.jkp.com

Library of Congress Cataloging in Publication Data
A CIP catalog record for this book is available from the Library of Congress

British Library Cataloguing in Publication Data
A CIP catalogue record for this book is available from the British Library

ISBN 978 1 78592 129 2
eISBN 978 1 78450 393 2

Printed and bound in the United States

For Carolyn and Elizabeth

Contents

TABLES

Acknowledgements

I would like to express my sincerest gratitude to everyone who offered me help and encouragement with writing this book and developing the programme described in it. It is not possible to name everyone here, but I would like to give special thanks to the people mentioned below.

Carol Gray, Peter Vermeulen and Jude Welton whose respective works in 1996, 2000 and 2004 (a and b) provided me with inspiring models of how to start explaining their diagnosis to children and young people with autism. I would also like to thank Jude for the personal support she gave me with getting this project off the ground by endorsing my proposal for this book with the publishers.

Everyone at Jessica Kingsley Publishers, particularly Hannah Snetsinger, Victoria Peters and Kara McHale, for providing me with plenty of much-needed support and guidance while I was working on this book.

My wife, Carolyn, and daughter, Elizabeth, not only for their patience, but also for the vast amounts of practical support and the encouragement they gave me during the lengthy period it took me to complete the book. Without their help, I doubt whether I would ever have got to the end, especially if Carolyn had not read through and commented on numerous draft copies of my work.

Pat Markwardt and Julie Foster, as the managers in the respective autism services I worked under as an advisory teacher. The encouragement, advice and knowledge that they both shared with me were invaluable. Pat provided me with my first opportunity to work specifically with children and young people on the autism spectrum. I am particularly grateful to her, first, for enabling me to attend the conference in 2004 where Jude Welton described the approach she took to tell her own son about his autism diagnosis, and then, for trusting me to initiate a similar work programme with individual children we knew. I am appreciative of the confidence Julie showed in supporting me to continue to develop and deliver this work when I moved to my next post.

Dr Glenys Jones for supervising my master's study at the University of Birmingham into the effectiveness of my own work using the programme. Besides sharing her vast knowledge of this subject, she helped me to develop the skills and confidence needed to write this book.

Suzanne Goddard, an excellent specialist autism teacher and colleague, for sharing her own experiences of teaching children about their autism with me and for contributing ideas to help further develop the programme. Her reading through and commenting on the main electronic resources which accompany this book was extremely valuable.

All the children and young people with autism with whom I have worked through this programme. Although the intention was for me to teach them about autism, I have learned so much about it from them! I am also extremely grateful to their parents. They all placed a massive amount of trust in me carrying out this sensitive and potentially life-changing work with their sons and daughters.

Part I

GETTING READY TO DELIVER THE PROGRAMME

Considerations, decisions and preparation

Chapter 1

INTRODUCTION

1.1 OPENING REMARKS

This book is based upon my experiences since 2004 of developing and using the *All About Me* programme (Miller 2014, 2015) to teach more than 250 individual children about their autism spectrum diagnosis. This programme was influenced by the earlier work in this area of Carol Gray (1996), Peter Vermeulen (2000) and Jude Welton (2004a, 2004b).

Telling children that they have autism and trying to explain what it means to them is difficult. The abstract nature of autism, its associated differences in cognition and its lifelong implications make it hard for children to understand, and finding out that they have autism could potentially cause some individuals emotional and psychological upset (Punshon, Skirrow and Murphy 2009; Vermeulen 2013; Whitaker 2006). Therefore, in some cases it could create more problems for an individual than it might intend to solve (Jones 2001).

Through my own work, however, I have found that sharing a child's diagnosis with them can frequently turn out to be a highly positive and enjoyable experience for both the individual concerned and everyone else who is involved in the process. The majority of children who first learned about their autism through the methods and approach described in this book have seemed to accept their diagnosis well. This has enabled their parents, and the other adults supporting them, to talk openly with these children about their autism. In many cases this led to them using knowledge of the child's autism jointly to help make practical improvements to the individual's daily life and involve them more in planning for the future. Many children were relieved to be told about their diagnosis and some have even gone on to regard its discovery as being a cause for celebration.

There are several reasons why it may prove vital to tell a child about their autism at the earliest stage possible and these are all put forward in Chapter 2. Not least, though, providing children with this self-knowledge might better protect their long-term emotional well-being and enable them to take up their legal rights to participate as fully as possible in making decisions affecting their lives. Despite wanting and needing to share the diagnosis with a child, parents and school staff can often be concerned that doing this themselves could damage their relationships, or they may feel that they have insufficient knowledge and skills to explain autism to a child on the spectrum (Miller 2015).

Given the situation described above, and the large rise in the numbers of children being diagnosed with autism (Walsh and Hurley 2013), it is perhaps surprising that very little practical guidance appears to have been written for professionals and parents on the subject of carrying out this much-needed work in telling children for the first time that they have autism (Fletcher 2013; Miller 2015). Conversations with autism practitioners across parts of England also appear to suggest that the provision of specialized professional support for this sensitive and challenging work may have been overlooked by some local authorities (LAs) and other service providers. I have also observed that education, health and care professionals who regularly work with children and young people with autism are not always able or available to offer this particular kind of help. This appears to include some specialist autism advisory teachers and staff working in specialist schools. Therefore, this book has been written to add to what literature is available for those professionals and parents who are contemplating the prospect of having to tell children about their autism diagnosis themselves and are looking for assistance and guidance on how to go about doing it.

After clarifying the definitions of some of the most frequently used terms in the book, the rest of this chapter will provide background information about the programme, an overview of the book and a summary of research into the effectiveness of my own use of this work with children.

1.2 TERMS AND DEFINITIONS USED IN THIS BOOK

1.2.1 Introduction

This section has been included to provide definitions and clarify the intended meanings of some of the key terms and expressions which are used frequently in this book. Any limitations these explanations might have are also considered. Terms referring to children, parents and other adults are clarified first. The book and the programme's shared approaches towards describing and defining autism are explained after that.

1.2.2 Terms and expressions used to describe people

All About Me has been delivered to children and young people across a broad age range; therefore, to keep things simple, the terms *child* or *children* are used to describe all individuals of school age who have not yet reached adulthood. This includes primary and secondary school students as well as those aged below 18 years who are continuing their education at colleges and other post-16 settings such as sixth form centres.

To simplify matters again, *parent* or *parents* includes all adult carers who have taken on similar legal responsibilities for looking after and bringing up children. *School staff* is used as an umbrella term for those working with children in any type of educational establishment; *professionals* refers not only to them but to anyone else who is employed by outside services to support children in a paid capacity (e.g. specialist advisory teachers, therapists and psychologists).

Gender-neutral pronouns are used exclusively throughout this book on grounds of equality, except when referring to individuals whose gender may be obvious either through their names or the ways in which they are described. It should also be noted that whereas authors and film presenters are referred to by their real names in this book, all the other children, parents and professionals mentioned are fictitious or have been assigned pseudonyms to protect their anonymity. All the schools that are referred to have also been given alternative names.

People-first language is used to refer to children and adults who have been diagnosed with autism. They are described as people *with*, or *who have*, *autism*, rather than as *autistic people*. This wording is not only applied in the book; it is also used consistently while teaching children about their autism and throughout the narrative of the booklet which is produced with the child during the programme sessions. Children are taught that they *have* autism. This choice is reflective of the terminology that is currently used by the Autism Education Trust (AET) in its national training programmes and other support resources for educational settings and professionals in England (e.g. Autism Education Trust 2012).

This decision has also been taken out of respect for the wishes of most of the parents with whom I have worked, but it must be acknowledged that this stance is not accepted by all individuals with autism. Clare Sainsbury (2000) and Jim Sinclair (1999), for instance, have raised objections to the use of people-first language. They have asserted that they wanted to be called autistic people. This is because they saw their autism as being something that could not be separated from who they are as people. Sinclair's online article argues that using people-first language implies that autism is 'so bad that it isn't even consistent with being a person'. Nonetheless, *All About Me* does not intend to communicate this message. The programme aims to describe autism positively as being a form of neurodiversity. This is done in the programme through presenting each child's autism to them as being a way of positively describing a type of person with whom they share similar patterns of strengths and differences.

1.2.3 The approach towards describing and defining autism

At present there is no agreed generic term for describing conditions on the autism spectrum. Government publications, LAs, voluntary and private sector services, authors and academic researchers variously apply the terms *autism, autistic spectrum disorder, autistic spectrum condition* and *autism spectrum* (Department for Children, Schools and Families 2009; Jones *et al.* 2008). *Autism* is used throughout this book to describe all conditions on the autism spectrum since this also corresponds with the terminology used by the AET and the LA service for which I worked most recently. When working directly with children, however, their condition is referred to as either *autism* or *Asperger syndrome* (AS). This is to avoid confusing children and to clearly reflect the wording of the formal diagnosis an individual has been given and lives with. Broader accounts of the different ways in which autism is described to different children are provided in later chapters.

Autism's complexity makes it difficult both to define and describe what it means (Frith 2003; Vermeulen 2013). Moreover, there is a disparity between the most recent revisions of the internationally recognized autism diagnostic criteria, published by the American Psychiatric Association (APA) in 2013 and the World Health Organization (WHO) in 1992. There are also very wide variations in how, and the extent to which, each characteristic of autism manifests from one individual person to another (AET 2012; Jones 2002; Wing 2002). For the purposes of this book and *All About Me*, a decision has been made to define autism as being:

> a lifelong neurological condition within which individuals have their own unique and innate developmental differences across all four of the following areas:
>
> • social interaction
>
> • social communication

- thinking and behaving flexibly

- sensory processing.

For readers who are interested, this working definition was arrived at by considering the currently used formal diagnostic criteria alongside: the earliest descriptions of autism, first by Leo Kanner (1973, first published 1943) and then by Hans Asperger (translated into English by Frith in 1991, first published 1944); later works by experts in autism (e.g. AET 2012; Bogdashina 2003; Boucher 2009; Frith 2003; Wing 2002); and my own professional experience.

The AET's descriptions of autism (e.g. 2012) had a particular influence on the development of this definition. It portrays autism as being a condition characterized by sets of differences. Much of the other autism literature refers to autism as being a disorder and uses more negative language such as *deficit* or *impairment* to describe its features or symptoms. The approach taken in this book has been adopted deliberately to present the diagnosis positively both to children with autism and the people around them. This is in agreement with Jean-Paul Bovee's assertion that although he and other people with an autism diagnosis may do things differently, they are 'not broken and do not need to be "fixed or cured"' (cited in Sainsbury 2000, p.30). *All About Me* is meant to offer children reassurance that although their diagnosis does make some things much harder for them, it is okay to be a person with autism.

Although the broad definition of autism given above identifies four key areas of difference which are common to all individuals with an autism diagnosis, it is limited in how far it can go towards describing what any of these differences are. Autism is a complex and diverse spectrum condition (Boucher 2009; Frith 2003; Wing 2002). As such, it is not possible to describe the manifestation of each of these areas of difference in global terms. These can be vastly different and uneven for every individual in each area. For example, taking just the area of expressive communication, a child with autism's differences could range anywhere from an individual using no language at all to an individual being able to apply a broad and mature verbal vocabulary when talking about certain subjects that interest them (Wing 2002).

I have concluded from my own work that every single child on the spectrum has their own personal version of autism, regardless of how their diagnosis is worded. Within this, the individual and combined manifestation of each child's differences across the four main areas described above is unique to each of them and therefore merits its very own description. Hence, any overall definition of autism, like the one given above, can only identify the areas in which those diagnosed might be different to typical (i.e. neurotypical, or not on the autism spectrum) people rather than state what form those differences take. This underlines the importance of adults taking time during the pre-programme work (described in Chapter 3) to gain an accurate understanding of the child's own unique manifestation of autism.

1.3 HOW *ALL ABOUT ME* CAME ABOUT

The approach and content chosen for *All About Me* was initially inspired by a description of how Jude Welton, a psychologist and author, explained his diagnosis to her own son who had AS. She presented this to a conference which I attended in 2004(a) shortly after the publication of her book called *Can I Tell You about Asperger Syndrome?* (2004b). She wrote this book to help children and adults, including those with a diagnosis, understand what having AS means. Her presentation also pointed to earlier work by two other authors in this area. The first was an article called 'Pictures of Me' by Carol Gray (1996), which explained how to write a *Social Story*™ to introduce children with AS or high-functioning autism to their diagnosis. The other was an autism workbook for children called *I Am Special* by Peter Vermeulen (2000). That workbook was targeted at individuals with around average intelligence who were aged ten and over, or those with below-average intelligence who were older than 12. I concluded that an ideal way to go about disclosing their diagnosis to most of the children I worked with might be to produce a unique booklet with each individual which contained a personalized narrative about themselves and framed their autism in the context of their personal attributes. The booklet, which would be different from a Social Story™ or workbook, could be written with a child by completing an electronic template which would involve working through this series of steps:

- drawing the child's attention to and listing their positive personal qualities

- listing and emphasizing their various areas of strength

- gently reminding them of the things which they find harder or do differently to other children of their age

- using all the above information about themselves to tell the child in a matter-of-fact way that they have autism

- explaining what their diagnosis does and does not mean, while relating this to their own strengths and challenges

- informing them that other people also have autism

- reassuring them that they have a network of very supportive people around them who love and value them for being the way they are

- highlighting the positive aspects of their diagnosis.

Much of this process was already familiar to me as it was very similar to social studies work that I and other colleagues carried out during the 1980s and 1990s with typical children as mainstream teachers in culturally diverse primary schools. This had included children exploring and being encouraged to value how they were similar and different to each other as people, both on the outside and the inside, as well as in their areas of strength and challenge.

This approach towards teaching *All About Me* appeared to offer a framework which could be used to present autism safely to different children across the spectrum and with minimal risks of negative outcomes. The whole process could present a child's autism to them in a positive, matter-of-fact, calm and reassuring manner, as just being a part of who they are as a person. Moreover, explaining autism in the context of a child's personal attributes makes allowances for autistic ways of thinking. In particular, children with autism tend towards interpreting things which they see and hear at literal levels (Frith 2003; Vermeulen 2013; Wing 2002). This approach to explaining autism in the context of what a child can do well and the things that they find more challenging seemingly makes it much more literal and tangible to an individual than any description that aims to explain the abstract formal diagnostic criteria. In turn, this could make it easier for adults to explain autism to children and help children gain a better understanding and acceptance of their diagnosis in the first instance. At the same time, this might also allow for the explanation of any child's autism to be individual to them, thus giving them more of a sense of ownership over their diagnosis.

Importantly, the whole process could also be broken down into a series of clearly structured steps which seemed easy to follow. They lead calmly up to the point where the disclosure is made and go on smoothly through the subsequent initial explanation of what having autism does and does not mean. If written carefully, the content of the text in the booklet and the discussions about it could be used continuously to create opportunities to offer the child reassurance that it is okay to have autism while the work progresses. It could be stressed throughout the disclosure process that the child is a good person who is loved by the people around them for being who they are, and it can also be made clear that autism is not something dreadful. Furthermore, producing a booklet would provide a child with a treasured end product which could be used by adults later to help consolidate what the individual has been taught.

This approach was also potentially transferable to a diverse array of children on the autism spectrum across the school age range who were working at various cognitive and developmental levels. If electronic word-processing templates of the booklet's narrative could be created, these tools might have the flexibility to be adapted on a computer in many ways. This would mean that the design and content of the children's booklets could be altered to make them engaging, relevant and accessible to more individuals. The resulting booklets would be unique to each person and their own autism in ways that might not be possible when using generic workbooks about autism.

1.4 A SHORT DESCRIPTION OF *ALL ABOUT ME* AND WHAT IT INTENDS TO DO

Work with children should only ever commence if the child's parents formally agree to it and once the pre-programme work detailed in Chapter 3 has been thoroughly completed. The exact nature and quantity of the pre-programme work is likely to vary in different circumstances. This might, for example, be determined by the role of the person leading the work, their prior familiarity with the child and their background experiences in working with children with autism. This pre-programme work is deemed essential to reaching informed decisions on whether the programme is suitable for individual children, and, if so, to planning how take the work forward in a bespoke manner. Doing this thoroughly appears to have helped to make the programme safe and accessible for a large group of very different children (Miller 2014, 2015).

The programme itself is usually delivered individually over the course of three sessions, which the child's parents also attend, lasting approximately one hour each. Part II of this book gives more precise details on the programme's content and delivery methods. In summary, however, the child is helped to identify and discuss their personal attributes in Session 1 (Chapter 5). This is done to create the context for positively disclosing and then explaining the child's diagnosis to them during Session 2 (Chapter 6). Information from these two sessions is used to complete a template to produce the unique printed booklet with the child, which contains personal information about themselves and their autism. The child's completed booklet is read and discussed with them in Session 3 (Chapter 6). The booklet is then presented to the child for them to keep and for their parents and other adults to continue using with them. Telling children that they have autism is always done against the background of the child having been taught first about their individual strengths and differences as well as having the reassurance that they are a good person who is loved by the supportive people around them (Miller 2015).

Besides Carol Gray (1996), Peter Vermeulen (2000, 2013) and Jude Welton (2004a), it should be acknowledged that other authors and practitioners have described work that involves similar approaches towards teaching children about their autism in the context of their personal attributes (e.g. Attwood 2006, 2008; Faherty 2006; Fidler 2004; Fletcher 2013). Furthermore, the approach described in this book continues to be used, in some form or other, by colleagues employed in services and schools that I have previously worked for as well as by those who it has been shared with in other ways (e.g. at networking meetings and conferences). Therefore, this book stakes no claims of ownership over this approach. Rather, the book has been written as a means of sharing what I have learned from adapting this approach to my own practice and using it with success to teach a large group of very different children. This is so that others might be able to provide similar support to children with autism as well as their families and schools.

The programme itself has three principal objectives for helping children, and these are to:

- positively introduce each child to their autism diagnosis for the first time (or reintroduce participants who already know something about it)

- provide each child with a personalized explanation of their autism which is appropriate to their level of understanding at the time, and

- start each child off on a continuous journey of learning to understand and accept their diagnosis so that this knowledge can be used to help improve their lives.

It is intended that children will not be unduly upset by finding out about their diagnosis and that by the end of the programme they might regard themselves as being different in a positive way, rather than as being broken or defective. It is also hoped that by understanding the reasons behind the support they receive they might go on to learn to engage with it better and take up their rights to be involved in making important decisions which affect their future lives – as enshrined in Articles 12 and 13 of the United Nations Convention on the Rights of the Child (United Nations 1989). Finally, *All About Me* is meant to be an autism educational programme rather than an intervention. It makes no attempts to intervene in any child's autism or to try to normalize them. It aims to provide children with accurate and honest information that might help them to live happily with their diagnosis and maximize their potential through knowing and accepting themselves for who they are.

1.5 WHO *ALL ABOUT ME* CAN BE USED WITH

Experience has shown that *All About Me* can be used successfully in some form with most children who have been given an autism diagnosis, have some understanding of language and have developed an effective means of expressing themselves. This is provided the work is carefully planned in detail, differentiated appropriately to the child's learning preferences and carried out at the right time. This opinion is based on my own unpublished research into the programme's effectiveness, which is the subject of the final section in this chapter, and my direct experiences of delivering it to children (Miller 2014).

The large group of more than 250 individual children with whom I have led this work has included girls and boys from diverse ethnic and cultural backgrounds. The programme has been delivered mainly to children who had no prior knowledge of their autism as well as to some who had already been told but needed to learn more about their diagnosis. Their ages were between six and 18 years, with the majority being in their final year at primary school or their first year of a secondary placement (aged 10–12). These children have included some individuals who were very able academically as well as others who attended special schools and inclusion units for children with special educational needs (SEN) or autism. It has proved possible to adjust the programme to include individuals who presented challenging behaviours despite these often meaning that they were much more easily distracted and harder to engage.

1.6 AN OVERVIEW OF THE BOOK

1.6.1 The purpose of the book and who it is for

This book aims to provide professionals and parents with a framework which they can work through to introduce different children on the autism spectrum to their diagnosis. It sets out to equip them with the theoretical information, practical guidance, teaching instructions and necessary resources for delivering the programme it describes in the absence of more specialized support. In educational settings, this book might be used by staff with the following roles:

- the special educational needs coordinator (SENCo)

- the inclusion manager

- learning support/SEN teachers

- class teachers in specialist schools and inclusion units.

Besides school staff, this book is also intended for outside professionals who could be supporting children with autism in similar capacities to these:

- local authority SEN and autism advisory/outreach teachers

- therapists

- educational psychologists

- mental health professionals.

There may be some readers who find certain parts of this book overly detailed and that a number of points are repeated. This has been done intentionally to cater for anyone who might be relatively new to learning about autism and how to work with children who have a diagnosis, as well as those who might have an academic interest in some of the topics that are explored. Therefore, several lengthier sections in the book are summarized in tables or bullet-pointed lists.

1.6.2 How to use the book

It is strongly recommended that the whole book is read before attempting to implement the programme for the first time. This is essential for gaining a clear overview of exactly what the programme entails, the key issues that could arise and how these might be prevented from occurring or be managed if they do. From then on the book can be used as reference material.

This book is accompanied by an extensive set of printable electronic resources, which can be accessed online at www.jkp.com/voucher using the code QLspdxjP. Some of these resources are intended to illustrate the instructions given in the book for carrying out the programme, and for completing two of the follow-up initiatives which are described in Chapter 8. These are also meant to provide examples of possible outcomes of the work and as such cannot be altered.

All the other resources are designed to support the planning and delivery of the programme as well as some of the suggested follow-up work. Most of these resources, such as the templates for making booklets with children, can be edited for use with different individuals as advised in the relevant parts of the book. Each template is also embedded with supplementary written instructions to aid its preparation and completion. Instructions that need to be carried out before or after working with a child are printed in red, and everything that should be completed while the individual is present is printed in blue.

Although all the electronic resources are brought together in Chapter 9, each of these is also referred to in the sections of the book that describe the programme stages in which they may need to be used or where they are mentioned for illustrative purposes. It is therefore advised that the relevant resources are viewed alongside the text referring to them while reading the book.

There are five resource sections in the online area, which are labelled from A to E, in the chronological order that their contents might be required for use in the programme or are referred to in the book. Similar categories of resources have been grouped together in each section. The pre-programme information-gathering tools are all in Section A; illustrative fictional examples of children's *All About Me* booklets are in Section B; Section C includes the adaptable templates needed for making the booklets; prompts to support children's participation in the work are in Section D; and resources to support follow-up initiatives are in Section E.

The titles of the individual resource files are prefixed both by the corresponding letter of the section in which they are located and a number. For example, the two files in Section A are referred to as A1 and A2 and the contents of the five files in Section B are numbered B1 to B5. This is how they are referenced whenever they are mentioned throughout the book.

1.6.3 An overview of the content of the book

The book is divided into two parts. Part I contains the first three chapters and provides some initial background information about *All About Me*. It then focuses on the key processes and decisions that may need to be worked through before everyone involved in the programme is ready to start carrying out the work with an individual child.

The current chapter introduces the topic of sharing the diagnosis with children and provides background information about the programme and this overview of the content of the whole book. Although disclosure can have positive outcomes, there have been reported cases of it having had significant long-term negative emotional and psychological consequences for the recipient (Vermeulen 2013; Whitaker 2006). Chapter 2 has therefore been included to help parents and other adults weigh up these and other potential risks against the possible benefits of a child being told about their diagnosis, before they make a subsequent decision on whether or not to disclose it. The main arguments for and against sharing the diagnosis are presented, as are the potential consequences of deciding to continue withholding a child's diagnosis from them.

Chapter 3 describes the pre-programme work and offers advice on how to answer several important practical questions which may need to be addressed before deciding whether to go ahead with the work and start planning its delivery. Importantly, it begins by offering pointers which might help readers identify the signs that it might be the right time to start talking to a child about their diagnosis. Advice is also given on the processes that parents might need to progress through themselves before they feel ready to start contemplating the idea of sharing the diagnosis with their child. Guidance is then offered on how professionals might be able to help parents reach that stage more easily. Following on from that, recommendations are made on how to decide who might be the most appropriate person to lead this work with the child and how other adults who support the individual could be involved. This chapter also identifies the kind of knowledge that the person leading the work might need to acquire about the individual child and their autism before they plan the programme, and offers advice on how to go about obtaining that information. The programme's inclusion criteria are also presented along with advice on how to decide which children this work might be suitable for. Finally, assuming it is decided that the work should go ahead, guidance is offered on practical matters such as how to select and set up an appropriate work space, scheduling the work so that it takes place at times best suited to the child, and how to explain the purpose of the work to the child before it happens.

Part II of this book is made up of six further chapters which do the following: describe how to teach the programme to different children; identify and advise on how to address potential issues that could arise during the work; and suggest ways to continue helping children to understand and live with their diagnosis after the programme has been completed.

The first part of Chapter 4 presents the programme's main teaching methods and explains the rationale behind their choice. This is followed by a brief overview of the programme's content and the ordered framework which needs to be worked through when teaching it across its usual three sessions. Chapter 5 then provides generic, step-by-step teaching instructions for the first session, while Chapter 6 covers Sessions 2 and 3. These two chapters also explain how to produce the personalized booklet about the child and their autism. Besides this, these chapters both identify key issues that can sometimes affect various stages of the work as it unfolds and then advise on adjustments that can be made when working with different children, before, during or after the programme, to help prevent these problems or ameliorate their effects. Chapter 7 provides more specific advice on how to differentiate various overall aspects of the entire programme to cater for and include individuals who might be operating outside either end of its generic levels in cognition, communication and literacy. Strategies are also suggested for adjusting the work to accommodate the needs of some children whose behaviour could otherwise prevent them from participating.

Chapter 8 considers what can be done to consolidate and follow up the work with children once they have completed the programme. This not only recommends various resources and initiatives that can be used with a child to continue developing their understanding, acceptance and engagement with their diagnosis, but also considers who else might need to be told about the individual's autism and offers guidance on how to go about doing this with various groups of people. This includes discussing how to share the child's diagnosis with their siblings and other family members, school staff and classmates.

The final chapter draws together all of the electronic resources that accompany this book. They are listed in full and further information is provided, where necessary, to supplement the guidance that would have already been given in the parts of main book that refer to the stages of the work where each one of them might need to be used or turned to as examples.

1.7 RESEARCH INTO THE EFFECTIVENESS OF *ALL ABOUT ME*

Much of this book has also been based on the findings from a research dissertation that I undertook while studying for a master's degree in autism and children at the University of Birmingham (Miller 2014). This was a retrospective study of my own experiences during the first ten years of developing and using *All About Me* with more than 200 children. Like this book, the study aimed to evaluate and describe the programme, identify the key issues related to sharing their autism diagnosis with children, and offer guidance to others who might be considering doing similar work. While wanting to avoid repetition, some readers might find it useful if this chapter were to end with an outline of the study's main research findings. It should be noted, however, that much of what is written below will need to be reiterated when explaining the rationale behind points that are covered later in this book.

First, it was found that no two instances of this work have ever turned out to be identical; nor has the content or format of any of the booklets that were produced with participating children. This supported my initial view that this type of work might be best done on an individual basis rather than with groups or pairs of children. It also offered support for the use of electronic templates to create customized booklets with children as opposed to more generic workbooks. The variety of outcomes and the different ways the work was delivered also underlined the necessity for carrying out adequate pre-programme work before starting this work with each child. This appears to have been essential to tailoring the work to each child's own needs and their unique situations.

As might be expected when working with children across the autism spectrum, a broad and diverse range of behaviour and learning support strategies and resources were found to have been used. These adaptations were judged essential to enabling various children to participate in and complete the work; examples of these are described in detail in later chapters. This perhaps demonstrates again how this initiative cannot be delivered uniformly or without the person leading the work learning enough about how best to teach each individual child beforehand.

Most importantly, it was concluded that the overwhelming majority of children appeared to have responded positively when their diagnosis was first disclosed to them. Instances where children appeared to respond negatively to being given their diagnosis made up less than 5 per cent of the total number of cases. These incidents mainly involved children appearing to be anxious, withdrawn or tearful, but none escalated any further. Interestingly, these were mainly older children who, while not knowing about their own autism, had already encountered negative views about it through the media or elsewhere. No situations arose where a child's behaviour became unmanageable.

The dropout rate from the programme was found to be very low. Occasions when this work has not been completed, once started, have turned out to have been extremely rare. Moreover, this has always been for reasons other than a lack of cooperation or inappropriate behaviour on the part of the child. This seemed to suggest strongly that *All About Me* does offer a safe and engaging method for sharing their diagnosis with most children with autism, especially when the work is not left too late.

During the programme itself it was found that children often exhibited difficulties when trying to carry out the self-assessment work that was required to create the initial context for disclosing and explaining their diagnosis. This has since led to additional adjustments being made to parts of the first session to support some children with identifying their own personal attributes and in gaining a generalized view of what type of person they are.

Difficulties inherent in the children's autism also made it harder to assess the extent to which some children went on to understand and accept their diagnosis. Nevertheless, it was clear in some cases that children had not achieved this by the time the programme had been completed. It should also be noted, however, that other authors appear to have concluded that it can take some individuals a long time to reach an adequate understanding and acceptance of their diagnosis no matter how they are told about it (e.g. Vermeulen 2013; Whitaker 2006). This finding has proved helpful, as it has resulted in much more thought being put into how to continue supporting children, and those around them, after the individual has completed the third session.

Chapter 2

ARGUMENTS FOR AND AGAINST TELLING CHILDREN ABOUT THEIR AUTISM

2.1 INTRODUCTION

As stated in Chapter 1, telling a child about their autism can often turn out to be a highly positive event for the individual and their family; however, this is not always very easy or risk-free. The outcomes vary from one child to another (Miller 2015; Pike 2008), and in certain cases this sensitive work has the potential to create more problems for the child than it was originally intended to solve (Jones 2001).

It is my personal view that all children who are able enough and ready should be told about their diagnosis at the earliest available opportunity. However, I also believe that this should only happen when it is thought that doing so might improve a child's everyday life and not pose any severe and long-lasting threats to their emotional and psychological well-being. Each decision on whether to tell a child about their autism should always be thought through very carefully on an individual basis and never taken lightly.

Personal experience has shown that this potentially life-changing decision can be very stressful for those involved, particularly parents. In some instances, parents who have already concluded that their child does need to be told about their autism have still worried that it might not turn out to be in their son or daughter's best interests (Duprey 2011).

Despite the difficulties involved in taking this decision, there appears to be very little published guidance for parents and professionals to turn to for help. Not much has been written specifically about the various ways children could respond to being told about their autism. However, a great deal of information about this subject can be found scattered in different places in the contents of literature and other sources related to autism in general. This chapter aims to make it easier for parents and professionals to make balanced and informed decisions on whether individual children should be told about their autism by bringing together and examining some of this information in one place.

This chapter also intends to help readers who might already have decided to go ahead and tell a child. I have found that having an increased awareness of what might go wrong because of this work has helped in planning how to prevent some of these problems from arising in the first place, or, if these problems do arise, in mitigating their effects on the child and others. This knowledge has also provided insight into what further kinds of support some children, families and professionals might need to be offered after this work has been completed.

The information and views presented in this chapter are based upon the reported life experiences of individuals with autism, other relevant literature and sources of information about autism, as well as my own experiences of teaching children about their autism and the discussions that I have had with parents, school staff and other professionals.

The next section provides a brief review of some of the background literature that has been drawn upon to write this chapter. This is then followed by three separate sections which respectively explore the potential benefits of sharing the diagnosis with children, the potential risks this carries and the possible consequences of deciding to withhold a child's diagnosis. For comparative purposes, tables have been drawn up to summarize the main conclusions from each of these sections (Tables 2.1, 2.2 and 2.3). Each table lists the relevant benefits or risks which are identified in the main body of the text, alongside references to the sources providing the information that these conclusions are based on; some of these are additional to those referred to directly in the text.

2.2 A BRIEF REVIEW OF THE LITERATURE SURROUNDING INDIVIDUALS' RESPONSES TO FINDING OUT ABOUT THEIR AUTISM DIAGNOSIS, OR HAVING IT WITHHELD

2.2.1 Background

This review has been written especially for readers who might have an academic interest in exploring the background literature to how individuals with autism could respond to being told about their diagnosis or how they might be affected by having it withheld. This is additional information which is not necessarily essential for understanding the main issues discussed in the rest of this chapter.

Earlier authors on this subject have remarked on how very little has been written about the issues associated with telling children that they are on the autism spectrum (Fletcher 2013; Jones 2001; Whitaker 2006). More recent literature searches of my own appear to confirm that this is probably still the case. In particular, there seems to be an ongoing paucity of academic research into this topic. Whitaker (2006) commented on there being a lack of research data available in relation to some very basic and important questions. Nothing is known about the proportion of children who have been told that they have autism, how old these children were when they were told, and why adults decided to share their diagnosis with them in the first place. Little seems to be known either about the number of parents who have chosen to withhold their child's diagnosis from them or, perhaps more importantly, their reasons for doing this (Whitaker 2006).

This missing information could all be helpful to parents and professionals who need to make their own decisions about telling individual children. Just as urgently, though, descriptions of practice in this area also seem scarce (Fletcher 2013; Miller 2014). This leaves very little for others to refer to for guidance on how to carry out this much-needed but equally challenging and potentially risky work with children. These gaps in the literature stress the need for further research as well as the publication of a broader range of theoretical and practical books like this one.

Starting with the few academic studies that have been conducted so far, the next two parts of this section briefly identify, review and pull together some of the sources that form the basis of the main discussions in this chapter.

2.2.2 Academic research into the effects of disclosing or withholding a child's autism diagnosis

So far, only two recent research studies, by Huws and Jones (2008) and Punshon *et al.* (2009), appear to have investigated the effects of receiving the diagnosis from the perspectives of individuals with autism. Both studies identified a range of positive and negative psychological responses that have been triggered by disclosure, and might therefore offer useful insights to anyone who is contemplating telling an individual themselves.

Significantly, each study concluded that disclosure can have a number of destabilizing effects on an individual's self-identity and that negative outcomes seem more likely the later it occurs. However, as isolated studies with small sample groups made up of older participants, generalizing their findings to the autism child population is difficult. Huws and Jones interviewed just nine college students, while Punshon *et al.*'s ten participants were all diagnosed as adults. Moreover, both studies will have limited usefulness for anyone who is looking to come up with a safe method for disclosing the diagnosis. Describing how their participants received their diagnosis or what they were told about autism was outside the scope of both studies. Therefore, neither paper provides any sort of insight into how particular disclosure methods might influence outcomes.

My own research into the effectiveness of *All About Me* (Miller 2014, 2015), which has already been described in the opening chapter, aimed to help address the gap in practice-based studies through describing and evaluating direct work carried out with a large and diverse group of children. It also provided descriptions of some of their responses to what they were taught. As stated, the study found that the programme methods and framework, described later in this book, appeared to work well with the majority of these children, and it could usually be adapted to cater for their various individual differences and needs. Although a few children were upset to find out about their diagnosis, none of the most extreme reactions, described later in this chapter, have ever materialized during an instance of this work. Nor have they been reported to have happened later. In common with the findings of the two studies that have already been described, it was also discovered that the least successful psychological and emotional outcomes appeared to occur when the work was left until later.

This research also identified that, as a short programme, there is a risk that some children will not develop a sound understanding or acceptance of what they are taught about autism by the time the work is completed. This highlighted the importance of the types of follow-up initiatives that are described in Chapter 8.

Although the overall findings of this study suggest that *All About Me* could offer a safe way to introduce many children to their autism, this research was not without limitations – not least because it was conducted by a proponent of the programme's approach. Since the study only evaluated a single short-term method for introducing children to their autism, it shed no light on whether there might be any better ways of telling children about their diagnosis and helping them to understand it. Moreover, it cannot advise on whether there are any other methods that might be harmful and therefore best avoided.

Although not focusing directly on the topic of disclosing the diagnosis, Cassidy (2015) recently carried out important research into suicidality among the adult autism population in England. This study, which was based on questionnaires completed by a total of 367 adults, identified a possible causal link between suicidal behaviours and receiving the diagnosis late.

This is something that definitely needs to be taken into consideration before deciding whether to withhold a child's diagnosis, particularly since all of the studies mentioned so far have proposed that later disclosure could increase the probability of more negative psychological outcomes. What constitutes late disclosure might vary from one individual to another; Chapter 3 therefore includes guidance on how to judge when an individual child might have reached the stage at which they are ready to be told (see 3.2).

Lastly, a doctoral study by Duprey (2011) appears to be the first of its kind to explore the processes that parents might go through before they decide to disclose their child's autism diagnosis. Notably, it found that some participants expressed surprise at how indifferently their children reacted to being told about their diagnosis. However, this was a small isolated study into what is perhaps a large and previously unexplored area. Therefore, as it was based on interviews with the parents of only ten children, it would also be hard to generalize any of its findings.

Given the numbers of children with autism, this work's sensitive nature and its potential difficulties, it would appear that there is an urgent need for much more research into the effects of disclosing their diagnosis to individuals with autism and into different methods for doing this. As argued already, the paucity of relevant and reliable academic research makes it difficult for parents and professionals to weigh up accurately the possible benefits of disclosure against its potential risks. Moreover, it offers them little if any outcome-based guidance on the best ways of doing this work with children and how to address any problems it could create.

2.2.3 Other literature and sources related to sharing or withholding a child's autism diagnosis

Despite the current lack of relevant academic research into the effects of disclosing a child's autism diagnosis, much useful information can be obtained from across a variety of other sources, all of which might prove helpful when trying to weigh up its potential benefits and possible risks. This is not just limited to published literature, but includes resources such as short films and conference presentations.

Alongside what little research is currently available, this book calls upon the written and verbal accounts of people with autism, such as Gunilla Gerland (1997), Luke Jackson (2002), Iain Payne (2012), Clare Sainsbury (2000) and John Simpson (2007). The AET produced a DVD in 2011 containing a series of short films made by teenagers and young adults in which they talk about living with their autism. These books, articles and film clips offer valuable first-hand insights into how their authors felt they benefited from being given their diagnosis. In several cases, individuals have also described the psychological effects of having their diagnosis delayed.

Meanwhile, expert theoreticians and practitioners have advised on things such as the potential benefits and risks associated with sharing a diagnosis, and possible methods for doing it. This book and the ongoing development of *All About Me* have been influenced in particular by the work of Tony Attwood (2006, 2008), Ingrid Fletcher (2013), Carol Gray (1996), Glenys Jones (2001), Peter Vermeulen (2000, 2013), Jude Welton (2004a, 2004b, 2014) and Philip Whitaker (2006). Except for a single chapter by Jacqui Jackson (2006), however, nothing else currently appears to have been written about the experiences of sharing the diagnosis with their child from a parent's perspective.

Although not directly addressing the topic of sharing the diagnosis, various publications have been written by government departments and other organizations, such as the United Nations (1989), which imply that children need to be taught as much as possible about their autism. This is echoed in the United Kingdom government's recent drive towards making LAs and schools in England include all children with special educational needs and disabilities (SEND) more fully in making decisions about their support (Department for Education (DfE) and Department of Health (DoH) 2014).

2.3 POTENTIAL BENEFITS OF DISCLOSING A CHILD'S DIAGNOSIS

2.3.1 Introduction

It is not uncommon for people with autism to experience some degree of disappointment and upset when they are first introduced to their diagnosis. However, individual accounts of people who have had these initial feelings appear to show that, given time and relevant information, they can go on to benefit hugely from having been told that they have autism (e.g. Beadle 2011; Hood 2012). This section therefore tries to identify and explore the various psychological and practical advantages children might gain from learning about their diagnosis, so that these can be balanced against the possible negative consequences which are discussed later. These possible advantages are summarized in Table 2.1.

2.3.2 Potential psychological and emotional benefits of disclosing the diagnosis

First-hand and indirectly reported experiences of people with autism appear to offer much proof that being given their diagnosis can have a hugely beneficial effect on an individual's overall emotional and psychological well-being. Their accounts suggest that finding out about their autism can provide an individual with better self-understanding and greater peace of mind. In turn, this can improve their self-concept and raise previously low self-esteem. Learning about their autism has even helped some individuals get past extremely serious mental health issues, including severe breakdowns (Simpson 2007) and suicide ideation (Payne 2012).

Through my own work, I have seen how children can regard the discovery of their autism as cause for celebration (Miller 2015), and some people have even expressed anger at not having been told about it sooner (Attwood 2006; Gerland 2000; Punshon *et al.* 2009). Various individuals have described how this knowledge gave them an enormous sense of relief (Aston 2000; Attwood 2008; Gerland 1997). At the age of 12, Luke Jackson wrote:

> I had finally found out why people classed me as weird. It was not just because I was clumsy and stupid. My heart lightened instantly and the constant nagging that accompanied me all of my life (not my mum) stopped immediately. (2002, p.34)

For many others like Luke, the discovery of their diagnosis has helped put their difficulties and previous life experiences into perspective (Aston 2000; Beadle 2011; Gerland 1997; Sainsbury 2000). They were able to make better sense of their lives. A college student renamed Jemma, who participated in Huws and Jones' study (2008), said it was only after being told about her diagnosis at the age of 13 that she understood why she was treated differently as a child. Another student who took part in the same research said that having his diagnosis helped him realize why he had struggled at school and often been in trouble.

Being told about their diagnosis has therefore provided many individuals with much-needed answers to important questions such as why they previously got things wrong, did not fit in socially and had no friends, were treated differently to siblings and peers, or were singled out by others for teasing, name-calling and bullying. Being given a tangible explanation for their differences has provided some individuals with a sense of exoneration for past incidents and mistakes (Huws and Jones 2008; Punshon *et al.* 2009). Indeed, Paula Johnston's advice to other people with autism was that knowing their behavioural differences are biologically based should take away feelings of guilt that they may have (MacLeod and Johnston 2007). Likewise, Luke Jackson wrote, 'I finally knew why I felt different, why I felt as if I was a freak, why I didn't seem to fit in. Even better it was not my fault' (2002, p.35).

Disclosure has also helped individuals learn to realize that negative labels that had been applied to them by others were in fact untrue, and that they were not stupid or weird as they had repeatedly heard in the past (Sainsbury 2000). Furthermore, some individuals have been relieved to find that difficulties they had with coping in certain situations were not down to them having some form of insanity or brain damage as they had falsely presumed (Gerland 1997; Payne 2012; Sainsbury 2000). I worked with an eight-year-old boy called Hugh who had wanted to know why he was constantly distracted by intrusive thoughts about his favourite cartoon and movie characters. He was delighted to find out that this was for neither of these reasons, as he had previously assumed (Miller 2014). Having the diagnosis might also offer some individuals an equally more acceptable explanation for any distress they experience as a result of their sensory processing differences (Sainsbury 2000; Helen 2011). As Tony Attwood put it, disclosure can provide the recipient with a much-needed sense of relief by knowing that they are 'not weird, just wired differently' (2008, p.330).

Many individuals with autism found that learning about their diagnosis helped them to identify with its more positive aspects and to value their areas of strength. This in turn made them more accepting of themselves for who they were (e.g. Beadle 2011; Grandin 1997). Moreover, knowing why they found certain things much harder than the people around them relieved some people from the pressure and anxiety caused by wrongly supposing that their difficulties might yet be overcome and that they could become 'normal' through trying harder (Gerland 1997; Sainsbury 2000). Following his own diagnosis as an adult, Iain Payne, whose social isolation had caused him to become severely depressed and consider suicide, said, 'I am happier now that I know why I am different from most people and I now know my strengths and differences, and I don't have to try to be someone I am not' (2012, p.34).

Communicating, interacting socially and forming relationships with others are far more effortful and challenging for people with autism. This all too often leads to them being socially excluded both as children and adults. Consequently, people with autism can experience feeling a deep sense of rejection, alienation, isolation and loneliness. These emotions, caused by being on the edge of society, have frequently had adverse effects on their overall mental health and well-being (Aston 2000; MacLeod and Johnston 2007; Sainsbury 2000).

For many people with autism, then, the discovery that there are others like them has been highly welcome and encouraging news. Being told about their diagnosis made them aware that they were not alone. They were able to gain comfort from the fact that other people like them do exist and that many of them lead successful lives. Once told about their autism, children participating in *All About Me* are shown pictures of notable people with autism and told about their achievements. Children have usually said in their feedback that this was their favourite part of the programme, and some have been pleasantly surprised and reassured to find that there were other children like them at their own schools.

Knowing that they have autism has enabled many individuals to seek out and make contact with other people like themselves. They have often done this through internet forums or in person at autism support groups. Disclosing the diagnosis has also allowed parents, teachers and support staff to introduce children to other individuals with autism. In one LA where I worked, an autism youth club was set up for teenagers from the mainstream schools in the area to attend once they knew at least something about their diagnosis and the reason they would be going there. Several individuals went on to form positive relationships and friendships with other children after meeting them at the club.

Iain Payne (2012) described how he struggled to understand and interact with the people around him throughout his childhood and adult life prior to finding out about his autism. He said that sometimes he even felt as if he did not belong to his own parents because they were so different from him. Being in the presence of other people and crowds made him feel highly anxious and under threat. After discovering that he had autism at the age of 36, he joined several email lists and then went on to meet other adults with autism, having found a group of people that he felt he could understand and relate to.

Paula Johnston described how she joined an adult autism support group after receiving her diagnosis because she was curious about meeting other individuals with similar difficulties and experiences. In everyday circumstances, she found it hard to socialize, but in the company of other people with autism, she said that she could do this freely and without the constant worry of getting things wrong (MacLeod and Johnston 2007).

One further psychological benefit of telling a child about their autism is that it removes any risks of them receiving their diagnosis accidentally. Telling a child about their autism in a planned, structured and supportive way will perhaps reduce any potential harm disclosure may present to their psychological and emotional well-being (Whitaker 2006). The possible consequences of unplanned disclosure are considered later in this chapter.

It needs to be said here, however, that, on the basis of my experience, children who find out about their autism abruptly seem more likely to regard their diagnosis negatively.

2.3.3 Potential practical benefits of disclosing the diagnosis

The knowledge that comes with disclosure also has the potential to offer a child a whole range of practical benefits if it is used well (Jones 2001). Various people with autism have argued that all individuals have an absolute right to be told about their diagnosis at the earliest possible opportunity. This is on the grounds that doing so can provide them with the type of self-knowledge that is important to them in gaining greater control over their lives and having a sense of ownership of their diagnosis (e.g. Gerland 1997; Jackson 2002; Sainsbury 2000). This information is essential to children with autism fully benefiting from the same fundamental legal rights that have been afforded to all other children, as well as those that apply specifically to children with SEND.

Under Articles 12 and 13 of the United Nations Convention on the Rights of the Child, all children are entitled to the right to a voice and having their views considered whenever decisions are being made that might affect their lives (United Nations 1989). Similar children's rights underpin the SEND Code of Practice in England (DfE and DoH 2014). This clearly states that LAs are required to ensure that the views, wishes and feelings of children with SEND are properly taken into account when decisions are being made about their support. It also says that LAs must try to ensure that children with SEND can participate as fully as possible in the discussions leading up to making these decisions. Alongside this, the Code places a duty on LAs to provide children and parents with any relevant information and support that they might need to enable them to access these rights (DfE and DoH 2014, p.19). Arguably, this must include LAs having to take on an active role in helping parents inform children who are able enough about their autism.

Knowing why they receive support seems fundamental to children participating effectively in any discussions and decisions about it. Learning about her autism proved beneficial in this way for a young woman called Helen (2011). In a film she made, she described how, from an early age, she was able to attend the meetings where her support was discussed. As a non-verbal learner, she used a communication aid to self-advocate, talking about things that she thought might be useful to her and which would help her to live the kind of life she wanted to. This was no doubt easier because the adults in her life could talk openly about autism in her presence and she could ask them questions about it too. Such discussions would have been much more difficult and limited with someone like Jemma, mentioned in 2.3.2, since she knew nothing about her autism before she became a teenager and had no idea why she was educated in a special needs unit (Huws and Jones 2008).

For many children, learning about their autism can be vital to them accepting and gaining any benefit from school-based support which is judged vital to them: achieving their academic potential, developing positive coping strategies and acquiring important communication, social, self-help and independent living skills. Increasing a child's awareness about their own strengths and the challenges they face might also be applied to helping them to make more realistic choices in relation to their future educational placements, career options, living arrangements and lives in general (Jones 2001).

Although having knowledge of their autism can help some children engage better with their school-based support, it can also lead to them accessing and taking up support offered by more specialist professionals and services (Punshon *et al.* 2009), as well as attending support groups or youth clubs. Joining a group might not only offer an individual the chances to socialize that were described earlier, but can also provide them with incidental opportunities for learning important life skills (MacLeod and Johnston 2007).

Once a child knows that they have autism, and they are able enough, their parents, school staff and other professionals will be able to openly share or signpost them towards a wealth of support literature and other resources that are relevant to their differences and needs. Some of these are referred to in 8.2.3, and include books written by adults who have autism themselves. An increasing number of self-help and guidance books offering advice on how to cope and live with having autism are also becoming available for teenagers and young adults.

As a final point, although learning about their diagnosis does appear to offer a broad variety of practical advantages for individuals with autism, it has to be accepted that because of their differences and needs, many children may not be able to take up all of these benefits independently. Autistic thinking will make it harder for them both to understand what their diagnosis means (Miller 2015; Vermeulen 2013) and to apply whatever they have learned about it spontaneously in different situations. Parents in Duprey's study (2011), for example, remarked on how being given the diagnosis seemed to have little apparent effect on their children's involvement in planning for their future lives. After receiving their diagnosis, many children will no doubt need ongoing support with learning how to use what they were taught about it in their everyday lives, and this may include some of the initiatives described in Chapter 8.

Table 2.1: Potential benefits of disclosing a child's autism diagnosis

Benefits	References
Raising an individual's self-esteem	Beadle 2011; Helen 2011; Jones 2001; Payne 2012; Vermeulen 2013
Providing an explanation for an individual's differences and past negative life experiences	Aston 2000; Beadle 2011; Brett 2011; Gerland 1997; Jackson 2002; Payne 2012; Punshon et al. 2009; Sainsbury 2000
Raising an individual's awareness of not being alone (this allows for joining support groups, developing friendships, gaining encouragement from the achievements of successful people with autism)	Attwood 2006; Helen 2011; Jones 2001; Kershaw 2011; MacLeod and Johnston 2007; Ministries of Health and Education (MHE) 2008; Punshon et al. 2009
Explaining why an individual is treated differently to their siblings and peers	Attwood 2008; Fidler 2004; Jones 2001; Punshon et al. 2009; Whitaker 2006
Supporting an individual's rights to self-knowledge and ownership of their diagnosis	Gerland 1997; Jackson 2002; National Initiative for Autism: Screening and Assessment 2003; Sainsbury 2000
Strengthening a child's voice in decision-making, self-advocacy and explaining themselves to others (as required by DfE and DoH 2014; United Nations 1989)	AET 2012; Jones 2001; Punshon et al. 2009
Avoiding the negative psychological consequences of accidental disclosure	Jones 2001; Lawrence 2010; Whitaker 2006
Helping an individual to develop appropriate coping strategies and the skills needed to lead more independent lives	Jones 2001; Kershaw 2011; MacLeod and Johnston 2007; Payne 2012; Vermeulen 2013
Helping an individual to identify, access and engage with specialist literature, professionals and support services	Jones 2001, MacLeod and Johnston 2007; MHE 2008; Punshon et al. 2009
Helping an individual to make realistic education, career and life choices as required in England under the SEND Code of Practice (DfE and DoH 2014)	Jones 2001

Source: Miller 2014, 2015

2.4 POTENTIAL RISKS OF DISCLOSING A CHILD'S DIAGNOSIS

2.4.1 Introduction

Although it could offer the recipient numerous possible benefits, it must not be forgotten that sharing an autism diagnosis with a child can involve taking some risks, which could pose threats to the well-being of both the individual and the people around them. This section tries to identify and evaluate the most common psychological and practical problems that could arise from an instance of this work, so that adults can factor these into their decisions on whether to tell individual children. These risks are summarized in Table 2.2.

2.4.2 Potential psychological and emotional risks of disclosing a diagnosis

In common with some parents whose children have other lifelong disabilities and chronic conditions, those who have children with autism may decide against telling their child about their diagnosis to protect them from possible emotional distress (Duprey 2011; Gallo *et al.* 2005; Heeren 2011; Jackson 2006). Some parents and professionals may also be concerned that sharing the diagnosis with a child could cause the individual to become angry and upset with whoever tells them about it and that this in turn could have lasting and damaging effects on their future relationships (Miller 2015). These concerns are not without foundation since reported cases seem to show that disclosure can trigger a range of different negative psychological reactions (Huws and Jones 2008; Punshon *et al.* 2009; Whitaker 2006).

Hearing about their diagnosis for the first time may well have destabilizing effects on an individual's overall self-identity and adversely affect their future life plans and expectations (Murray 2006; Punshon *et al.* 2009; Whitaker 2006), perhaps more so if the individual was previously unaware of the existence of their differences (Huws and Jones 2008). Individuals who are able to understand its implications can feel disappointed by their diagnosis and find it hard to come to terms with the realization that its implications are going to be lifelong (Kershaw 2011; Lawson 2006). The diagnosis has left some individuals feeling sad and bereft of hope since they regarded it as effectively signalling the end of any chance they ever had of overcoming their difficulties and becoming 'normal' (Gerland 1997; Lawson 2006; Sainsbury 2000).

Given that the diagnostic criteria for autism comprised a series of deficits and impairments (APA 2013; WHO 1992), an individual who is able enough to understand this might easily conclude that autism is something bad and shameful or that it makes them defective in some way. This may be reinforced due to the inherent nature of autism which means that any explanation of the diagnosis will at some point have to involve sharing the individual's areas of difficulty and their weaknesses with them (Miller 2014; Murray 2006; Vermeulen 2013).

Against this background, cases have been reported where being given the diagnosis has elicited severe feelings of shock, anger, fear and stigmatization

(Attwood 2006; Huws and Jones 2008; MHE 2008; Punshon *et al.* 2009). Some individuals have then refused outright to accept the validity of their diagnosis or discuss the matter any further (Jones 2001; Vermeulen 2013; Wing 2002). The impact of these reactions can cause some people to develop lower self-esteem or long-term mental health conditions such as depression (Jones 2001; Whitaker 2006) and, in the most extreme cases, at least briefly contemplate suicide (MacLeod and Johnston 2007). At the same time, a disproportionately high number of people with autism are already thought to suffer from depression and attempt suicide (Cassidy 2015).

Although it needs to be taken seriously, the risk of a negative psychological reaction need not necessarily be seen as a reason for deciding not to share a child's diagnosis with them. Like Tony Attwood (2006), I have concluded from working with a large group that most individuals seem to accept their diagnosis well when it is presented to them calmly and positively in the context of their overall personal attributes. Furthermore, initial negative reactions to disclosure can often fade quite quickly once an individual has had time to absorb their diagnosis (Beadle 2011; Jones 2001).

Whenever this work does go ahead, though, it normally ought to be on the proviso that it does not coincide with an individual going through an exceptionally challenging and traumatic time. Steps should also have been taken to ensure there will be adequate support in place for the child if they do experience a negative backlash. It must also be remembered that having autism means that, regardless of the level of their communication, many individuals could have difficulties with expressing their feelings and requesting help when it may be urgently needed. It is essential therefore that the typical people around a child are extra vigilant in monitoring their behaviour for changes and any outward signs of increased distress in the period after they have received their diagnosis.

2.4.3 Potential practical risks of disclosing the diagnosis

Explaining autism is difficult, so parents and school staff can often be uncertain about how to go about doing it. In the absence of professional support or other practical guidance, they might decide to avoid telling a child altogether. In these circumstances, adults may be anxious that they could upset the child by getting things wrong (Jackson 2002). Additionally, many adults may well feel that they do not have the skills and knowledge needed to explain autism in a way that a child on the spectrum would be able to make sense of (Miller 2015). It is hoped that reading this book and using the accompanying resources will help some readers overcome these barriers.

The risk that a child might not understand much about their diagnosis when they are first told about it is genuine. They could find it confusing irrespective of who explains it to them or how it is done. It can take some individuals a long time whereas others might never manage this. Autism is complex and is difficult to explain in simple terms to anyone, let alone a child with a diagnosis. Their cognitive differences and tendency towards making literal interpretations make it harder for children on the spectrum to understand autism's abstract nature (Vermeulen 2013). After all, the diagnosis is based on sets of behavioural and psychological traits rather than any tangible physical symptoms (Whitaker 2006). In my personal experience, helping children to have a clear understanding of their diagnosis has often turned out to be the hardest part of this work.

Assessing children's understanding and acceptance of what they have been taught about themselves and autism has never proved to be straightforward either. This does not only relate to children with fewer expressive language skills; autistic thought processes imply that even when an individual can clearly describe what they have been told about themselves and their diagnosis, this should not necessarily be taken to signify that they have identified with that description or recognized how it might apply to them. As suggested by Vermeulen (2013), they may simply be echoing what has been said about them without giving much thought to its meaning.

The risk that a child might not understand or identify with their diagnosis straight away does not have to be a valid reason for deciding not to introduce most children to their autism through this programme. If need be, the programme allows for the initial description of a child's autism to be reduced to just a single headline sentence that simply tells them that having autism describes someone whose overall strengths and differences are similar to theirs. Moreover, guidance is given in 8.2.1 on how parents and other adults can use the personalized booklet, made with the child during the programme sessions, as a tool for consolidating the initial work and gradually adding to the child's knowledge of autism later.

There are, of course, some children with autism who have quite severe learning difficulties. For them, even the simplest explanation of autism is likely to be beyond the reach of their understanding. This work would be unsuitable for them, given *All About Me*'s inclusion criteria, presented in Chapter 3.

A further risk that cannot be discounted is that of children deciding to tell other people about their diagnosis. This concern is shared by parents who have children with other chronic conditions (e.g. Gallo *et al.* 2005; Heeren 2011). Their worry may be that their child could expose themselves and other family members to name-calling, bullying and stigmatization.

In my experience, although this has happened on a few occasions, the children I have worked with rarely seemed to go around telling others about their diagnosis afterwards. Given their differences in theory of mind – the ability to attribute mental states to themselves and others (Baron-Cohen, Leslie and Frith 1985) – it might not occur to some children that they would need to tell other people (Frith 2003). Furthermore, even the most able children with autism tend to have very few friends to talk with and find it difficult to initiate contact with those around them. Besides, plenty of children whom I have met said that they did not want other people to know about their autism anyway.

When parents and school staff feel that there is a reasonable risk of a child telling others, the individual can be told, both verbally and through an additional written statement in the narrative of their booklet, which people it is okay for them to talk with about their autism, and that they should try not to mention it to anyone else until told otherwise (also see 6.15.5). This, coupled with close monitoring by school staff and other adults, has generally seemed to work in the past.

Another option could be for the adults to pre-empt the possibility of this situation causing problems for the child at school by sharing the diagnosis with their classmates themselves. The main issues that need to be considered before telling classmates about a child's autism are explored in 8.6, which offers advice on how to go about it. I have usually found that peer work can have positive benefits for everyone concerned, without it resulting in a child being stigmatized or treated badly in other ways because of their autism. Nevertheless, work like that comes with its own risks and must never be undertaken without careful planning and consent from the child's parents.

Finally, adults can sometimes worry that telling a child about their diagnosis could lead to the individual developing lower overall self-expectations and becoming more non-compliant. Based on their knowledge of the child, they may become concerned that they might try to use their autism to excuse inappropriate behaviour or as a means of explaining their way out of having to do certain things that they might find more challenging or less motivating (Vermeulen 2013; Whitaker 2006). This could include them saying that they cannot possibly do things like school work or household chores because they have autism. Although parents and professionals have occasionally raised these issues beforehand, few have later reported children adopting this type of behaviour after the programme has been completed. In instances where they did, the difficulties this had created usually seemed manageable, and therefore this issue ought not interfere with a decision to pass on the child's diagnosis to them.

Table 2.2: Potential risks of disclosing a child's autism diagnosis

Risks	References
The diagnosis having negative destabilizing effects on an individual's self-expectations and future life plans (through them being aware of the negative and lifelong implications of an autism diagnosis and that normality cannot be achieved)	Gerland 1997; Huws and Jones 2008; Kershaw 2011; Lawson 2006; Murray 2006; Punshon *et al.* 2009; Sainsbury 2000; Whitaker 2006
A child developing a negative perception of their autism and believing that it makes them defective	Miller 2014; Murray 2006; Vermeulen 2013
A child being angry at the people who informed them about their diagnosis (leading to damaged relationships with the adults from whom they will need support)	Attwood 2006; Gerland 2000; Punshon *et al.* 2009; Sainsbury 2000
Disclosure triggering short- or long-term negative emotional and psychological reactions, leading to lower self-esteem and possible separate mental health issues (e.g. depression and suicide ideation)	Gerland 1997; Jackson 2002; Jackson 2006; Jones 2001; MacLeod and Johnston 2007; Paul 2011; Simpson 2007; Whitaker 2006
A child feeling stigmatized by their autism label	Huws and Jones 2008; Punshon *et al.* 2009; Sainsbury 2000
A child rejecting their diagnosis and avoiding all attempts to discuss it further	Attwood 2006; Huws and Jones 2008; Jones 2001; Paul 2011; Pike 2008; Sainsbury 2000; Vermeulen 2013; Whitaker 2006; Wing 2002
Mistakes could be made by the person leading the work (due to inexperience and an absence of published guidance and specialized professional support)	Miller 2015
An individual not understanding and assimilating their diagnosis	Miller 2015; Vermeulen 2013; Whitaker 2006
An individual disclosing their diagnosis to others (leading to possible ridicule, bullying or stigmatization of themselves and other family members)	Gallo *et al.* 2005; Heeren 2011 (Note: these are both studies based on research into disclosing other serious medical conditions to children)
An individual developing lower self-expectations and using their autism label as an excuse for not doing certain things or behaving inappropriately	Duprey 2011; Vermeulen 2013; Whitaker 2006

When it has been thought that a child might behave like this, a few extra sentences have been included in the narrative of their *All About Me* booklet. This has advised the child about the inappropriateness of this kind of behaviour and suggested what they should to try to do instead (see 6.3.2 for examples of how to do this). Although this measure is intended to prevent this behaviour from arising in the first place, it also provides a visual reminder for adults to bring a child back to if any problems occur later. Adults also need to be mindful of how they could unwittingly cause or reinforce this type of behaviour themselves through using a child's autism to explain why they are not allowed to do certain things (Vermeulen 2013).

2.5 POTENTIAL RISKS OF WITHHOLDING A CHILD'S DIAGNOSIS

2.5.1 Introduction

Despite its possible benefits, telling children about their autism is clearly not risk-free. In some instances, it might be felt that the threats to a particular individual's well-being could outweigh any possible advantages they would be able to take up from knowing about their diagnosis. Even so, accounts of individuals with autism offer proof that delaying disclosure is also something that has the potential to create far more problems than it might be intended to prevent (Aston 2000; Gerland 1997; Jackson 2002; Sainsbury 2000). This being so, if any doubts exist over whether a child should be told, it is vital that the possible problems that could emerge as a consequence of witholding their diagnosis are also fully explored.

This section considers both the practical difficulties of trying to conceal the diagnosis from a child and the possible long-term effects that not knowing about their autism could have on an individual's emotional and psychological well-being. Table 2.3 provides an ordered summary of the main risks that are identified from this.

2.5.2 Practical difficulties caused by withholding the diagnosis from a child

Needless to say, not telling a child that they have autism would deny them any of the practical and psychological benefits that might come from knowing about their diagnosis. Early disclosure is thought to lead to better overall outcomes for children with autism (Jones 2001). Unnecessary delays waste valuable time that might be better used helping a child to start coming to terms with their autism and learning to deal with its practical challenges. Besides this, withholding the diagnosis leaves a child exposed to the risk of finding out about their autism accidentally (Lawrence 2010; Whitaker 2001).

For individuals who are be able enough to understand the significance of what it might mean, there are a number of theoretical ways that an unplanned disclosure could occur at any time, without warning and possibly without anyone else knowing that it had happened. Despite everyone's best efforts to keep the diagnosis concealed and repeatedly avoid answering any questions raised by the child, it cannot be discounted that they will not accidentally come across it through any of the following ways:

- overhearing adults discussing their autism at home, school and elsewhere

- finding and reading copies of professionals' reports and other paperwork about their autism, if these are left unattended at home or on a teacher's desk

- hearing the diagnosis being referred to in meetings about their support

- an adult mentioning the diagnosis without realizing the child has not been told about it

- being told, perhaps unkindly, by siblings, classmates or other children who have already been informed or guessed for themselves that the child has autism

- working out the diagnosis for themselves based on information that they come across in the media or elsewhere, as experienced by Gary Aston (2000)

- observing the behaviour of other children with autism and concluding that they are the same.

Even if it proves possible to withhold the diagnosis in the meantime, in most cases it will be very difficult to do so for much longer once an individual has reached the age of 18. Like the rest of the population, as an adult, they would have a legal entitlement to access all their personal medical, educational and care records.

An unplanned disclosure can be problematic and distressing for everyone concerned. The timing is always going to be unpredictable and it is doubtful that adequate support mechanisms would be in place to support the child with any adverse reactions to it (Whitaker 2006). Moreover, vital relationships between the individual and those on whom they depend for support could be damaged as a result. It has already been said that negative outcomes seem more likely for individuals who are made to wait too long for their diagnosis, no matter how they eventually do find out. This can result in them reacting angrily towards people who held information back or did not truthfully answer any questions they may have previously raised about their differences. They may even conclude that important people in their support network are liars who are no longer to be trusted (Gerland 1997; Sainsbury 2000) and consequently disengage from working with them at the very time they need them the most.

2.5.3 Potential psychological and emotional risks of withholding a child's diagnosis

Most children with autism attend mainstream schools (Jones 2002). In England, for example, this is thought to be around 70 per cent of all children with autism (DfE 2014). It is probable that a large proportion of these children will notice that they are different to their classmates while they are still at primary school (Vermeulen 2013; Whitaker 2006). This raises the possibility that not offering these children an explanation for their differences could have adverse effects on their self-esteem and overall psychological well-being (Jones 2001). Furthermore, as discussed in Chapter 3, it is not always easy for adults to detect when a child is developing concerns about being different (Wing 2002). Luke Jackson's mother, for example, said that she decided to wait for five years before telling him about his autism. She did this to spare his feelings, only to find later that he had been worrying all along about why he was different (Jackson 2002).

As stated earlier, in the absence of adequate explanations for being different, some individuals (e.g. Aston 2000; Gerland 1997, 2000; Jackson 2002; Sainsbury 2000; Tammet 2007) have variously described how they assumed that they must have been either mentally ill or had brain damage instead. Not having a label for their differences led them to come up with alternative and unpleasant words of their own to describe themselves and they even applied some of the hostile names given to them by others.

Gary Aston (2000), Gunilla Gerland (1997) and Clare Sainsbury (2000) have all written about being in anxious and confused mental states. Despite worrying that something was terribly wrong with them, they simultaneously believed typical people's reassurances that everything was fine. Consequently, they wrongly believed that they needed to keep trying harder to be normal. Finding out much later that this was untrue caused Gunilla Gerland (1997) a great deal of anguish and anger at having needlessly spent her entire childhood and much of her adult life in a futile struggle trying desperately to fit in and be like everyone else.

Many people with autism have described how not knowing that there were others like them made them feel alone, alienated and lacking any sense of belonging. Clare Sainsbury (2000) spoke about how as a child she felt like an alien from another world and hoped that a spacecraft would come and take her off to live among the type of people she belonged with. Iain Payne (2012) felt similarly isolated and apart from those around him, not understanding why his efforts to join in playing with other children usually went badly wrong and ended in him being ridiculed; as mentioned earlier, he also had difficulty relating to his own parents.

In the most extreme cases, the long-term anxiety and frustration caused by not having a suitable explanation for being different has resulted in individuals developing separate mental health disorders (Payne 2012; Punshon *et al.* 2009; Sainsbury 2000) or becoming involved in drug and alcohol abuse (Aston 2000). John Simpson (2007), for example, was hospitalized by a mental breakdown while he was still at secondary school and said that things only started making sense for him after he received his formal diagnosis later. Moreover, no decision on whether to delay telling someone about their autism should be finalized without giving due consideration to recent research which claims that late diagnosis can be a key risk factor for suicidal behaviours among individuals with autism (Cassidy 2015).

The final word on this matter must go to an eight-year-old boy who wrote after participating in *All About Me* that if 'children don't know about their autism they will believe their life is awful and be miserable' (Miller 2015).

Table 2.3: Possible risks of withholding a child's autism diagnosis

Risks	References
Poorer overall outcomes for a child caused by the delay in them being able to access the potential benefits of knowing about their diagnosis	Jones 2001
An individual finding out about their diagnosis accidentally	Lawrence 2010; Whitaker 2006
An individual developing low self-esteem, anxiety, depression and other mental health conditions	Gerland 1997; Jackson 2002; Miller 2015; Sainsbury 2000; Simpson 2007
Anxiety caused by an individual falsely concluding that something must be terribly wrong with them (i.e. they are weird, unintelligent, insane and/or have brain damage)	Attwood 2006; Gerland 1997; Jackson 2002; Miller 2015; Sainsbury 2000; Simpson 2007; Tammet 2007

Risks	References
Distrust of and anger with their family and other people in their support network for having concealed the diagnosis	Gerland 1997; Sainsbury 2000
Emotional consequences of an individual falsely believing they can achieve normality by trying harder	Gerland 1997; Payne 2012; Sainsbury 2000
An individual feeling socially isolated and alienated	Aston 2000; Gerland 1997; MacLeod and Johnston 2007; Payne 2012; Sainsbury 2000
An individual accepting negative labels applied to them by others and/or applying their own	Jackson 2002; Payne 2012; Punshon et al. 2009
Drug and alcohol abuse	Aston 2000
An individual being at increased risk of a negative emotional and psychological reaction to disclosure when it occurs later	Huws and Jones 2008; Miller 2015; Punshon et al. 2009
An individual being at increased risk of suicidal behaviours through late diagnosis	Cassidy 2015

2.6 CONCLUSION

This chapter set out to bring together and examine key information that parents and professionals might find useful when they are trying to decide, in principle, whether it might be in a child's best interests to be told about their autism. Although some of the risks carried by this work are clearly serious and cannot be ignored, it has been argued that, on balance, children who are able enough should usually be told about their autism as soon they are thought ready.

In the majority of cases, the possibility of the problems described in this chapter materializing once children have been told may well be outweighed by the positive practical and psychological advantages that can come from learning about their diagnosis. Furthermore, the more serious reactions seem to be rare, and when individuals are initially upset by their diagnosis, these feelings often subside fairly soon afterwards.

It cannot be ignored either that withholding the diagnosis can have its own significant psychological risks, and it cannot be guaranteed that the child will not find out about their diagnosis anyway. Not having their diagnosis seems to have caused some individuals constant and prolonged emotional distress throughout virtually the whole of their childhood and well into their adult lives. This has caused some individuals to develop more serious mental health problems. Withholding arguably wastes valuable time that could be spent helping a child get on with learning to live with the challenges of their autism and so is therefore only likely to store up more problems for everyone later on.

My own experience has shown that children nearly always accept having their diagnosis shared with them well when this is done through the methods suggested in this book (Miller 2015). There have been no reported cases of *All About Me* having had any of the more harmful long-term psychological effects by itself on the children with whom I have worked with (Miller 2015). I have learned that with good timing, careful planning and sensitive delivery, the risks described in this chapter can usually be averted or mitigated and the child can start being helped to profit from the advantages that can come from knowing about their diagnosis.

In the end, each decision on whether a child should be told also needs to be based upon thorough knowledge of the individual and their own unique circumstances. Regardless of the views of professionals, it is for each child's parents to decide if and when they should be introduced to their autism. When a decision has been made to share the diagnosis, the potential risks of doing this dictate that the programme should then only commence once the work has been carefully planned for, relevant support is in place to deal with a possible negative reaction and it is judged that the child and everyone else involved are all ready for this to happen.

Chapter 3

THE PRE-PROGRAMME WORK

3.1 INTRODUCTION

Once it has been decided in principle that it would most likely be in a child's best interests to be told about their autism, adults can then move on to the pre-programme work. This is an information-gathering and decision-making stage which is intended to lead to the adults involved suitably familiarizing themselves with the child and agreeing on a number of important practical issues related to the work itself. Before commencing with the programme, decisions will need to be taken on whether the child and everyone else has reached the stage at which they are ready for this work to take place, as well as whether this programme is suitable for the child and, if so, how it will need to be differentiated to meet their individual needs. If a decision is then made to go ahead, other important practical matters will also need to be resolved along the way. These include: who should take the lead role in telling the child; who else needs to be involved; where and when the work should happen; and what the child will need to be told about it beforehand.

Each child's circumstances and those of the people around them will be different. This makes it impossible to provide parents and professionals with definitive answers to all the questions that are explored in this chapter. Instead, the intention is to help readers reach their own conclusions through providing information that is relevant to each issue and guiding them towards what they might need to find out about the child. A series of questions are then posed in the concluding section of the chapter to help readers assess whether they are ready to move on to the planning and teaching stages of the programme. It must be noted, however, that it will not be possible to answer all of these questions fully without first reading the subsequent chapters (4–7) which describe what the programme involves and how it can be differentiated.

The advice given in this chapter is based primarily on work that I have carried out as an external specialist professional and so is presented mainly from the perspective of someone who might never have met a child before.

That said, most of the content should be relevant to anyone who is thinking about sharing an autism diagnosis with a child, regardless of their current relationship with the individual.

Sharing a child's diagnosis can be both challenging and risky, so it needs to be carefully planned (Whitaker 2006). Experience has shown that the best outcomes occur because of detailed pre-programme work and having consequently obtained thorough knowledge of the child and their situation. Therefore it is strongly recommended that readers always take time working through this stage and never contemplate cutting corners or missing it out.

Chapter 2 presented arguments that might be made in favour of, or against, sharing the diagnosis with children. The next section picks up from there by discussing when might be the right time in a child's life to start talking to them about their autism.

3.2 DECIDING WHEN A CHILD SHOULD BE TOLD ABOUT THEIR AUTISM AND IDENTIFYING IF THEY ARE READY

This section contains guidance that is intended to help readers judge for themselves when individual children might be ready to start learning about their autism. A more focused discussion on how to decide on whether *All About Me* might be a suitable programme for individual children appears in a later section in this chapter (see 3.7).

Individuals aged between six and 18 years have participated in *All About Me* and the overwhelming majority of these individuals responded well to being given their diagnosis in this way. The vast diversity of individuals with autism means that there can be no set chronological age for telling a child about their own diagnosis (Jones 2001; Vermeulen 2013; Whitaker 2006). The lack of research into this work, referred to in Chapter 2, offers very little information for adults when they are trying to decide on an approximate time or possible reasons for sharing the diagnosis. No research data is available into the ages at which children are usually told about their autism or why adults decide to tell them (Whitaker 2006).

Telling children too early in their development could run the risk of confusing them. Younger children might acquire skewed views of what having autism means. On the other hand, the small amount of research literature available cautions that the risks of more negative psychological reactions could increase the longer an individual is kept waiting for their diagnosis (Cassidy 2015; Huws and Jones 2008; Miller 2014; Punshon *et al.* 2009).

Experienced practitioners have advised that children should be informed about their diagnosis while they are still at primary school (Attwood 2008;

Lawrence 2010; Vermeulen 2013). This seems sensible since most children with autism attend mainstream schools and during this time tend to develop an awareness of being different to the typical children around them (Whitaker 2006). It has also been argued that to reduce the risk of more negative outcomes, children ought to be introduced to their diagnosis well before they reach adolescence (Fletcher 2013; Pike 2008; Whitaker 2006). I have found that this work appears to have had its most successful outcomes when it has happened within this timeframe.

Whenever possible, introducing children to their autism should be timed to pre-empt any of the potential negative consequences that could develop while the work is being delayed. Some of the reported experiences of people with autism referred to in Chapter 2 suggest that it needs to happen before an individual starts to reach false conclusions about their differences and needs, or accepts and adopts any inaccurate negative labels that others might apply to them. Moreover, responses from participants in research by Punshon *et al.* (2009) and children I have worked with (Miller 2014), as described in Chapter 2, appear to imply that disclosure of their own diagnosis really needs to happen before a child begins to develop negative perceptions of autism in general. Arguably, this work should also commence before the challenges presented by an individual's autism become overwhelming enough to force disclosure in difficult circumstances and for negative reasons (Fletcher 2013; Shore 2003).

A child questioning or expressing concerns about their differences is regarded by many as being a clear indication that they are ready to be told about their autism diagnosis (e.g. Fletcher 2013; Pike 2008; Vermeulen 2013; Whitaker 2006). Individuals querying things such as why they are the only child in their class who has an adult sitting next to them in lessons, their difficulties coping in noisy and crowded situations, or why they have no one to play with, have often proved to be good starting points for including children in *All About Me*.

On the strength of this, some adults might decide to defer conversations about autism until a child starts to raise these matters by themselves (Jackson 2006; Sainsbury 2000), but this should only be done with caution. An individual not mentioning their differences must not be taken as definitive proof that they are unaware of having them and are not anxiously awaiting some sort of explanation (Jackson 2002; Pike 2008; Sainsbury 2000; Whitaker 2006). Their differences in social communication can leave children unable to articulate and express their concerns to others. Gunilla Gerland said that she simply lacked the words needed to do this (cited in Sainsbury 2000, p.126). Similarly, given their differences in theory of mind, it might not necessarily occur to some children with autism that they would need to approach another person to notify them of their worries (Frith 2003). Children with autism can find it far more stressful than typical children to talk about things that they find emotionally upsetting and so may choose to avoid mentioning their anxieties about being different (Whitaker 2006).

In the meantime, a child could be waiting anxiously for months or possibly years for much-needed answers and reassurance (Gerland 1997; Jackson 2002; Sainsbury 2000). Philip Whitaker (2006) therefore urges that situations where children do not voice concerns or enquire about their differences require that adults monitor their behaviour for any outward signs of frustration or distress. Even so, as Lorna Wing (2002) proposed, it can be very difficult to detect how aware some children might be of the effects of their autism. In my experience, the facial expressions and body language of children with autism can often betray how they are feeling on the inside.

Overall, based upon the success of my own work, knowledge of the emotional harm that withholding a child's diagnosis risks and the possible consequences of accidental disclosure, I agree in the main with Clare Sainsbury's assertion that 'Any child who is old enough to understand a simple explanation of their condition is old enough' (2000, p.126). *All About Me* is built upon my already stated belief that all children who are able enough have an absolute right to be told about their autism in an appropriate way at the earliest opportunity, provided that it is not thought that this would cause them unnecessary psychological distress at the time. To support this, *All About Me* offers ways of matching the explanation of autism to different individuals' ages, stages in development and overall levels of understanding, as explained in Chapter 7.

This work could turn out to be damaging to a child if it is carried out against the background of an individual going through a particularly stressful and traumatic period. In these circumstances, it would be wise to consider delaying disclosure until things have calmed down if the general consensus among adults is that introducing the child to their autism at that point would make matters worse (Pike 2008). But the risk of the child finding out accidentally or reaching false conclusions about the cause of their problems in the meantime needs to be factored into this decision.

It might also be sensible to delay telling children who appear to have developed less awareness of their own attributes and how people might differ from each other (Vermeulen 2013). Given that this programme explains autism to children in the context of their overall strengths and challenges, not having this understanding will make it harder for them to accept and make sense of their diagnosis. Introducing an able child simultaneously to a range of challenges they were previously unaware of having could prove shocking and cause them to deny or disbelieve their diagnosis (Huws and Jones 2008; Miller 2014). I have also found that more literal children who lack similar self-insight usually appear to react indifferently to being given their diagnosis. Disclosure appears to have little meaning for them. In most cases, any delays caused by these issues need not be for too long if suitable preparatory work can be carried out to gradually introduce these children to their own attributes. Suggestions on ways to do this are offered at various points in Chapter 5.

If mistakes are made over the timing of this work, however, the structure of *All About Me* still allows for it to be ceased or deferred at any time during the first session, should it becomes obvious that a child is not ready to be told after all. The child would not have been told about their diagnosis at this stage and so it is unlikely that any harm would have been done. A decision like this could be taken if a child appears to be overly confused by the work or if they show signs of becoming traumatized as their challenges start being brought to their attention. To promote the best outcomes for children, this work should always be reviewed collectively by the adults at the end of the first session before thinking about how to move forward, as explained at the end of Chapter 5.

In summary, the best times to start telling children about their autism could be:

- before they reach adolescence

- while they are going through a relatively calm emotional period

- when the child starts to query their differences, or appears frustrated and distressed by them

- as soon as they are judged able to understand a simple headline explanation of what having autism means.

3.3 IDENTIFYING WHETHER PARENTS ARE READY FOR THEIR CHILD TO BE TOLD, AND HOW PROFESSIONALS CAN HELP THEM REACH THIS STAGE

3.3.1 Introduction

Each child's parents will need to reach a point at which they feel ready for their son or daughter to be told about their diagnosis. The length of time this takes can vary widely. Although some have chosen to share the diagnosis very early (Helen 2011; Kershaw 2011; Shore 2003), others have decided to wait for several years (Jackson 2006; Jones 2001).

To be ready to pass on the diagnosis, parents will first need to have come to terms with their own reactions to it and then have developed a suitable understanding of what having autism means (Whitaker 2006). This seems vital regardless of whether a parent chooses to tell the child themselves or seeks professional help with this. Either way, once a child has been told, their parents will need to be able to provide them with accurate and truthful answers to any questions they might pose about their autism later (Vermeulen 2013; Whitaker 2006). Parents will also need to have reached the conclusion that, despite the risks involved, disclosure would be in the individual's best interests (Duprey 2011).

None of this is often easy, so this section offers some possible insight into the journeys that many parents might need to undertake from when they first receive their child's diagnosis themselves, up to the point where they feel ready to share it with their child. This section seeks to reassure parents that they are not isolated in their experiences and to help them to assess their own readiness for this work. It also aims to help school staff and other professionals who might be trying to advise parents who appear reluctant or ambivalent about telling their child about their autism. It is hoped that this will help them to better understand the barriers parents might need to be supported in overcoming along the way. Some simple but effective suggestions are then offered on how professionals can help parents with this.

3.3.2 Some of the processes parents may go through before they are ready to share the diagnosis with their child

Parents often find that obtaining an autism diagnosis for their child is a drawn-out and stressful process (Duprey 2011; Whitaker 2006). Their immediate reactions to then being told that their child has autism have sometimes included feelings of isolation and uncertainty (Dale, Jahoda and Knott 2006; Woodgate, Ateah and Secco 2008) as well as shock, anger, fear and disbelief (Moyes 2003). Such feelings can cause parents to deny the validity of their child's diagnosis (Moyes 2003). Each child's parents will have had their own unique starting point in the process of coming to terms with being told that their child has autism. Parents react to this news in diverse ways, even within the same families. A parent's initial reaction needs to be understood, since it could have a direct effect on the length of time that it will take them to reach a stage at which they feel resolved enough with the diagnosis themselves to even start to contemplate sharing it with their child.

A parent's reactions can be influenced considerably by their prior expectations of the outcome of the diagnostic assessment. Parents who seek an assessment because they already suspect that their child has autism will perhaps accept and engage with the diagnosis more readily. Receiving the diagnosis would validate what they already thought and could help them to access the support that they had felt their child urgently needed. Those who suspected that there was *something wrong*, but did not anticipate being told that their child's differences were attributable to a serious lifelong condition such as autism might find it harder to accept the diagnosis (Moyes 2003). Parents' initial responses can be further determined by how the diagnosis is announced to them. Parents are not always satisfied with the quality of the explanation or the amount of information they are given about the implications of their child's diagnosis and the support that might be available to them (Duprey 2011; Moyes 2003).

Having a child with autism usually means that families will have to go through what could be quite a lengthy period of adjustment while coming to terms with leading a very different type of everyday life (Moyes 2003). Parents have often described how their child's behaviours caused them constant stress and had disruptive effects across virtually every aspect of their lives. This can leave parents feeling 'raw and unprotected' (Peters 2011, p.19) and have a significant impact on what they can and cannot do as families. Parents often find that normal activities such as shopping, days out or having guests visit the home can become daunting. Furthermore, they can find it difficult to find child care that caters for individuals with their child's behavioural needs. Many parents can also experience years of regular sleep loss.

Parents have often commented on how their child's behavioural differences made them feel isolated or stigmatized among other parents and members of the community, as well as their own extended families. Consequently, parents may avoid social and public situations through fear that their child's behaviour would draw negative attention and thus cause them embarrassment. It is also not unusual for parents to go through a period of mourning, for the life that they had been expecting to share with their child. This can add to their sense of isolation further by leading them to avoid having the usual types of conversations that parents have with each other about their children (Moyes 2003).

In the absence of a better explanation for the cause of their child's autism, it is not unusual for parents to blame themselves and feel ashamed or guilty. Being told that their child's condition is lifelong can be hard to contemplate and could cause some parents despair. Understandably, this might take most people a considerable amount of time to come to terms with (Moyes 2003).

In trying to improve their situation, many parents can devote a great deal of their time and energy to gaining information about autism and learning how to adapt their parenting style to help their child (Duprey 2011). This often entails vast amounts of reading, attending courses and working through intensive intervention programmes with their child for a set amount of time each day. Furthermore, many parents have spoken of the emotionally wearing effects of going through constant battles with professionals and services while trying to obtain what they thought to be the right support packages for their child. Disputes like this can be protracted and leave many parents feeling even more isolated and excluded, particularly if they feel that their own knowledge of their child is being ignored (Woodgate *et al.* 2008). At the same time, parents can struggle to find any time for their other children and consequently feel guilty about this (Moyes 2003).

The physical and emotional resources parents need to devote to dealing with all of these issues simultaneously might push any thoughts they have of preparing to share the diagnosis with their child to one side (Duprey 2011). When parents do arrive at a point at which they feel ready enough to start thinking about introducing their child to their diagnosis, they may then debate whether or not it would turn out to be in the child's best interests. It is possible that they could become ambivalent towards progressing any further. Individual parents might believe that their child should be told about their autism while at the same time be concerned that any potential practical benefits of doing this would be outweighed by the possible risks of upsetting, stigmatizing, destabilizing or confusing their child (Duprey 2011).

Progress in this area and a parent's acceptance of a child's diagnosis could actually be delayed during periods when things are going well for an individual. Children's progress can sometimes be misinterpreted as proof that they are starting to leave their autism behind them (Barnes and McCabe 2012). In these circumstances, parents might decide that the child will not need to be told about their autism after all (Jackson 2006). On occasions, well-intentioned school staff can mistakenly contribute to this type of situation while they are trying to reassure parents. This might be through misguided comments which exaggerate the extent to which their child's support needs are diminishing without taking into account autism's lifelong consequences at the same time (Moyes 2003).

In conclusion, parents may need to work through the following processes themselves before they might be ready to consider sharing the diagnosis with their child:

- reaching a reasonable level of acceptance of their child's diagnosis

- obtaining the right support for their child and the rest of the family

- adjusting to the impact of the child's behaviour on everyday family life

- developing an accurate understanding of their own child's autism

- acquiring the skills needed to support their child's needs and manage their behaviour

- reaching the conclusion that it would be in the child's best interests to be told about their diagnosis.

When parents do decide that they and their child are ready for the diagnosis to be shared, they might then need to find a suitably skilled professional to help them with this, or, if this support is unavailable, come up with a suitable way of doing it themselves.

3.3.3 Some ways professionals can help parents

The remainder of this section contains advice for professionals working in schools and services who come into regular contact with parents of children with autism. Having said that, some of this guidance may help parents identify various types of support that they might want to seek out for themselves.

Professionals can offer a great deal of support to parents as they go through the processes of coming to terms with their child's diagnosis, learning enough about their autism and trying to reduce the amount of stress in their daily lives. These things can make big differences in helping parents reach the stage at which they are resolved enough with the diagnosis and have the necessary energy and resources to consider sharing it with their child. The ideas offered below mostly cost very little and require few resources other than time, information and a supportive approach.

It is my belief that fostering trusting relationships that are based upon sharing experiences, information and ideas honestly through genuine two-way communication should be fundamental to all work with parents of children with SEND. Within this framework, professionals should aim to support parents in identifying and appreciating the positive aspects of their child and their differences. It is important to be non-judgemental when discussing the more negative aspects of the child's diagnosis and to regard any issues that arise as being shared challenges which belong equally to the child's school and any other services involved. What is more, attention needs to be given towards finding alternative ways to share information with parents whose work arrangements or other commitments make it harder for them to meet or maintain contact with professionals.

I have found that working with parents in this way can provide vital insight into their home situations, their perspectives of their child's autism, the stresses they might be enduring, the types of help they want or need and what support they are prepared to accept. Hence building trusting relationships can facilitate parents and professionals identifying together any emotional and practical help individual parents might need to help them reach a point at which they are ready to think about passing on the diagnosis to their child.

Helping individual parents to meet others in the same position – for example, by providing details of parent support groups – could offer numerous advantages which might result in lowering their overall stress levels (Moyes 2003; Peters 2011). Meeting parents with similar children and sharing each other's knowledge and experiences can offer parents encouragement, emotional reassurance and hope for the future. Parents in these groups can advise each other and develop friendships. It can also be reassuring to know that they are not struggling alone and that their worries and concerns are genuinely valid. Besides providing incidental opportunities for learning from each other about how to cope with the challenges of their child's autism, some support groups run bespoke programmes of autism training and information workshops that focus specifically on the needs of parents. They often organize family activity days and social events too, where parents do not have to worry about what other people might think about their child's behaviour.

Parents who are not inclined to join large support groups can still be supported on a more informal basis. This could be through introducing them to other parents who have children with autism at their child's school. Many schools have helped parents feel less isolated in the school community by holding autism coffee meetings. On some occasions, specialist professionals have been invited to join them too, thus creating a more relaxed opportunity for parents to meet and discuss things with them.

Parents who do not feel that they have detailed or accurate enough knowledge about their child's autism could become fearful for the future and find it difficult to meet their child's needs (Moyes 2003). Informed professionals can help by sharing key information about autism with parents and signposting them towards appropriate literature, websites and parenting courses. Besides short courses, more in-depth parenting programmes may be available in some areas, such as the National Autistic Society EarlyBird and EarlyBird Plus Programmes in England (further details of these courses can be found at www.autism.org.uk/earlybird). Parents have said that attending lengthier courses like these gave them a clearer understanding of the underlying reasons for their child's behaviour. Some have said that they felt more empowered as their confidence increased in preventing and managing challenging situations both at home and when they were out in public. This in turn can lower parents' stress levels by making their day-to-day lives more manageable and closer to what they had been like before. Not only that, what parents can learn during these courses is likely to benefit them later when they set their mind towards explaining the diagnosis to their child.

Professionals can advise parents about the support available for them and their child in their area and how to access it. However, they will not usually be able to support them directly during any disputes that parents might have with LAs and service providers over their child's provision. In these circumstances, though, professionals could help instead by providing parents with information about local advocacy services. By doing this, parents might then gain access to one-to-one impartial advice and support from a professional such as a parent support advisor (PSA). Having someone alongside them who understands their situation and can offer them appropriate guidance on how to challenge the support system might alleviate some of the additional ongoing stress that parents can experience at such times.

Professionals can also help parents explore the different types of support that they and their child might be able to access from social care services and voluntary organizations. Referrals could be made for children to attend specialist after-school clubs and holiday play schemes. In some cases, children might be offered overnight breaks. This type of provision can create chances for families to do some of the things they might have previously enjoyed doing while knowing that their child is in a safe place and receiving specialized care. Parents could then devote some of this time more specifically to their other children; overnight breaks might also provide opportunities for families to catch up on their sleep. In certain cases, these services might also have the capacity to offer families support with managing the child's behaviour in the home.

Once parents seem to be reaching a reasonable degree of acceptance of their child's autism diagnosis and are coping sufficiently with its day-to-day consequences, professionals can then begin floating the idea of sharing the diagnosis with the child. Some parents might spontaneously decide to tell their child without needing to discuss the matter at all. Others can get stuck at this point, however, while they try to ponder whether it would be in their child's best interests to tell them (Duprey 2011). This might be a good time to meet for a matter-of-fact discussion about the main points raised in

Chapter 2 (as summarized in Tables 2.1, 2.2 and 2.3). Introducing ambivalent parents to other mothers and fathers who have already shared the diagnosis with their child could also be constructive.

Finally, a significant number of children are not diagnosed until they reach their teenage years. An early diagnosis allows parents more time to deal with the other issues that they might need to address more urgently first. The dangers that may be associated with telling children later or them finding out accidentally mean that the prospect of sharing the diagnosis with these children may need to be raised as a priority with their parents far sooner.

In summary, professionals can support parents in reaching a position at which they might be ready to start talking to their child about autism through doing the following:

- fostering and maintaining trusting relationships

- providing information about parent support groups and offering to put them in contact with other parents of children with autism

- sharing their own knowledge of autism and providing them with information about relevant literature, websites and parent training opportunities

- signposting them towards sources of support such as advocacy and social care services

- helping them to weigh up the pros and cons of sharing the diagnosis with their child.

3.4 HOW TO IDENTIFY WHEN THE PROFESSIONALS ARE READY TO TELL THE CHILD

3.4.1 School staff

Any school staff actively contributing to an instance of this work will need to have acquired an accurate enough understanding of autism and how it affects the child with whom they are working. Problems can arise if staff wrongly interpret children's behaviour from a typical perspective or understate the significance of the individual's differences. This can sometimes occur through staff having little specialist knowledge about autism or being genuinely concerned for the child's and their parents' feelings.

Experience has shown how easily a child's needs can be hidden from a less trained eye. A more passive individual's difficulties with interacting socially can be camouflaged to some extent by the presence of a supportive peer group who go out of their way to help the child and include them in their play activities. Children who can talk exhaustively about certain subjects might wrongly be thought of as having excellent communication skills. If a child's differences become less obvious over time, adults could even conclude that the individual's autism is regressing or has gone away (Barnes and McCabe 2012).

An important part of being ready to participate in this work must therefore be that the relevant school staff are able to recognize, agree upon and accept the child's autism-related differences. Staff members will also need to feel comfortable enough to discuss these openly with the child and their parents. This is important because if children are to gain anything from this work, then they must be made aware of their challenges and their support needs, even if there is a chance that they might find some of this information upsetting (Jones 2001). Differences in flexibility of thought mean that once children have been led to believe something about their autism is true, it may be very hard to teach them otherwise later.

School staff will also need to be aware and accepting of the potential issues that could arise as consequences of this work. Before commencing, they will need to have drawn up contingency plans for supporting the child in case they have a negative emotional reaction to being given the diagnosis.

Situations where school staff decide that they are not suitably prepared for being involved in sharing the child's diagnosis might necessitate delaying the work until they have undertaken further autism training or sought specialist advice.

3.4.2 Specialist professionals

Working with a large number of children has taught me how each instance of sharing a child's diagnosis needs to be regarded as a unique event and, as such, be prepared for in isolation. For external professionals to be ready to lead or contribute to this work, they will need to develop ample familiarity with the child and their circumstances first, during the pre-programme work. Despite any specialist knowledge of autism that they may already have, they will need to be fully aware of each child's own unique manifestation of autism and their personal learning preferences. To reach an appropriate stage of readiness, they will have to have first taken enough time to meet and get to know the child, their parents and school staff as well as gather all the types of information that are identified in 3.6.

3.5 DECIDING WHO SHOULD LEAD THE WORK AND WHO ELSE MIGHT NEED TO BE INVOLVED

3.5.1 Who should lead the work?

All About Me could possibly be led by a child's parents, a suitably qualified member of staff at their school or another qualified professional. Despite this, little is known about which adults do tend to lead autism disclosure work with children. Moreover, research provides no indication of how variations in the background of that person might affect its outcomes.

Many parents decide to tell their children themselves, however. Some may regard this as being part of their overall parenting responsibility and may not look elsewhere for support. In other cases, this may be because of a lack of specialist support in their local area or due to delays in accessing it at the time of need (Whitaker 2006). Decisions on who might lead this work are perhaps best taken on a case-by-case basis according to a child's circumstances and those of the surrounding adults. This may ultimately be determined by who is available at the time.

A few points need to be reiterated and reflected upon briefly at this point. Understanding something as complex as autism and then explaining it to a child with a diagnosis is not easy, nor is it free from risks. As such, teaching children about their diagnosis can be very intricate and stressful work (Jones 2001; Miller 2015; Vermeulen 2013; Whitaker 2006). To complicate matters further, children with autism are all very different from one another (Jones 2002). Importantly too, the subsequent processes children may go through while learning to understand and accept their diagnosis can extend over very long periods of time (Jones 2001; Punshon *et al.* 2009; Vermeulen 2013; Whitaker 2006).

In allowing for the above issues, I have discovered over time that anyone planning to lead a specific instance of *All About Me* is most likely to succeed when they possess all the qualities listed in the following person specification:

- an ability to regulate and disguise their own anxieties about the work so that these are not transferred on to the child

- an adequate understanding of autism's main characteristics

- sufficient familiarity with the child and knowledge of their unique manifestation of autism

- an understanding of the child's learning preferences

- a clear understanding of the programme framework and how to work through each of its stages to disclose and explain the child's diagnosis (as described in Chapters 4–6)

- the specific skills needed to differentiate and teach the programme to that child

- the ability to meet any challenges presented by the child's behaviour with confidence

- being accessible to the child for an extended period afterwards.

This book intends to help suitably qualified professionals and parents to arrive at a point where they might be able to meet most of the above criteria regardless of their current role in a child's life. It must be accepted, however, that this will not be possible in every single case and specialist support may still be needed anyway. Even after reading this book, parents and mainstream school staff may still feel that they do not have sufficient skills and confidence to carry out this programme themselves with certain children. I have worked with various children in mainstream schools, for example, whose successful participation in *All About Me* was only achieved by applying a range of specialized structured teaching and behaviour management techniques.

In other instances, parents may want their child to be told but might be concerned about how either they themselves or their child could react emotionally (Beadle 2011; Jackson 2006; Miller 2015). It may be preferable in these situations for someone outside the child's family to lead the work with the child (Pike 2008), while Whitaker (2006) advises that there might be more of a case for specialist professionals telling adolescents since there could be a greater risk of them experiencing an angry backlash.

I have been able to support many parents and schools by leading this work with children, but, like many specialist professionals, having a large caseload restricted what I was then available to do for individual children or their families and schools afterwards. This problem was solved, to a great extent, through adopting an apprenticeship approach. This involved at least one of the child's parents attending the three sessions so that they were aware of what their child was being taught and how this information was presented to them. I was then able to hand over the responsibility for continuing the work to the child's parents at the end of the programme.

The sensitivity and importance of this work and its associated risks have led me to conclude that anyone leading it in a professional capacity should be suitably qualified as a teacher, psychologist, therapist or similar. Parents place a great deal of trust in a person telling their child about their autism, so meeting this responsibility properly always requires detailed and well-researched planning, skilled teaching and professional accountability. Therefore, there is an argument for saying that this work falls outside of the remit of support staff such as teaching assistants (TAs), regardless of their experience and knowledge of autism or the child involved. However, this does not mean that support staff cannot make other significant contributions to this work.

3.5.2 Which other adults might be involved, and how can they help?

In common with other children with SEND, those with autism are usually supported at home, school and elsewhere by a variety of different adults. It would be impractical for all these people to attend the programme sessions. However, each member of a team around a child can make their own valuable contributions to making this work successful. They can do this first through exchanging information about the child with those planning to lead the work and then through helping the child to accept and make sense of their diagnosis on an ad hoc basis after the programme has been completed. Different people will have their own perspectives to share on an individual child, their autism, how it manifests in different contexts and how to meet their needs. They might all need to answer sensitive questions or discuss any concerns that the child might approach them with about their autism later.

Everyone in this team should be consulted directly where possible when deciding how the child's diagnosis will be presented and explained to them. On a practical basis, however, this is not always possible, so information may sometimes need to be exchanged via a single point of contact, such as the SENCo in the child's school.

Decisions on who should attend the work sessions may depend upon which person leads the work and where it will take place. If parents decide to tell their child themselves, then the work might just involve them sitting down together at home. It might be helpful nonetheless to create opportunities afterwards for the child to share their *All About Me* booklet separately at school or elsewhere with other significant adults in their lives such as their teachers, TAs, therapists, childminders and other adult relatives.

If someone else leads the work, it seems vital that at least one of the child's parents is present. By being there, they can offer emotional support to their child and be aware of what the child is told about their autism as well as how the individual responds to it. This will help them to support their child at home afterwards. The possibility that children will find this work emotionally upsetting also means that there are sound ethical reasons for parents being present. Their cognitive and communication differences create complications concerning children with autism giving informed consent or communicating its withdrawal. Therefore a parent being there could do this on their child's behalf if the individual needs a cessation in the work (Miller 2014).

It is recommended that the number of adults sitting in on each of the work sessions is kept to an absolute minimum. However, this work should never be carried out in situations where the child is left working alone with an unfamiliar adult. In the first two sessions of my own work, the group has been strictly limited to the child, their parents and me as an outside professional. The most sensitive work is carried out in these two sessions. It involves discussing the child's challenges with them, disclosing their diagnosis and then managing their reaction to finding out that they have autism while at the same time explaining its potential implications. The intention should therefore be to create as intimate and relaxed an atmosphere as possible. This should take into account the innate anxieties children with autism often endure when they are in the presence of other people. Furthermore, having fewer adults present limits the number of people speaking to the child, which is essential given the receptive language differences associated with autism and the confusion and anxieties these can create (Wing 2002).

The number of people present can be opened up slightly in the third session according to individual children's wishes and what they can realistically manage. No new work is presented at this point. This is a summary session during which the child's *All About Me* booklet is read through, discussed and reviewed. A member of the school's staff, who is close to the child and trusted by them, should usually be invited to attend this session as part of the process of bringing the school back into the work as it is taken forward. Children's siblings can join on occasions when it is thought appropriate. Again, wherever the work has taken place, arrangements have often been made for children to share their completed booklet afterwards with the other familiar adults living and working with them.

It is important that a summary of what occurs during each of the sessions is fed back to the adults who are not present, directly or via the child's SENCo. This should outline the child's responses and reactions to the work, any issues that occurred and how all of this might affect what needs to be done to support the individual next. Finally, before signing off an instance of this work, I have always provided parents and school staff with copies of the child's *All About Me* booklet. Adults are advised on how to use the booklet as a reference for themselves and as an ongoing support tool for the child in the ways described in Chapter 8. The information contained in a child's booklet provides the adults with a precise record of everything that the individual was told about their autism and how this was explained to them.

3.6 GATHERING AND SHARING ESSENTIAL INFORMATION ABOUT THE CHILD

3.6.1 Introduction

Every instance of *All About Me* has not only had to be taught differently, but has also turned out to be a unique event. Therefore, as proposed earlier, having a good general understanding of autism and previous experience of delivering this programme successfully to other children is unlikely to be enough to qualify someone to lead this work with further individuals unless they know them well enough. Also, the decisions that parents and other professionals need to reach on whether children should participate in this programme cannot be taken without them first fully considering the individual's circumstances and what the work might involve. Time needs taking during the pre-programme work to enable all the adults concerned to establish a detailed all-round picture of the child as an individual and how their autism affects them. This section therefore identifies the types of information that parents and professionals may need to collect and use before the programme starts for each of the following purposes:

- reaching an informed decision on whether the child is ready to be told about their diagnosis

- deciding whether this programme is suitable for the child

- identifying any other work that may need to be done first if it is decided that the child is not ready to take part in the programme

- differentiating and personalizing the programme delivery methods and its supporting resources to cater for the child's unique strengths, differences and needs.

The final part of this section offers some practical advice on how to gather the types of information that are described next in an efficient way.

3.6.2 What adults might need to know about the child

It is perhaps important to start off by trying to establish what a child already appears to know about their own differences and challenges before deciding whether to embark on this work. Knowing what questions or concerns an individual might already have voiced to the people around them about their situation may give an indication as to whether the child is ready to be told about their diagnosis and can also offer adults ways into the work. This information can be used to give children valid reasons for participating in the programme in the first place. It could also prove useful when the adults are trying to come up with a tangible way of describing what having autism means to the child (see 3.10). Having prior knowledge of how an individual feels about being different and whether there are any specific issues that they find upsetting to talk about can alert the adults to the possibility that a child could be likely to find learning about their challenges and being told about their diagnosis distressing. Contingency strategies can then be drawn up for managing any upset both during and after the sessions. Moreover, as stated earlier, a child appearing to know very little about being different could also signify that they might not be ready to be told about their diagnosis until after some preparatory work on developing their self-awareness has been undertaken (as described in Chapter 5).

The first session in *All About Me* involves helping children to draw up lists of their own personal traits, strengths and challenges. This part of the work is essential for explaining their diagnosis later, but can be disrupted if the child is unable to make many of their own contributions to these lists. Collecting information about children's attributes beforehand allows back-up lists to be drawn up by the adults which they can then refer to themselves to prompt the child during the session (see Chapter 5).

Planning this work also requires having insight into the child's special interests, hobbies and preferred items. Pictures and text related to these are normally included in children's booklets to add meaning to the work and make it more appealing to the child. Where necessary and practical, controlled access to children's favourite objects and activities can be planned into the sessions to motivate and reward individuals whose behaviour might otherwise prevent them from participating in the sessions (see 7.2). Moreover, as explained below (in 3.9), it is essential to know what the child's favourite activities are and when these usually happen, so that arrangements can be made to avoid sessions clashing with them.

Anyone leading this initiative will also need to have adequate knowledge and understanding of the effects of the child's sensory and perceptual differences. These are likely to be different in virtually every case (Bogdashina 2003). The child's own sensory irregularities will need to be explained to them as part of the programme. Knowledge of these issues will be vital when trying to identify and set up a suitably calm and structured environment for the work to take place in (see 3.8). Any sensory-seeking behaviours which could impact on a child's concentration and engagement in the work will also need to be identified and understood. This is so that controlled access to the relevant stimuli and equipment can be planned into the structure of the session as appropriate and when reasonable (as advised in 7.3).

Guidance is given later (in 7.2) on various ways that the generic programme and the supporting resources can be differentiated and personalized to cater for the needs of individuals who are working at different developmental levels in cognition, communication and literacy. This includes advice on how to choose the correct level booklet template and make further adjustments to its language, content and format so that the child will find it accessible and engaging. The template and the subsequent booklet are the main tools for working through and following up the programme. It is therefore important to customize the template before the sessions based on accurate knowledge of the child's reading accuracy and comprehension level. Information will be needed about the types of language and the formatting used in the books that the child understands best and prefers reading.

Successful completion of the programme is largely reliant upon children being able to answer questions about themselves and understand the verbal account of their autism. Those leading the work will need to be aware of the types and level of verbal language the child uses and responds to best, before deciding if the work can be differentiated sufficiently to enable their participation. The programme uses abstract language and concepts to describe children's personal traits. For some children, it might be necessary to pre-teach some of the vocabulary that they will need to understand and use during the first session (as advised in Chapter 5). Knowing how literally the child thinks will also help when deciding upon the amount of information the child will be given about their autism and how concrete this will need to be. It would also be useful to know what questioning techniques work best with the child so that these can be planned into the work. Some children, for example, may be able to answer open-ended questions more easily, whereas many others might need to be given a series of closed questions and offered choices of possible answers or asked to complete partial sentences instead.

Anyone carrying out this work will need to understand any emotional and behavioural issues that could disrupt a child's participation in the programme. Awareness of children's distractibility and how long they can remain calm for and engage with an adult agenda allows for adjustments to be made to the learning environment as well as the length and structure of the sessions. This information will help to determine which additional resources may need to be brought to the sessions, such as timers, rule prompts, reward charts and items that the child might find rewarding (see 7.2). It is also important to identify any challenging behaviours that may need to be managed in the sessions. If there are concerns that a child might try to use their diagnosis to excuse certain types of behaviour, this can be addressed in the programme by including relevant advice into their booklet (as advised in 6.3.2).

Children with autism have a strong need to know what is going to happen next and can have problems understanding how events are sequenced and time is organized. Consequently, they can become highly anxious when they are placed in unfamiliar situations, such as participating in this programme, particularly if there is a lack of a sense of predictability (Mesibov, Shea and Schopler 2004; Whitaker 2001). For this reason, as described in Chapter 5, each child is provided with both a visual guide detailing what the whole programme entails and individual schedules showing the sequences of steps they need to work through to complete each of the three sessions. The visual processing preferences and reading comprehension skills of children with autism can vary significantly from one individual to another, however. It is essential therefore that personalized adjustments are made to these resources so that each child can make sense of the information more easily if they need to be shown this while they are feeling anxious or distressed. For some children, this may mean using fewer written words as well as augmenting them with symbols or pictures. Others may prefer to work through schedules that are presented as written lists (Mesibov and Howley 2003). It is important therefore to try to establish beforehand what types of visual timetables and schedules are already being used with a child at their school and elsewhere, as well as assessing how effectively the individual is able to access them in their current formats. Where there is any uncertainty about the child's preferred visual medium, adults may need to consult with the child's speech and language therapist or another relevant professional specializing in autism.

It should be stressed that whoever leads this work should make every effort to try to acquire insight into the main strategies and resources that are being used to support the child successfully at home, school and elsewhere. When considered appropriate to this work, their use should be planned into the programme.

In summary, it is recommended that adults involved in leading or making decisions related to an instance of *All About Me* should first set out to obtain and collate comprehensive knowledge of the child in the areas listed below:

- the child's awareness of their differences and challenges and how they feel about them

- any sensitive subjects which could cause the child to feel distressed if they are discussed

- the child's personality traits and strengths, and things that they find harder than typical children

- the child's interests, preferred activities and favourite objects

- the effects of the child's sensory processing differences

- the child's learning preferences and the developmental levels at which they are operating

- how the child uses and responds to verbal and written communication and language

- any challenges presented by the child's behaviour and how these are usually managed

- the types of visual schedules and timetables that the child can make sense of most easily if they are feeling anxious or distressed

- key strategies and resources that are already being used successfully to support the child at home, school and elsewhere.

All the above information about the child also needs to be considered in the context of everyone having an overall understanding of what the programme involves.

3.6.3 Gathering and sharing the information

I have usually found that by asking the right questions, the kinds of information described above can be obtained through doing the following:

- observing and meeting with the child

- holding joint discussions with the child's parents, relevant school staff and other available professionals

- referring to reports by therapists, psychologists or other specialists who have recently worked with the child

- reading the child's current behaviour support and individual education plans.

The amount of new information that needs to be gathered by the person leading the work will depend upon their existing relationship with the child, how well they know the individual and what discussions they might have had previously with the other adults.

External professionals have not always met a child before and could often be starting this process from scratch. Professionals with large caseloads might be limited in their availability for attending meetings with the various people who have the knowledge they require and with whom they will need to share information about the programme. In my own case, this usually had to be accomplished in just one or two preliminary visits to a child's school. To address this problem, the pre-programme questionnaires included in the electronic resources (A1 and A2) were devised to maximize the amount of relevant information that could be gathered in whatever time was available respectively for the meetings with children and the other adults. Detailed instructions for using these forms are given later (in 9.2), but, briefly, each one contains an ordered series of questions that can be used to initiate focused discussions about each of the key areas identified above. At the same time, sharing printed examples of *All About Me* booklets, from the electronic resources (Section B), has made it possible to explain the programme more precisely to the other adults.

Although the main decisions about this work are usually taken in the meetings between parents and professionals, it is essential that the person leading the work observes and meets with the child first. Structured conversations using the child questionnaire have proved valuable for initiating rapport with children and gaining first-hand insights into how they perceive their own lives. These meetings can also offer informal opportunities for assessing the approximate developmental levels children are operating at, their communication skills and their behaviour as learners. Furthermore, this could enable the person who might go on to lead the work to explore what types of prompting the child may need in order to make their own contributions to the sessions. However, meeting an unfamiliar adult can be stressful for any child, and therefore an adult who the child knows well should also attend. This person should be briefed on the purpose of the meeting and the importance of them not prompting the child, speaking for them or attempting to correct anything that they say. Inaccuracies in the child's responses can be discussed with that person after the meeting.

3.7 CRITERIA FOR DECIDING WHETHER *ALL ABOUT ME* WOULD BE SUITABLE FOR A CHILD

In short, children usually participate in *All About Me* when their parents and the relevant professionals agree that the individual is ready to be told about their diagnosis, that they will be able to access the work and that introducing the child to their autism is more likely to improve their everyday life than cause them any significant emotional harm.

Although *All About Me* has been used successfully with many children, like any other initiative it should not be regarded as a generic programme that will benefit, or be needed by, every single child on the autism spectrum. For this reason, a set of inclusion criteria have been developed to guide adults towards making informed decisions about the suitability of this work for individual children. These criteria are presented in Table 3.1 and are based on my own past experiences as well as other practitioners' views (e.g. Fidler 2004; Vermeulen; 2013; Whitaker 2006). The information in this table should always be considered in conjunction with knowledge of the child concerned and an overall understanding of what the programme itself involves and how it can be differentiated.

Provided they already had a formal diagnosis and their parents had consented to the work, efforts have been made to try to find ways to include every child who has been referred for *All About Me*, even if at first glance their behaviour or their levels of communication and cognition appeared to indicate that they might not have met some of the essential criteria.

It has proved possible to differentiate the overall programme structure to an extent that would enable some individuals to complete all the work even though in normal circumstances their behaviour and distractibility made it harder for them to follow adult-led agendas for more than a few minutes at a time. Chapter 7 includes a description of how this can be achieved and also advises on how the complexity of the verbal and written language used to deliver the programme and characterize autism can be modified, reduced and augmented to make the work less cognitively demanding and more accessible for children who are operating at more literal developmental levels. However, the successful use of all these support strategies will depend very much on the expertise, training and knowledge of the person leading the work.

Decisions not to include a child should never be considered permanent. When it is judged that a child is not ready for the work, further discussions ought to be held between parents and professionals to explore ways of helping to move the individual forward. For example, as already stated in 3.2, if a child seems to have more limited self-awareness, the adults living and working with them could carry out some of the preparatory activities suggested at various points in Chapter 5 for broadening children's knowledge of their personal attributes.

Following Lorna Wing's advice (2002), children who have already found out about their autism elsewhere, but are too angry to discuss it further, should be given an appropriate cooling-off period before any attempt is made to try to engage them in this type of work. In the meantime, they can be told about the programme's existence and be offered an open invitation to participate in it later once they feel ready to find out more about autism. As advised earlier, a temporary delay in disclosing the diagnosis should be seriously contemplated if the work would otherwise coincide with an individual going through a particularly stressful phase.

Table 3.1: Inclusion criteria for the *All About Me* programme

Children are likely to be included in *All About Me* when:	Children might not be included in *All About Me* if:
• their parents feel ready and consent • the child can engage in the sessions and share attention with the lead person for the required amount of time (with appropriate visual, environmental or motivational support) • the child has developed the cognitive and communication skills needed to understand and discuss the concepts used in this programme to describe themselves and autism • the child has developed the literacy skills needed to read and understand the content of their *All About Me* booklet (with appropriate symbolic support and/ or reduced language) • the child is developing an awareness of their own personal attributes, those of others and how all people differ • it is felt that knowing about their autism would improve the child's everyday life.	• the child has not been formally diagnosed • the diagnosis is under question or is about to be reassessed • the child, their parents and the person leading the work are not all fully ready (in which case it should be deferred until they are) • the child is not questioning or raising concerns about their differences while presenting as being generally contented (however, the potential threat of accidental disclosure or negative responses to late disclosure *must* be considered) • the child is aware of their autism diagnosis but appears to be in denial/unwilling to talk about it (in which case they are informed that they can access the work when they feel ready) • the child is going through a period of emotional turmoil and it is thought that finding out about the diagnosis would make things worse (again the potential costs of accidental or late disclosure *must* be considered) • the child already has an adequate understanding and acceptance of their autism.

Source: based on Miller, 2014, 2015

3.8 DECIDING WHERE THE WORK SHOULD TAKE PLACE: IDENTIFYING AND PREPARING THE RIGHT ENVIRONMENT

Children with autism are likely to remain calmer and productive for longer periods in structured, low-arousal working environments (Jones *et al.* 2008;

Mesibov *et al.* 2004). It is important to apply this advice to *All About Me*, given the length of each session and this work's potential for causing children to feel anxious. The diversity of children with autism does mean, however, that each child will have their own individual environmental requirements (Bogdashina 2003) which adults involved in this work will need to be aware of.

In many cases, schools and parents will have already identified working areas that individual children with autism function well in and are using successfully. Some parents may have created work stations for their children at home, but, by their nature, home environments are generally not well matched to the demands of formally teaching children with autism. A child's home might offer a secure and familiar environment in which to introduce them to their autism, but it is also likely to provide them with easy access to many of their preferred objects and so can be full of distractions. Flexibility issues also mean that some children might stubbornly resist the idea of their home being used as a teaching and learning environment. In such situations, parents planning to lead this work themselves may need to think about doing it elsewhere.

In my experience, schools invariably do their best to try to allocate suitable areas for this work, but shortages of available learning spaces may mean that it will have to be carried out in less than ideal conditions. In many instances, the adult leading the work may need to make some creative temporary adjustments to the proposed work environment, wherever it is located. To avoid confusing the child, these modifications are best done before the individual enters the room.

On a purely practical level, whether teaching *All About Me* in the child's home, school or elsewhere, the room that is used will need to accommodate the child and all the participating adults comfortably. Each person will need an appropriately sized chair and enough personal space. Moreover, the work carried out in the first two sessions requires that everyone attending can view the same computer screen. There will need to be at least one table, which can be placed close enough to an electrical socket. Enough clutter-free table space will be needed for all the other resources that might be required to support the work. This is likely to include things like the child's visual schedule, rule cards and other prompts. Difficulties can occur when the work is carried out in cramped conditions, with inappropriate furniture, such as armchairs or swivel seats, and limited table space. Furthermore, some children may be using alternative types of seating at school to meet some of their sensory needs and this should be available to help them work calmly during the sessions.

The privacy of the work space is also important. The confidential and sensitive nature of this work can be compromised and children may become anxious if others are able to see or hear what is happening inside the room and if people enter the room to do their own work or retrieve property. Therefore, if this work needs to be carried out in a school or another public building, arrangements need to be made to secure the exclusive use of a suitably private room which has a door that can be closed. This work should never be carried out in corridors or open-plan areas. Where blinds or curtains are not available, it may be necessary to place large sheets of paper over windows if a child is likely to raise concerns about being seen by other people. If the work is taking place at the child's home, parents should consider doing this when siblings and other family members are not around.

Due regard needs to be given to any sensory processing differences which might cause particular children with autism to become excited, distressed or distracted. The nature of autism means that these issues are going to be different for everyone (Bogdashina 2003; Jones *et al.* 2008). This means that the work having gone well with one child in one place does not guarantee that the same environment will be equally supportive of others with autism. Consequently, different adjustments may need to be made to the layout of a workroom; if this is inadequate, a change of room will need to be contemplated.

In an ideal situation, this work would perhaps take place in a sound-proofed room where the visual and physical environment only contains the essential furniture and resources needed for the work itself, where blank walls are painted in neutral colours, and where windows allow in enough natural light yet cannot be seen through. Such an environment is highly unlikely to be found in any home or in most mainstream school settings.

Children with autism can find it harder to work in rooms that are normally used as office spaces, resources areas or group teaching areas. Typical children might have the flexibility needed to learn in these types of places, but the number of items they can contain might be over-stimulating and create too many distractions for children with autism, who find it harder to filter out irrelevant sensory input and so can have a fragmented and disordered view of the world. This makes it difficult for them to make sense of their surroundings and can cause them to become distressed and overwhelmed in regular environments (Bogdashina 2003; Frith 2003). Lawson (2011) also describes how hard it can be for people with autism to direct their attention away from things that they find interesting and how they can become totally fixated on particular environmental stimuli. Consequently, children could be distracted by items that they come across such as educational toys and games, interesting wall displays or things that they can see happening outside through a window. It is not always easy for these children to switch their attention back to their work. Children with visual sensory irregularities can become excited or distressed by effects caused by both artificial lighting and the sun shining through a window.

In the above circumstances, if no other room is available, it may be necessary to temporarily remove certain items from it before the session or to rearrange things within the room so that they cannot visually distract the child. This may involve shifting furniture or placing drapes over displays and shelves. Of course, when working at home, children will know where all their preferred items and activities can be found. So, to encourage some children to participate in the programme, both at home and elsewhere, it may need to be communicated clearly through their work schedules what they will need to do first before they can have controlled access to any of these things.

Some children's auditory hypersensitivities may cause them to become aroused and distracted by certain sounds that typical people would not necessarily notice or be bothered by. This could include telephones ringing in offices and clocks ticking or the effects of an echo within a room. Again, things occurring outside the room such as music lessons or children doing outdoor sports activities also need to be considered. Although it might be difficult to remove many of these sounds from the environment, and a quieter room might not be available, clocks can be removed and telephones in the room can be disconnected for the duration of a session. The sessions could be timed not to coincide with noisier lessons and activities taking place elsewhere. Parents doing the work at home will need to ensure that fun activities and things such as televisions and games consoles cannot be heard from other rooms in the house. If anyone else is in the house at the time, they should be reminded not to use domestic appliances.

Besides the visual and auditory environment, any hypersensitivities a child may have to certain smells as well as the temperature and ventilation in the room need to be taken into consideration. Scott (2009, p.36) advises that having 'knowledge and understanding of how they experience the environment and the objects within it' is essential to designing appropriate work areas for children with autism. The adults who live and work alongside children with autism may not always be able to detect sensory stimuli that might concern some individuals. This being the case, it seems sensible that wherever possible the child is consulted over where the work should take place and that they are introduced to the proposed work area for some other purpose on a trial basis beforehand to assess how well they respond within it. Doing so will also help to develop the child's familiarity with working in that space. A further advantage of this would be that when it comes to participating in *All About Me*, the child might feel somewhat calmer since going into that room to work would involve one fewer new experience for them.

In conclusion, the following factors should be considered along with the differences in the child's sensory profile and their other needs when identifying and setting up an appropriate space for the work to take place in:

- the privacy of the room

- having an adequate amount of space

- the suitability of the furniture

- the auditory and visual environment

- the temperature, any odours and the amount of ventilation in the room.

3.9 DECIDING WHEN THE WORK SHOULD TAKE PLACE: CHOOSING THE RIGHT TIME FOR THE SESSIONS

Prior liaison with staff, children and parents over the scheduling of the session times is vital when carrying this work out in schools. Failure to do this or sudden unannounced changes to children's timetables can lead to sessions coinciding with one of the child's few preferred activities. It can be extremely difficult to engage children in *All About Me* if they are withdrawn to do this work in these circumstances. Any anger or frustration this could cause would detract from this sensitive and life-defining work (Miller 2014). *All About Me* intends to introduce children to their diagnosis positively and so should never be associated with unnecessary emotional upset or a sense of disappointment.

On occasions, compromises can be agreed with children which lead to them agreeing to participate in the missed activity at a different time, but this may not always be possible. Sessions have had to be postponed at the last minute and rearranged. Parents' work commitments and the limited availability of professionals may create problems in rescheduling appointments quickly and this can have an adverse effect on maintaining the programme's continuity. In normal circumstances, this programme seems to run best when the three sessions are spaced approximately one week apart.

Parents carrying out the work at home are advised to be similarly mindful of potential clashes with a child's favourite television programmes or other things that they would normally enjoy doing at the time.

Some children can be resistant to doing this work at any time during the school day. They might be anxious that missing even one lesson will have a serious impact on their educational progress. Others, who already know that they have autism, may be convinced that the other children in their class would somehow know why they had left the room and what was being discussed even though no one has told them. If the child is willing, this may be resolved by arranging for the sessions to take place after the other children have left the premises at the end of the school day, or by moving the work to another venue such as a support service office or the child's home.

When scheduling the work, attention also needs to be paid to what the child might be doing after the session has ended. Issues can come up, for example, if a child is anxious about one of their lessons that is timetabled to occur later in the day. People with autism tend to have single fixed attention and so can be completely preoccupied by thoughts related to things that are worrying them. They often struggle to shift their attention away from their concerns and on to other things (Lawson 2011). For this reason too, adults may need to be prepared to cancel and reschedule sessions at short notice if something has already happened that day which badly upset the child.

Unsurprisingly, children seem to be more motivated to participate in this programme when they know that they are not missing the activities which they find enjoyable and do well in. Finally, children should always be given adequate notice and reminders of when the work is going to take place to avoid them becoming upset by an unannounced change.

3.10 DECIDING HOW TO PRESENT THE WORK TO THE CHILD

Anyone deciding to proceed with this work needs to give the child an honest and plausible reason for attending the sessions. Not doing this might make it difficult to engage some children as they may not see any point behind doing the work. Children who already know that they have autism can simply be told that they are going to be learning more about it. Children who do not know about their diagnosis will need to be given a satisfactory reason which does not include any mention of the word 'autism'.

Children have usually accepted having to do this work when they were provided with reasons that were tangible to their situation at the time. Links can be made to questions or concerns that individual children have already raised themselves by telling them, for example, 'We are going to make a booklet which will help you to understand why it's harder for you to make friends.' Some children do not mention or query their differences spontaneously (Whitaker 2006), so in these circumstances adults could link the explanation for doing this work to the child's additional support. Children have been told, for example, that their booklet would tell them why they need to have help from a TA. The reason for this work could also be associated with children coincidentally moving on to secondary school. They might be told that they are going to make a booklet to help the staff there get to know them.

3.11 CONCLUSION

This chapter has explored the practical questions and issues that usually need to be attended to during the pre-programme work. It is recommended that once readers have worked through this stage, they stop to consider each of the questions listed below on the basis of the guidance provided in this chapter.

- Is there sufficient evidence that the child you know is ready and needs to be told about their autism?

- Are the child's parents ready to share the diagnosis with their daughter or son?

- Are all the professionals who might need to play an active role in planning, teaching or supporting this work sufficiently familiar with the child and ready to do this?

- Has a suitable person been chosen to lead this work and have they reached the stage at which they are ready to carry out this responsibility?

- Have the roles of other adults supporting this work been identified and agreed upon?

- Has all the necessary information about the child been gathered and collated?

- Based on the programme's inclusion criteria and knowledge of the child, is *All About Me* a suitable programme for the child? (This decision should be regarded as being tentative until after considering details of what the programme entails in Chapters 5–7.)

- Has an environment been selected which meets the conditions necessary for this work to be undertaken successfully with the child?

- Have the child's most and least preferred times for doing this work been established?

- If the child does not already know about their autism, have the adults come up with a plausible reason that they can be given for doing this work?

Ideally, parents and the other adults should be able to respond positively to each of these questions before deciding whether to progress on to the planning and teaching phases of this work.

This concludes Part I of this book. Attention now focuses on the programme itself and how to teach *All About Me*. The next three chapters provide a detailed generic description of the programme and what it entails. This is followed up in Chapter 7 by examining how specific information collected about individual children during the pre-programme work can be used to personalize each aspect of *All About Me* and make it accessible to children with very diverse differences and needs.

Part II

TEACHING AND FOLLOWING UP
ALL ABOUT ME

Chapter 4

AN OVERVIEW OF THE PROGRAMME'S TEACHING METHODS, CONTENT AND FRAMEWORK

4.1 INTRODUCTION

This chapter is organized into two main sections which summarize how the programme introduces children to their diagnosis, what it teaches them about their autism and the stages that need to be worked through to do this successfully.

The first of these sections (4.2) provides an overview of the programme's design and its principal methods for sharing the diagnosis with children while also explaining the rationale behind their choice. It begins by describing how the programme uses an exploration of the child's personal attributes to create the context for disclosing and explaining their diagnosis. Issues also considered are other ways to present autism to children on the spectrum, what types of language should be used and the programme's preferred teaching approaches. The section ends with an explanation of the main method for delivering and following up the programme, which is the joint production of the booklet containing the personalized narrative about the child and their autism.

The second section (4.3) provides a brief description of what children are usually taught during each stage of *All About Me* and provides a structured framework for others to follow later when they are teaching it. This is a shorter section that is intended to provide an overview of what should be taught while working through the teaching instructions and processes detailed in Chapters 5 and 6.

4.2 THE PROGRAMME'S DESIGN AND TEACHING METHODS

4.2.1 Exploring the child's attributes to create a positive context for disclosing and explaining their diagnosis

Autistic ways of thinking and behaving can create significant barriers to children being able to participate in and understand this type of work. Pragmatic language differences mean that, to varying degrees, children with autism tend to interpret things literally (Frith 2003; Wing 2002). They are all likely therefore to find the abstract language and concepts that are generally used to define and describe autism confusing. Furthermore, as noted in Chapter 2, those who do gain a clear enough understanding of their autism could initially find its disclosure destabilizing and upsetting, especially if it is presented to them as being a series of deficits. The design of any programme for teaching children about their autism therefore needs to accommodate the group and individual cognitive, communicative and emotional differences inherent in autism. Furthermore, it should aim to support children over time in learning to cope with their differences, develop a positive self-image and reach a manageable level of acceptance of their diagnosis (Vermeulen 2013).

There seems to be a consensus among various theoreticians, practitioners and individuals who have autism that, in order to achieve this, the explanation of a child's diagnosis should be framed positively within the overall context of who they are as a person. This should place strong emphasis upon things such as the child's positive personal qualities, strengths and challenges (e.g. Attwood 2006, 2008; Beadle 2011; Fidler 2004; Fletcher 2013; Gray 1996; Paul 2011; Vermeulen 2013; Welton 2004a, 2004b; Whitaker 2006). Therefore, *All About Me* uses a *personal attributes* method for teaching children about their autism. This approach is supported by the teaching framework, described later.

This method of disclosure involves helping children to explore and discover key information about themselves as unique individuals first before making any attempt tell to them about their autism. This is done by guiding children through the self-assessment processes described more fully in Chapter 5. Each child is supported in exploring who they are through drawing up separate lists of their own personal characteristics and areas of strength, as well as the main situations and activities that they find more challenging than most children of the same age (e.g. finding someone to play with).

Successful outcomes to the programme will depend upon devoting enough time to work through these stages of the programme thoroughly before moving on to use what is learned there to tell the child about their diagnosis. The order in which this is carried out is highly important. In the interests of enhancing the child's self-esteem, the things that they find challenging should only be raised with them after their positive personal traits and areas of strength have been identified and affirmed. This is reflected below in the ordering of the programme framework.

Adults leading this work should next use the lists of the child's attributes to help the individual reach and record an overall conclusion about themselves in each of the three areas noted above, such as:

- 'I am a good person who is loved by my family.'

- 'I am good at doing certain things on my own like using computers and electronic gadgets.'

- 'I can find it harder to work and play with other children.'

These summaries ought collectively to provide the key types of information that will be needed for composing a simple and precise personalized headline explanation of their autism that the child can be given later to contextualize their diagnosis. Taking the example summaries of a child's attributes given above, the headline definition of autism given in a booklet made for an individual with similar attributes might state that 'Having autism describes a person like me who is good at using things like electronic gadgets and can find it harder to work and play with other children.'

This approach allows for the child's autism to be explained to them primarily in more tangible and, arguably, less confusing terms, as simply being a word that can be used to describe a kind of person who could happen to have similar patterns of strengths and differences to theirs. This attribute-based method has usually allowed children to be given their diagnosis and have it explained to them meaningfully in a positive, calm and matter-of-fact way (Miller 2014, 2015). A single headline sentence, like the one shown above, has also been included in children's booklets because it was previously found that some individuals were unable to explain to others what they had been told their diagnosis meant after the programme had ended. Of course, the majority of children are given broader explanations of what having autism means during the rest of *All About Me* and this is reflected later in the instructions for teaching the second session given in Chapter 6.

4.2.2 More about the programme's approaches towards describing autism to children

There are various subtypes of autism and each of them has its own diagnostic label. Whilst *autism* is used in this book as an umbrella term for all conditions on the spectrum, it is important to give each child whose diagnosis is described differently the exact wording at the outset. This is to avoid risks of children wrongly concluding later that they were lied to or given incorrect personal information. Some may think that they have been diagnosed with an additional condition, or that they do not have autism after all. This could perhaps occur if they read reports and other written information about themselves or if the formal wording of their diagnosis is referred to by someone else in passing (e.g. by a professional in a review meeting).

In most cases children are told that they either have *autism* (if their formal diagnosis includes the word 'autism'), or *AS*. Children who have been given a diagnosis with more complex wording (e.g. *pervasive developmental disorder not otherwise specified* or *pathological demand avoidance syndrome*) are first told that this is the case and their formal diagnosis is written verbatim on the page in their booklet where it is first disclosed (i.e. 'I have pathological demand avoidance syndrome'). However, to keep things as simple as possible at this early stage, it is written and said immediately afterwards that 'This is a type of autism.' From then on the word 'autism' is generally used to describe the child's condition throughout the rest of the programme and in the narrative in their booklet.

All About Me aims to provide every child with a positive initial explanation of their autism which is as concrete and tangible as possible in their personal situation and does not cause them any undue emotional distress or lead participants into believing they are defective. Hence, as described above and in the opening chapter, the explanation of each child's autism is personalized for them on the basis of the summary of an individual's personal attributes which is drawn up in Session 1. Their autism is presented to them positively, focusing on it being a difference rather than something that is either disabling or tragic. At this stage, children are not referred to any of the definitions of autism that are characterized in the formal diagnostic criteria. Besides using abstract terms, these are specifically based on generalized descriptions of autism's negative deficits and present it as a disorder (APA 2013; WHO 1992).

Although *All About Me* focuses on explaining each child's autism to them in the context of their own strengths and differences, it is important to regard it as being a transactional condition. As such a child's differences should not be thought of as attributes which belong solely to them. It can be argued that the level of a child's autism-related challenges is also determined by what steps the typical people around them take to make themselves and the environment more accessible and autism-friendly. There is broad consensus among practitioners and theoreticians that typical people can help make things easier for individuals with autism by modifying their own behaviour and communication while also maintaining a sense of calm by making themselves less arousing (e.g. Clements 2005; Whitaker 2001). This being so, the child's attributes and their autism should not be considered in isolation (Jordan 2005). Therefore, *All About Me* incorporates a social model of disability (as described by Oliver in 1990) as its basis for explaining their autism to children. Within this approach it is made explicit to children that the extent to which they find some things harder than other people is not purely down to them. Children are told that things that they find challenging and frustrating, such as talking, working and playing with classmates and other typical people, can be equally challenging for these individuals when they try to initiate similar contact and interact with people on the autism spectrum. It is explained that while typical people can generally socialize with each other freely, they usually find it harder to understand how to respond to individuals with autism and that they may need some support in learning how to do this better.

4.2.3 Choosing the right words

People with autism tend to try to understand what the words mean when they are listening to speech rather than what the speaker is meaning to say. This often leads to them interpreting what they hear literally or missing the point that is being made (Jordan 2005). Telling a child about their diagnosis risks causing them significant emotional upset or confusion. It is crucial therefore that these joint factors are accounted for in a programme for teaching children about their autism. Anyone carrying out this work needs to be mindful of which words and phrases they choose to express themselves with, both verbally and in the written narrative of a child's booklet. Careful consideration needs to be given at all times as to whether what adults are intending to say could possibly be interpreted differently from an autistic viewpoint and thus unwittingly cause the child to misunderstand their diagnosis or become more anxious and distressed by its possible implications.

Positive, idiom-free and matter-of-fact language should be used as a matter of course, especially when discussing more difficult issues. Cognitive differences between typical people and those with autism mean that, no matter how hard they try, those carrying out this work are bound to get things wrong sometimes. It is essential therefore that adults try to build in frequent opportunities for assessing how accurately children are understanding what they are being taught over the course of the programme. Depending on the child, this can be done by asking open or closed questions about certain aspects of the work or, better still, asking able enough children to try to restate what they were told in their own words. However, adults will need to consider whether the child's responses are simply echoing what they were told (Vermeulen 2013). Furthermore, each page in the finished booklet needs to be checked, line by line, for words and expressions that could be open to misinterpretation before handing it over to the child.

Each child's challenges need to be discussed with them openly and honestly. *All About Me* is intended to help children identify and understand their challenges and the reasons behind them, so that they might work towards making progress in those areas and learn to collaborate with the people supporting them. Some children can find these discussions distressing, so the programme has been refined to ensure that certain words such as 'difficult', 'hard' or 'tricky' are no longer used. Interpreted literally, words like these could be taken to imply a state of permanence. They might suggest to the child that they will never be able to make any progress with the things they find challenging and could lead to them developing lower self-expectations and poorer self-esteem. This is why words such as 'deficit', 'impairment', 'difficulty' or 'disorder' are not used in the programme either. This applies equally to children who might be capable of understanding and using these words themselves. Their use might not only have the potential to leave some children feeling devoid of hope or motivation, but could also cause them to believe that they are permanently defective or broken. An 11-year-old boy called Alexis, for instance, told me that autism must be 'something bad' because he had read about it being a 'disorder'. He then added that he had reached this conclusion because he knew that disordered computers are broken and do not work properly (Miller 2014).

Instead, children's challenges are referred to more reassuringly through using comparative descriptive language. The child's challenges are not avoided or ignored; rather, they are described to them as being things which they find *harder* or *more challenging* to do. In the interests of being truthful, it is made explicit that having autism does mean that at least some of the issues the child currently faces are always going to present them with challenges and a certain degree of anguish. The child, however, is also told that, while autism is a lifelong condition, like everyone, they can make improvements in their weaker areas and learn to become better at coping with things that cause them more upset. Emphasis is placed on the value of accepting and engaging with their support.

All About Me has been designed with the intention of giving every child with autism the clear message that their diagnosis has its positive aspects, presents challenges and is not something bad, and that it is okay to be a person with autism. For this reason, the use of 'but', 'although', 'besides' and similar connectives is kept down to an absolute minimum. 'But' and comparable words and phrases are always substituted wherever possible with 'and' or another relevant neutral conjunction. Telling a child, for instance, that they are 'good at science *and* find playing with other children harder' seems preferable to saying that they are 'good at science *but* find playing with other children hard'. Arguably, the wording in the former example offers the child a more matter-of-fact and acceptable way of presenting their challenges.

In common with other initiatives for telling children about their autism (e.g. Gray 1996; Vermeulen 2000, 2013), the narrative in each child's booklet is usually written as if it is coming from the individual's own perspective. A strong emphasis is placed on the use of first-person language to describe the child and their autism. In this case, it is done deliberately to describe the child's diagnosis to them personally in a way in which it is hoped they might internalize more easily and which will provide them with some sense of ownership over it. The booklet is, after all, meant to be a record of the child's own exploration of themselves as a person and where having autism might fit into their overall self-identity. Occasionally, however, some personal information about children has had to be presented to them in the third person. As noted in Chapter 5, this has usually been when individuals disagreed with certain things that needed to be written about them. In those circumstances, it was noted that those parts of the narrative reflected other people's views (i.e. those of their parents or other people supporting them).

4.2.4 The preferred teaching approaches

The broad diversity of children on the autism spectrum is evident through wide variations in how their autism manifests (Wing 2002), as well as their cognitive abilities and the developmental levels they are working at (Jones 2002; Jordan 2001). Besides that, each child has their own unique personal traits. This leads to everyone having their own distinct differences and needs which call for the person-centred teaching approaches proposed in this book (Jordan 2005). In recognition of these differences, *All About Me* is always carried out on an individual basis rather than as a group activity. Even siblings, including twins, who are referred for the work at the same time are taught separately so that they can be offered their own personalized account of their autism and be given the specific types of support that they will need to access the work. This does not mean that children should not become involved in more generalized group programmes about autism later, after they have developed an initial understanding of what it means for them.

In most cases it is advised that anyone leading this programme implements an inductive teaching approach. This approach is reflected in the teaching instructions described in Chapters 5 and 6. Children are provided with questions and prompts which are intended to lead them towards making their own discoveries about themselves rather than having this information given to them. In this programme the approach is used when trying to help children to compile the lists of their own attributes and detect overall patterns in them. This process is meant to help each child reach their own understanding of who they are as a unique person and, in doing so, create their own context for receiving their diagnosis. Again, it is intended that this will maximize the child's ownership of their diagnosis and make the description of their autism seem less abstract and more relevant to them. The same approach is used to try to help children understand the reasons for their support. By using this method, children should better understand and internalize both what having autism means and why they might need support because it will have been grounded in their own findings about themselves (Vermeulen 2013).

It is acknowledged that not all children will be working at developmental levels that would make this approach fully suitable. Individuals may variously require more deductive teaching approaches wherein adults provide increased amounts of prompting or supply children with more of the information about themselves and ask them to comment on its validity. Furthermore, the questioning techniques used by adults will need to be differentiated to allow for each individual's communication preferences.

4.2.5 Making a unique booklet about the child and their autism

As already stated, *All About Me* principally involves supporting children through the process of completing an editable computer template to produce a unique narrative about themselves and their autism rather than write a Social Story™ or complete a generic workbook. The finished product is presented to the child in the form of a personalized printed booklet which their parents and other adults can then use to consolidate and follow up the programme (as advised in 8.2.1).

Having this type of end product is important because *All About Me* is a short programme and it can take some individuals a long time to learn to understand their diagnosis regardless of how it is shared with them.

Furthermore, working from a computer screen, producing a booklet and the possibility of being able to augment the text with symbols and pictures all acknowledge the strong preference most children with autism have for learning through visual media (Mesibov *et al.* 2004).

The electronic templates accompanying this book will need some preparation, but they can have several advantages over the use of readymade workbooks. These templates do not have set content nor do they involve working through prewritten generic worksheets and tick lists by hand. As editable resources, the appearance and content of each booklet can be designed uniquely to match the requirements of the child it is written with (as can be seen from the examples provided in Section B in the electronic resources). Furthermore, its completed narrative will provide an uninterrupted personal description of the child and their autism.

Being produced on a computer means that a booklet needs only to include information that is directly relevant to the individual concerned and the effects of their own manifestation of autism. Facts about autism that are not pertinent to the child can be omitted or deleted from the narrative as appropriate. This removes any need to cross things out, miss out pages or discuss things that are not applicable. It need not be stated, for example, that some people with autism can have issues with eating or sleeping if the child does not exhibit those kinds of behaviour. To minimize confusion, specific details about autism that are irrelevant to some children can be set aside, at least for the time being.

The flexibility of these templates means that the content of each child's booklet need not be limited to that provided by the programme author either. For instance, further information and guidance relevant to an individual's needs or behaviour can be added to the narrative. This method also allows the child and their parents to add their own contributions to the content. Moreover, photographs, pictures and text related to the child's special interests, cultural background and everyday life can be pasted into their booklet. This will enhance the narrative and make the booklet more relevant and engaging for the child. If done well, the finished booklet can have the appearance of a published resource, while being free from distractions such as adult guidance sections and handwritten entries.

Most importantly, however, the electronic templates provided have been proven to help make the programme more accessible as a whole to children across a broad age range with differing abilities and learning preferences, many of whom might not otherwise have been included. This is not only because different versions of the templates have been produced for children working within three broad developmental levels. As advised later (in 7.2.2), the content, format, written language and other visual features in each template can all be differentiated still further, in numerous ways, to make them accessible for children with very different needs.

Many children with autism have strong interests in technology and computers. Using a laptop computer to produce the booklet can provide the motivation needed to encourage some children to participate in the work in the first place, but some individuals may want to use the computer themselves. Because of their tendency to having single focused attention (Lawson 2011), the processes of recording the work can distract children from attending to what they are meant to be learning about autism. Work can be delayed if children lack appropriate touch-typing skills or become distracted by the computer's other programs and functions. To prevent these problems from arising, it has therefore become usual practice for the person leading the work to do all the typing. From the outset, it needs to be communicated clearly that the leading adult is the only person permitted to input data into the computer. I have found that children generally adhere to this rule when it is explained to them clearly beforehand. To further minimize distractions and avoid potential disagreements, it is advisable to use a computer that cannot be used to access the internet.

4.3 A BRIEF OVERVIEW OF THE PROGRAMME CONTENT AND FRAMEWORK

Table 4.1 contains a summary of the programme's framework for introducing children to their autism. The table lists the programme's main teaching and learning objectives and outlines the stages that are usually worked through to help children meet them. This framework is under constant review and has been adjusted frequently based on my own experiences of teaching children about their autism. The current version of the framework shows how the programme is delivered generically over three sessions, lasting for around one hour each and spaced approximately a week apart.

Table 4.1: *All About Me* **programme framework**

Session number and title	Content	Main teaching points and learning objectives
1. All about me	**Introducing the child to the programme** **Stage 1: Me on the outside** • Taking a photograph of the child. • Discussing how all people look different on the outside. **Stage 2: Me on the inside – my personality** • Discussing the concept of personality and how everyone is different on the inside. • Identifying, listing and exploring patterns in ten of the child's personality traits. **Stage 3: My strengths** • Discussing how everyone has different strengths. • Identifying, listing and exploring patterns in ten of the child's areas of strength. **Stage 4: Things I find harder** • Discussing how everyone has different challenges. • Identifying, listing and exploring patterns in around five of the child's main autism-related challenges. **Session summary**	• To enable the child to be aware that all people are unique on the outside and on the inside too. • To raise the child's awareness and acceptance of their own individual and overall attributes (personality traits, strengths and challenges). • To emphasize that the child is a good person whose family loves them and is proud of the child for who they are.

Session number and title	Content	Main teaching points and learning objectives
2. About me and my autism	**Introduction and recap of the previous session** **Stage 5: I have autism or AS** • Disclosing the diagnosis: telling or reminding child they have autism or AS in the context of their overall personal attributes and them being a good person. **Stage 6: Other people with autism or AS** • Providing the child with information about other people on the autism spectrum (including famous and notable examples). **Stage 7: Information about autism or AS** • Explaining how autism/AS got its name. • Sharing information with the child about what having autism does and does not mean in the context of their overall personal attributes. • Providing the child with a personalized headline definition of their autism. • Discussing the child's differences in social communication, managing change and sensory processing. **Stage 8: People who help me** • Reminding the child of the people who make up their support network: at home, school and elsewhere. **Stage 9: The good things about autism or AS** • Discussing the child's special interests. **Stage 10: Who am I?** • Reading the final page of the booklet to summarize the work so far and positively reaffirm the child's personal attributes.	• To tell or remind the child they have autism or AS in a positive, matter-of-fact way, framed in the context of their personal attributes and without causing the child upset. • To enable the child to be aware that others have autism and AS and that the child can lead a happy and fulfilling life. • To enable the child to be aware that having autism or AS is just a way of describing a person with similar personal attributes to their own and that it is a difference. • To provide simple basic information about what autism or AS is and is not, including a personal 'headline' sentence which defines the child's own autism or AS. • To enable the child to be aware that typical people have reciprocal challenges in initiating contact and interacting with individuals with autism. • To make the child aware of who the members of their support network are and its function. • To explain how autism/AS got its name. • To share information with the child about what having autism does and does not mean in the context of their overall personal attributes. • To discuss the child's differences in social communication, managing change and sensory processing.

3. My booklet	• Presenting the child with their completed booklet. • Reading through and discussing the completed narrative in the booklet. • Considering what to do next.	• All of the above. • To assess how well the child has accepted and understood what they have been taught about their own autism or AS and identify possible follow-up work.

Source: Compiled by Miller 2014, 2015

Working through the stages described in Table 4.1 and using the methods described above, all of the necessary information about a child's attributes is gained from them during the first session. This information is used in the second session to calmly disclose or reaffirm the child's diagnosis and then explain to them positively what it means. As already stated above, autism is presented to children in the context of each of them being a good person who is loved by the supportive people around them and of autism being a way to describe someone with similar patterns of strengths and differences to theirs. The content of this framework is also intended to raise children's awareness of some other important points such as the child not being alone in having autism; how their support is meant to fit in with their diagnosis; and that there are positive aspects to having autism.

As will be explained in more detail later, each of the programme's teaching stages are worked through while helping the child to read, discuss and fill in the gaps in the corresponding sections of their booklet. The final session is used to summarize and review everything that the child would have learned from the previous two sessions. This involves reading through and discussing the completed booklet's narrative with the child, while also trying to evaluate their understanding of the work, before considering what to do next.

This framework was originally designed to fit around the commitments of external professionals with limited time. However, if the adults involved have the availability, the work could be scheduled more flexibly to match an individual child's concentration span, the pace at which they learn and their prior level of understanding of some of the programme's key concepts. For instance, spreading the work over more sessions would allow certain aspects of it to be explored in more detail if an individual had significant gaps in their knowledge of them (e.g. their awareness of their own strengths and differences). It is possible to break down the content of each of the first two sessions into smaller portions and teach it over a series of shorter meetings for children whose behaviour makes it harder for them to concentrate and settle for longer periods of time. Alternatively, each session could have regular inbuilt breaks to accommodate these needs. Advice on all these scheduling issues is given at various points in the next three chapters, but it must be stressed in the meantime that once a child has been told about their diagnosis for the first time, that particular session should not end without the child having been given at least the headline description of what autism means and a recap of their positive attributes. Not doing this heightens the risk of the child drawing negative conclusions about their diagnosis or finding harmful or misleading information about autism from the internet or elsewhere before the next meeting.

The overview of the programme given above is followed up in detail in the next three chapters. Generic instructions are given for working through each stage of this framework with different children in Chapters 5 and 6. Practical advice is offered for dealing with any key issues that could arise at various points in the work. Chapter 7 then provides guidance on ways in which the overall programme might be differentiated to support and include children whose behaviour and learning needs might prevent them from participating in the generic programme.

Chapter 5

TEACHING SESSION 1: CREATING THE CONTEXT FOR DISCLOSING THE CHILD'S DIAGNOSIS

> The programme resources for this chapter can be downloaded from
> www.jkp.com/voucher using the code QLspdxjP

5.1 INTRODUCTION

This chapter contains the generic instructions for preparing for and delivering Session 1. This is when children are introduced to the programme and are guided through its first four stages (as shown in Table 4.1) to explore their personal attributes and create their own context for being told about their autism. This chapter also identifies the key issues that can arise during each stage worked through in this session and advises on how adjustments can be made to support children who could experience similar difficulties. This includes ideas for preparatory work with individuals who are judged not ready to participate in some of the activities that take place in this session. Finally, guidance is offered on how to evaluate children's responses to the work covered in this session and then decide whether they should still participate in the rest of the programme and thus be told that they have autism.

The instructions in this chapter, and the next, describe how all of this work is usually carried out with children aged between eight and 12 years who are considered to be of around average intelligence. Despite this, chronological ages do not tend to accurately reflect the levels that children with autism might be operating at in different areas of their development. By making some of the individual adjustments described later, the same model can be applied successfully to working with younger children with more advanced cognitive and communication skills, as well as to older children who are working at earlier developmental levels. Moreover, the advice in Chapter 7 suggests possible ways of meeting some of the needs of less and more able children who are working outside the programme's generic levels.

The teaching instructions in this chapter are illustrated by a generic (Level 2) *All About Me* booklet about a fictional 11-year-old girl with autism called Kim. Although neither this booklet nor the instructions for producing it refer directly to work carried out with a real child, both are grounded in my own first-hand experiences of teaching a large group of individual children about their autism. Many of these girls and boys were quite like Kim, so I have tried to use this experience to create a broad generalized example which arguably reflects best practice.

Kim's booklet needs to be read alongside the teaching instructions that are given below. For convenience, these instructions contain frequent quotations from its narrative. A copy of Kim's booklet has been included in the electronic resources (B2) so that it can be read separately, in full and in its intended format. As children with autism are very different from one another, four other booklets about fictional children with autism and AS, working at different developmental levels, are also presented in Section B as examples of how the outcomes of this work can vary. A copy of the generic (Level 2) template that was used to produce Kim's booklet is also available (C2), as are copies of those which were used to create all the other examples (in Section C). The front cover and first four pages of that template correspond with the programme stages that are worked through in this session, while the remaining pages relate to everything that is usually taught during Session 2. Template C3 is provided for use with children who are diagnosed with AS rather than autism, and who are operating within the same levels as Kim, but there are no differences in any of the pages and activities or instructions that are worked through during this session. It is advisable to refer to printed copies of Kim's booklet and its template for clarity while reading the teaching instructions in this chapter.

It should be acknowledged again that the narrative in Kim's booklet and some of the advice given in this chapter are also based on similar work by other authors and autism practitioners. Notable among these are Carol Gray (1996), Peter Vermeulen (2001, 2013) and Jude Welton (2004a, b). As already stated, this book makes no attempt to claim ownership over any of the methods described in it. The intention is to share my own experiences of teaching a large number of children about their autism with others who need to carry out this difficult and much-needed work.

5.2 TEACHING AND LEARNING OBJECTIVES FOR SESSION 1

This section recaps on the session's main teaching and learning objectives, which are as follows:

- to develop the child's awareness that all people, including themselves, are unique on the outside and on the inside, and that this is okay

- to raise the child's awareness and acceptance of their own individual and overall attributes; including their personality traits, areas of strength and the things they find more challenging or harder than typical children of their age

- to affirm that the child is a good person who is loved by the supportive people around them and that they are all proud of the child for being who they are.

These objectives are intended to prepare children for being told about their autism calmly during the second session. It is hoped that by the end of this session children will have developed an enhanced positive understanding of themselves and how everyone has their own unique attributes.

5.3 REQUIRED RESOURCES

5.3.1 Introduction

This section goes through all the equipment and learning materials that might be needed for teaching Session 1. This includes standard resources essential to virtually every instance of this work. Additionally, it describes support tools which might need to be gathered in support of individuals who could find it harder to formulate and express answers to the types of questions that children are posed in this session or are likely to find it difficult to concentrate on the work and understand what it means. This section also explains the reasons for choosing these resources. Guidance on their use is provided later in the relevant sections which describe how to teach the various parts of the programme in which they could be needed. A complete checklist of all the resources described below has been added to the end of this section.

5.3.2 What is needed and why

A computer with word-processing capability is needed throughout Sessions 1 and 2 to work through the template to produce the booklet about the child. Many children with autism have special interests in technology and so can find this motivating. However, computers usually contain a variety of distractions which might affect some children's concentration on their work. A computer must be treated as a type of working environment and, as such, be adjusted according to individual learners' needs. For children with autism, this means clarifying its use and making it as distraction-free as possible. Children need to be told explicitly at the start of each session what the computer will and will not be used for. Web browsers and other attractive and non-essential applications, such as games, ought to be hidden from sight. This can be done easily by deleting their shortcuts from the computer's desktop or by moving them temporarily into a hidden folder before the child is aware of their existence. I have always used a laptop computer without internet connectivity for carrying out this work.

This advice may be obvious, but not having the correct power cable and mains adapter for a laptop computer can create unnecessary problems. A session may have to be postponed at the last minute or end prematurely and abruptly if the computer's battery runs out. It is also wise to check that the battery is fully charged beforehand, even when using a mains electricity supply, so that the work will not be disrupted in the event of a power failure.

Following the advice in 7.2.2, the adults involved in this work should go through the sample booklet templates contained in Section C of the electronic resources and select whichever one appears best matched to the developmental levels at which the child is working. Further adjustments may need to be made to that template's language and format to make it more accessible for the individual concerned. A word-processing file containing the front cover and the first four pages of the adjusted template will need to be saved on to the computer, ready for use at the start of the session. Each template contains embedded adult guidance for completing all the gaps in its narrative and this should be deleted before the session to reduce clutter on the screen and avoid confusing the child.

Once it has been prepared for use with the child, it is advisable to print a paper copy of the booklet template to take along to the session as a precautionary measure. This could prove useful if there are any last-minute technical problems with the computer itself or if a child experiences unforeseen difficulties when working with it. If either of these things occurs, the paper copy can be worked through instead. Information gathered about the child in the session can be handwritten into the spaces on the paper copy and typed into the electronic template later. This way the child can still work through the programme and be presented with a printed booklet at the end of it.

A digital camera is needed for taking the photograph of the child which illustrates the front cover and first page of their booklet. This photograph should be uploaded to the computer during the session; a compatible USB connection cable will therefore be needed if the computer does not have a suitable memory card slot. It is also advisable to have a spare set of charged camera batteries. Furthermore, collecting portrait photographs of a few people who the child is familiar with can also be useful. These photographs can be used alongside the picture taken of the individual in the session to support those children who find it difficult to reach the conclusion that all people's facial features are unique to them.

A notepad can be an indispensable resource in all three sessions. Notepaper can be used to provide children with visual explanations and representations of language and concepts which are difficult for them to comprehend. Children can use a notepad themselves to express their own thoughts and ideas in writing or pictorially if they are unable to do this verbally. Literate children who may feel anxious about saying certain things aloud or who do not feel like talking on the day of a session can be asked to write down what they need to say instead.

Adults involved in this work are advised to draw up their own collective lists of the child's strengths and challenges during the pre-programme work (see 3.6.2). This is mainly so that they can refer back to these lists during this session if the child gets stuck while trying to identify their own attributes and requires prompting. In addition to this, the sets of *Personal trait*, *Strength* and *Challenge* cards, provided in the electronic resources (D1, D2 and D3 respectively), can be offered to children who might need more visual support to complete any of the self-assessment tasks that need to be worked through during the session. An *Easiness rating scale* has also been included in the electronic resources (D4). Based on work by other practitioners, including Buron and Curtis (2008), this scale can be used to help children assess their own strengths and challenges in different areas.

Children can sometimes find various aspects of this work distressing. At the same time, having autism makes it harder for them to recognize and express their feelings, regulate their emotional responses and spontaneously ask others for support in doing this (Whitaker 2001). Moreover, it is not always easy for adults to detect when a child on the autism spectrum is feeling anxious and could be about to lose control of their behaviour before it is too late (Wing 2002). Consequently, alternative communication systems should be made available during all three sessions for children who are known to find it harder to verbally express their feelings or request help when they are under stress. For this reason, an *Emotions rating scale* (similar to the *Easiness rating scale* described above) has been included in the electronic resources (D5). As advised by Attwood (2008) and explained later in this chapter, scales like this can be used at various points during each session to help children rate their emotional states numerically and communicate their feelings to the adults who can then act accordingly.

Help and break card systems are often used in schools to support children on the autism spectrum as well as other individuals who have communication difficulties or emotional and behavioural challenges. These can be useful for some participants in this programme. They can be made from two pieces of different-coloured card (about the size of standard playing cards) with the word 'break' written on one of them and 'help' on the other. Children can then be told how to hand the relevant card to an adult, or point to it, if they need to ask for assistance with any of the activities or request a short break from the work for calming purposes. A sand timer, or a similar device, should be available for use alongside a break card to regulate the duration of any breaks that are taken and to show the child when they must try to resume working.

Regardless of their ages and abilities, children with autism tend to have a strong need to know what is going to happen next. They are likely to become anxious in environments that lack a clear sense of predictability and where there is uncertainty over what is expected of them. This is more likely to be the case in unfamiliar and novel situations (Whitaker 2001), such as participating in this programme. Simply telling them what will happen is unlikely to suffice, however. Most children with autism prefer having information presented to them visually and need a permanent means of being able to see and recall what will happen. These needs can be met by providing each child with a visual guide to the whole programme as well as separate schedules which show all of the steps they will need to progress through in order to complete the current session.

Details of how to populate the contents of the programme guide and the schedule for this session are provided in the next two sections. In most cases these are both presented to children on notepaper as written checklists. However, the possibility that this work could upset children means that those leading it must try to ensure that each child is provided with the types of schedules that they can quickly process and make sense of when they are feeling emotionally aroused. Therefore, some children will need to have their schedules and other visual resources, such as rule prompts, presented in more pictorial or symbolic formats, as advised on later in this chapter and again in 7.3.3.

Provided it does not become a distraction for the child, having a clock or timer in a format that they can understand is very important for some individuals. This can help children stay calm by being able to see, or be shown, what time the session is due to finish at. Children can also find it reassuring to know that they have not missed one of their preferred activities if it is due to take place later the same day.

Finally, anyone leading this work should try to ascertain what further resources are used to support the child in staying focused on and engaged in adult-directed activities so that these can be incorporated into the sessions as needed. This might include things like personalized rule prompts, alternative communication aids, sensory aids such as fidget toys and specialized seating, items that the child finds motivating and rewarding as well as any timing devices that are used to manage the child's access to them.

5.3.3 Resources checklist

In summary, some or all of the items on the two checklists below will need to be gathered and prepared before the first session is delivered:

Essential resources:

- laptop computer (with power cable and adapter)

- a personalized electronic copy of the cover and pages 1–4 of the booklet template chosen for the child from Section C

- digital camera with available memory

- USB lead for the camera (if the computer does not have a memory card slot)

- notepad and writing implements

- draft lists of the child's strengths and challenges (drawn up by the adults during the pre-programme work)

- a visual programme guide listing all three sessions (formatted to match the child's visual preferences – see the box on page 111 for an example)

- a visual schedule ordering the activities to be completed in Session 1 (formatted to match the child's visual preferences – see the box on page 113 for an example).

Recommended resources:

- a paper copy of pages 1–4 of the booklet template

- spare camera batteries (charged)

- a selection of photographs of people familiar to the child (for children who are unlikely to realize that everyone has a unique facial appearance)

- sets of *Personal trait*, *Strength* and *Challenge* cards (D1, D2 and D3) (for children who might have difficulty describing themselves verbally)

- the *Easiness rating scale* (D4) (for children who have less awareness of their strengths and challenges)

- the *Emotions rating scale* (D5) (for children who have difficulty identifying, expressing and regulating their emotional state or requesting help)

- a help card (for children who have difficulty requesting help verbally when under stress)

- a break card (for children who have difficulty requesting help verbally and could become upset or anxious)

- a timer (for children who might need short breaks or controlled access to rewarding items or activities)

- a clock that the child can understand (provided this will not create a distraction)

- any other communication aids and rule prompts that the child relies upon using on a regular basis (as required by the individual)

- items that the child finds motivating and rewarding and an appropriate timer (as needed by the individual)

- fidget toys and specialized seating (as needed by children who exhibit sensory-seeking behaviours).

5.4 INTRODUCING THE CHILD TO *ALL ABOUT ME*

5.4.1 How to introduce the programme when it is taught over the usual three sessions

At the beginning of this session, children need to be given a short explanation of what the programme entails and the main reason for participating in it. Children should be told that this work will take place across three meetings so that they can complete a programme called *All About Me* and make a booklet about themselves which they will then be given to keep. If the child already knows about their diagnosis, they can be told that the programme and the booklet are intended to help them have a better understanding of their autism or AS. If the child is unaware of their diagnosis, they should be given the alternative explanation agreed upon by the adults during the pre-programme work.

The child is then referred to the programme guide to provide them with a visual overview of what is going to happen over the course of the three sessions. This should contain brief details of the dates, times and titles of each session as well as inform the child about who will be attending them. It is usually set out similarly to this example:

THE *ALL ABOUT ME* PROGRAMME

We will meet three times to make a booklet all about me. When the booklet is finished, it will be mine to keep.

Session 1: Finding out about me
(2pm: Tuesday 28 June 2016, in the Rainbow Room)
Me, Mum, Dad and Andrew Miller

Session 2: More information about me and why I have extra help at school
(2pm: Tuesday 5 July 2016, in the Rainbow Room)
Me, Mum, Dad and Andrew Miller

Session 3: My booklet
(2pm: Tuesday 12 July 2016, in the Rainbow Room)
Me, Mum, Dad, Andrew Miller and Mrs Jacobs (my teacher)
This is when I will take my booklet home.

Children should be referred to this guide at the start and end of each session so that they can track their own progress in working through the programme towards its completion.

For children who need additional visual support, this guide may need to be produced on a computer so that it can be augmented with symbols. It could also include photographs of the people who are going to attend each session.

Children with autism can become alarmed by unannounced changes or being in unpredictable and unfamiliar situations, especially if they are expecting that something else is going to happen instead. They often find managing transitions from one activity to another just as upsetting. Because of the sensitive nature of this work, it is vital that children arrive for each session feeling as calm as possible. Adults looking after and working with a child can support their successful participation in the programme by including each of these sessions in any timetables and schedules which the child uses at home, in their classrooms or elsewhere on days that the work is due to take place. That way, being taken from their usual routine will not come as a totally unexpected surprise. The sessions should also be recorded in any diaries or calendars that the child uses. Furthermore, children need to be warned in advance of any possible changes to the proposed dates and times of the sessions as well as to who will be attending them. Their programme guide should be amended accordingly.

After going through the programme guide, the child is offered a brief explanation of how the booklet will be produced on the computer from the template. It is stated unambiguously at this point that although everyone will need to pay attention to the screen and read from it throughout most of the first two sessions, only the lead adult is permitted to input data into the computer. To avoid some of the potential arguments described later in this chapter, it should be made clear now that although the booklet is about the child and is being written for them, the adults are going to have the final say on what information will be included in its narrative.

If it is felt that the child may need to use a help or break card at some point, they should be given them and told how to use each of them. It is explained that although it is hoped that the child will enjoy doing most of this work, if they do find anything too challenging or stressful, they can ask for help or a short break either verbally or by handing the relevant card to one of the adults instead. However, it is also made clear that it will be up to the adults to decide whether to grant any requests for breaks. The child should also be shown the timing device that will be used to regulate the duration of any breaks so that they are aware that they will need to try to carry on with their work after a set period of calming time (e.g. five minutes).

5.4.2 How to introduce the programme if it is being taught over more than three meetings

As mentioned in Chapter 4, this session can be adjusted and broken down into a series of two, three or even four discrete sessions of their own if the adults have enough time and it is agreed that the child needs this. The second session can also be divided into two separate parts. This is on the proviso that the child is given an initial explanation of their diagnosis before the end of the meeting in which they are first told about their autism. Session 3 should stay as it is, however, because it only involves reading through and discussing the finished booklet and this is often completed in less than an hour anyway. Changes to the number of meetings will need to be reflected in the programme guide. If, for example, it is decided that the work should to be taught over five sessions the guide might be presented to the child like this:

ALL ABOUT ME PROGRAMME

We will meet together five times to make a booklet all about me. When the booklet is finished, it will be mine to keep.

Session 1: Me on the outside and on the inside
(2pm: Tuesday 7 June 2016, in the Rainbow Room)
Me, Mum, Dad and Andrew Miller

Session 2: What I am good at doing and what I find harder
(2pm: Tuesday 14 June 2016, in the Rainbow Room)
Me, Mum, Dad and Andrew Miller

Session 3: More information about me and why I have extra help at school
(2pm: Tuesday 21 June 2016, in the Rainbow Room)
Me, Mum, Dad and Andrew Miller

Session 4: Some more information about me and why I have extra help at school
(2pm: Tuesday 28 June 2016, in the Rainbow Room)
Me, Mum, Dad and Andrew Miller

Session 5: My booklet
(2pm: Tuesday 5 July 2016, in the Rainbow Room)
Me, Mum, Dad, Andrew Miller and Mrs Jacobs (my teacher)
This is when I will take my booklet home.

5.5 INTRODUCING SESSION 1

5.5.1 Using a schedule to introduce the session in its usual one-hour format

Having given the child an overview of the programme as a whole, they should then be shown what is going to happen during this session by referring them to their work schedule. The child's schedule should contain an ordered list of the activities they are going to have to complete during the session; tell them when the session will finish; and, to help them manage the transition at the end of session, say what they will be doing immediately afterwards (e.g. going back to their classroom for a lesson, having lunch or going home from school). The schedule for this session is usually presented on notepaper in the form of a written checklist. An example of how this might appear is shown below:

ALL ABOUT ME SESSION 1: FINDING OUT ABOUT ME

    1. A photograph of me
    2. My personality
    3. Things I am good at doing
    4. Some things I find harder
    5. What I have learned today.

Back to class to do science (*around* 2.15pm).

There are differences in the ways that children with autism process visual information which could prevent some individuals from making adequate sense of a schedule that is presented using the above language and format, particularly when they are anxious. Some children may need to have the activities on their schedule labelled in fewer words (Mesibov and Howley 2003), so, if given as a written list for this session, it may have to be simplified to read as follows:

SESSION 1:

    photograph
    personality
    strengths
    harder things
    what we learned
    classroom

Children with stronger visual learning preferences and less developed literacy skills may also need to have the words on their schedule augmented with symbols or pictures to help them understand it more clearly (Mesibov and Howley 2003). Where appropriate, individual children's schedules will also need to communicate the timing of any planned breaks in the session for children who need to have managed access to their preferred activities, favourite objects or certain types of sensory stimuli and this is considered further in 7.3.4.

While being referred to each item on the schedule, the child is also provided with a verbal explanation of what will happen at each point in the session. The script written below has been included as an example for anyone planning similar work. Whatever is said will need to be adjusted on the basis of knowledge of the child's receptive language skills. In this case, dots have been included in the text to show where there might need to be pauses to allow a child enough time to process what they have just heard.

Today we are going to make the first part of your booklet on the computer…

First we will use the camera to take a photograph of your face…
When we have taken the photograph, I will upload it to the computer…

Next, we are going to find out about your personality…
This means that we will be finding out about what you are like as a person…

Then we will find out about your strengths… These are the things that you are good at doing…

After that we will find out about some things which you find harder…

Last, we will talk about what we learned about you today…how you are a good person…and how we are all different…how it is okay to be different…

We will finish at *around* 2.15pm…
We might finish a few minutes before that…
or we might finish a few minutes after that…
When we finish, I will walk with you to your classroom…
Then you will do your science work…
Mr Cohen will be there to help you… He will show you what you will need to do.

The fact that this is quite a lengthy script underlines the need for the child to have a schedule as a visual means of recording what will happen and to help them to retain or be reminded of this information. In my experience, if the schedule is not used correctly and consistently throughout the whole session, it is unlikely to be fully effective and problems are more likely to occur. The session schedule can be an effective tool for keeping children of all ages and abilities engaged with this work and for refocusing them if they become distracted, start asking repetitive questions (such as 'When am I going back to class?'), go off topic while talking or lapse into other inappropriate behaviours. It is recognized as being good practice to prompt children to tick, cross out or remove each of the activities on the schedule themselves once they have been completed, before showing them what needs to be done next. This is to help children calmly switch their attention and focus away from one activity to the next during transitions. It is also intended to make children aware of their progress towards completing the session (Mesibov *et al.* 2004). Children should be referred to their schedule as a matter course if it appears that they could be about to experience a difficult moment.

After going through the schedule with the child, it is important to specify what time the session is planned to end and show them this on a clock or a timer that they are able to understand. However, as in the example given above, children should always be made aware that the session could end a few minutes earlier or later than the specified time. Literal thinking and inflexibility can cause children to exhibit agitation if this is not explained properly and the work does not finish at precisely the time that they were told it would.

5.5.2 Introducing the Session 1 content when it is being delivered over more than one meeting

If necessary, the four stages covered in this session can be worked through at a rate of one or two at a time, on up to four separate occasions. If it is decided to do this, then it is vital that these four stages are still taught in the same order and that the child is given a thorough recap of all the main teaching points that came up in the earlier meetings when starting each additional session. This is to protect the child's self-esteem and maintain the programme's continuity. In these circumstances, children are provided with separate schedules for each meeting to reflect how the programme is restructured. When splitting this session into two parts the schedules might appear like this example:

ALL ABOUT ME **SESSION 1: FINDING OUT ABOUT ME**

    1. A photograph of me
    2. My personality
    3. What I learned about me today

Back to class to do science (*around* 2pm).

ALL ABOUT ME **SESSION 2: FINDING OUT MORE ABOUT ME**

    1. What I have already learned about me
    2. Things I am good at doing
    3. Some things I find harder
    4. What I know about me now

Back to class to do art (*around* 2pm).

Once the child has been shown what they will be doing during the first meeting, they can move on to the first stage of the programme.

5.6 STAGE 1: EXPLORING THE CHILD ON THE OUTSIDE

5.6.1 Introduction

This section explains how to work through and complete the front cover and the opening page in the Level 2 template for children with autism (C2). This is illustrated by the corresponding parts of Kim's booklet (B2). The aim of this stage is to help children recognize that everyone's external appearance is unique and perhaps conclude that it is okay to appear different. This involves working through the following steps:

- taking a photograph of the child and uploading it on to the computer

- inserting copies of the child's photograph on to the front cover and page 1 of the booklet template

- discussing how everyone, including the child, has a unique facial appearance

- reading the text on the first page in the template

- referring the child to the session schedule to show them that this stage has been completed and what they will be doing next.

5.6.2 Instructions and explanation

Although it is possible to insert an existing photograph of the child into the template before the session, taking a new picture now helps to involve the child as fully as possible in producing the booklet and provides them with a visual record of what they looked like on the day when they started this life-changing work.

The photograph needs to focus on the child's facial features and so should be a portrait rather than a whole-body picture. It also needs to be free from other distractions and so should be taken against a blank background, such as a light-coloured wall, and not include any other people or show the child engaging in an activity.

Before taking the child's photograph, it is important to be mindful that some individuals with autism have visual hypersensitivities or can be frightened by sudden and unexpected exposure to certain sensory stimuli. It is advisable to switch off the camera flash and reassure the child that this has happened in case they are anxiously anticipating its effects.

Once copies of the photograph have been added to the cover and first page in the template, the child can be shown what the front of their booklet will look like when it is finished. The photograph on page 1 is then used to initiate a discussion with the child aimed at helping them recall, or learn, that no two people's facial appearances are exactly identical. This conversation can be prompted by telling the child to look at their photograph while asking an exploratory question such as 'How many people do you know who have the exact same face as you?' or 'Who else do you know who looks exactly like you?' Not all children come up with a suitable answer the first time, so comparisons may need to be made between the facial appearances of the people in the room, members of the child's family, staff who work with them and other children in their class. It may be useful to take portrait photographs of a few of these people and bring them to the session for the child to compare at this point. The discussion should then be completed by reading all of the text on the first page, which says:

> **ME ON THE OUTSIDE**
>
> This is a photograph of me on the outside. It was taken on Tuesday 28 June 2016 [i.e. the date the session takes place on].
>
> We all look different on the outside. No one else in the world looks exactly like me.
>
> We all look different on the outside so it must be okay to be different.

Differences in understanding language can make it harder for children with autism to realize when generalized statements which contain words like 'everyone' might also apply to themselves. On this occasion and at other times in the programme when similar statements are made, children who are working at more literal levels will need to be told explicitly that what is said refers to them as well.

Children who are conscious about their differences and are aware that others treat them differently can find this upsetting and may therefore put a great deal of effort into trying to fit in and appear normal within their peer group (Gerland 1997; Sainsbury 2000). For this reason, it is important to stress the final sentence on this page before moving on to the next stage. This starts the process of presenting children with a logical and matter-of-fact argument which proposes that, since all people are unique in various ways, it must be okay for them to have their own differences.

5.6.3 Key issues and adjustments

The main issue that tends to occur during this stage is with children not being able to understand or recognize that everyone has unique facial features. Due to their neurological differences, individuals with autism do not tend to process facial information in the same ways as typical people (Attwood 2008; Boucher 2009; Frith 2003). Furthermore, they do not always make observations and deductions that are obvious to others (Blackburn 2013). For example, a ten-year-old boy called Ricky, who was very good at recognizing the people he knew at home and school, said that 'everyone has the same face'. When he was asked to explain why he had said this, he responded literally by saying that 'everyone has two eyes, a nose and a mouth'.

Children who might be referred for this work can also have difficulties with matching names to faces. Some may only be able to name a few of the people they regularly meet at school, despite having known them all for several years. Furthermore, they may not necessarily use facial appearances to recognize those they do know. Many children with autism pay minimal attention to other people's faces and seldom look at them directly unless prompted to do so.

Children with these types of needs will require support in developing an awareness of facial differences. Preferably, time should be taken to start doing this before they participate in the programme so that they might have a more tangible understanding of what is being taught. The child could be helped to produce a photograph album containing portraits of familiar people. Pairs of photographs could also be used in matching and sorting activities. At first, however, a child might only be able to manage these kinds of activities by being given pictures of the same few people to choose between each time. The number of people can then be increased gradually according to the child's success. As well as being able to put people's names to photographs, children might have to be taught to generalize this skill into everyday situations where they will need to recognize and name people when they meet them in person. This might be done over time through supporting a child with running errands such as handing out exercise books and delivering messages as well as by prompting them to greet familiar people by name.

Besides bringing a selection of photographs of familiar people for a child to compare in the session, copies of some of these pictures could also be included in the first few pages of their *All About Me* booklet. This would enable their parents and other adults to continue reinforcing how people appear different when they are using the booklet together after the programme has ended.

For some children, the difficulties described above could be caused by them having prosopagnosia. This is a separate neurological condition which reduces an individual's ability to recognize and compare faces. In effect, this can make an individual *face blind* to all but the most familiar people in their lives (Bogdashina 2003). In the most severe cases, no amount of prompting is likely to help a child who also has autism to conclude that all people's facial features are unique to them. They may need to be taught this as a given fact so that the programme can progress. However, this is unlikely to have any concrete meaning for them. Given more time before starting the programme, individuals with prosopagnosia can perhaps be taught to see how various people they know appear unique in other ways. This could be done through exploring a combination of their other external physical attributes such as their hair and skin colours, heights and finger prints. Putting this programme aside, these children are going to need some level of support in learning how to develop and use a variety of different recognition systems (e.g. the sound of people's voices, their hairstyles or their gait) so that they can function more effectively in everyday social situations (Bogdashina 2003).

5.7 STAGE 2: EXPLORING THE CHILD AS A PERSON ON THE INSIDE

5.7.1 Introduction

This section provides the instructions for working through and completing the second page in the template (C2) as illustrated in Kim's booklet (B2). This stage is intended to help develop children's understanding of how everyone also has their own unique internal characteristics before guiding them towards coming up with a description of their own personality and reaching the overall conclusion that they are a good person. This involves working through the following sequence of steps:

- explaining that everyone has unique internal qualities and what the word 'personality' means

- reading the title and the first five points on page 2 of the template

- supporting the child to draw up a list of ten words and phrases to describe their own personality and recording them in the template

- guiding the child towards reaching the overall conclusion that they are a good person who is loved by the supportive people around them

- referring the child back to their session schedule.

5.7.2 Instructions and explanation

The child should be told, or reminded, first that besides everyone being different on the outside, all people, including them, have various internal features which collectively make each of us unique individuals. Whereas this is perhaps obvious to most typically developing children, individuals with autism may need to be taught this explicitly. Differences in theory of mind mean that this may never have occurred to them or that it would have little tangible meaning for them anyway (Frith 2003).

The child should be asked to say what they think the word 'personality' means. If they are unsure or give an inaccurate answer, it should be explained as being a term for describing who each of us is as person on the inside. Children are told that someone's personality is made up collectively of the ways in which people think and feel about things as well as how they behave. Some children appear to understand this better when they are presented with a rough sketch of a human body which shows them where the brain is located. Labelled arrows can then be added pointing to the brain to indicate that this is where everyone's thoughts and feelings take place. Discussing and comparing the likes, dislikes and characteristics of the people in the room or the child's siblings or some of their classmates is a way that has often been used to demonstrate this point. This discussion is then followed up by reading and discussing the following points which are already written in the template:

MY PERSONALITY (ME ON THE INSIDE)

Just as people look different on the outside, we are all different on the inside too.

We all have different things that we enjoy and don't enjoy.

We all have different things that we find easy and things that we find harder.

Like everyone, I have a **unique** personality.

Everyone has a different personality so we are all different and that is okay.

Here are some words to describe my own personality: …

The child is then asked to try to think of some words that might describe who they are as a person and say what they are. The aim is to guide the child towards producing a list of ten of their own positive personal traits and record this in their booklet. Although the adults might need to suggest one or two traits to start things off, the rest of this information ought to be provided by the child so that they can have ownership of the description of themselves. The list in Kim's booklet is as follows:

- friendly
- funny
- clever
- hardworking

- messy
- caring
- kind

- helpful
- talkative
- polite.

In addition to Kim's list, Table 5.1 offers some real examples of words and phrases that children have been helped to come up with to describe their personalities. The table presents the outcomes of recent work with four very different boys of primary school age whose names have all been changed to protect their identities.

Whoever is leading this work needs to be aware of how children's differences in understanding and using language can affect the outcome of this activity. Children with autism often interpret things very differently from typical people and this can be in subtle ways that may be hard to detect. It is essential therefore to always try to ascertain the reasons why children choose each of the words or phrases with which they describe themselves before deciding whether to type them into the template. Experience has shown that this approach must be taken with all children, regardless of their age, intelligence or how obvious a word's meaning may seem at first. For instance, Ricky described himself as being 'loving'. He was then asked to give an example of something he does that shows that he is a loving person. Rather than saying something like hugging or kissing his mother (who was expectantly looking on and waiting for him to do this), he surprised us by saying, 'wearing glasses…I love wearing people's glasses' (Miller 2014, 2015).

Simply asking children on the autism spectrum whether they understand what something means is not enough by itself. Individuals have often thought and said they had understood things when this was not so, or, like Ricky, they had interpreted it in a different way to how the adults had assumed. Instead, children should always be asked to try to describe a situation in which they have exhibited that trait. If, for example, a child says that they are helpful, then they should be asked to think of and describe something that they have done recently that was helpful. This can be made less open-ended and more specific if the adults ask contextualized questions such as 'What did you do for me today that I said was helpful?' or 'What had you just done yesterday when I told you that you were a kind person?' This is something that participating parents and school staff can contribute to much better in the session than a visiting professional.

A distinction needs to be made in the types of attributes which should be included in this list. It should contain those which relate to the child's behaviour and mannerisms rather than to their areas of strength and challenges. Those types of attributes are explored respectively in their own discrete areas during the next two stages. If the child goes on to mention an attribute that falls into one of those categories, they should be told that their contribution is valuable and that it will be recorded later when they reach the relevant page in the template.

Table 5.1: Words used by children to describe their own personal attributes

	Phil	Hugh	Ricky	Alexis
Personality traits	• funny • loud • cheerful • honest • helpful • friendly • fair • kind • polite • confident • assertive	• friendly • loud • active • hardworking • funny • messy • loving • gentle • helpful • talkative • anxious	• messy • loud • friendly • funny • hardworking • loving • helpful	• tidy • shy • anxious • perfectionist • serious • honest • cheerful • helpful • active • hardworking • polite • organized
Strengths	• art • design • construction • swimming • playing musical instruments • public speaking • computer games • cycling • reading	• darts • chess • using an iPad • using a computer • video games • working out how televisions work • swimming • construction • art • reading	• reading • playing on my Xbox • using tablets • using computers • badminton	• cricket • rugby • PE • computer coding • using computers • using gadgets • history • organization • processing visual information • listening • public speaking
Challenges	• learning names • making friends • meeting new people • team games • recognizing people's moods • personal space	• thinking about school work instead of my toys and movies • listening to things other people want to talk about • managing my feelings • putting up with other people	• literacy • making new friends • talking to people I don't know • waiting • changes to routines	• predicting how people will behave (e.g. when meeting new people) • tolerating things other people say or do • staying calm when other people interfere • rules not being applied rigidly • crowds and confined spaces

Source: Miller 2014, 2015

After compiling this list, children are asked to try to use it to identify an overall pattern in their personal traits so that they acquire an overview of what type of person they are as a whole. The list should be read back with the child before asking them a question such as 'These words describe you and your personality... What type of person do you think these things all make you?' or 'If we add these words together, what type of person do they describe?'

For the purposes of this work, it is intended that children will be able to arrive at the overall conclusion that most of their individual traits are positive and therefore recognize that this makes them into a good person. However, many children can find it difficult to make this deduction without the structured support suggested later in this section (in 5.7.3). Assuming that the child has been helped to do this successfully, though, they should then be asked to read the sentence on page 2 of the template, which says:

> I am a good person, who my family love very much and they are very proud of me!

All the adults concerned with the child should treat this as being the single most important fact about the child as a whole. Differences in theory of mind and picking up on other people's non-verbal communication make this statement's inclusion essential. Individuals with autism are less likely to know what others think about them unless they express this explicitly and give the child regular feedback on their actions and behaviour. Moreover, this sentence will be used later to positively frame the child's diagnosis when it is disclosed. The child should be referred back to this statement frequently throughout the rest of the programme, especially before moving on to any of its more sensitive stages or if the individual shows signs of becoming upset and anxious. This stage is then completed by recapping on these key points:

- all people are different on the outside and on the inside so it must be okay to be different

- the child is a good person who is loved by their family and the supportive people around them for being who they are.

5.7.3 Key issues and adjustments

The following issues have been known to occur during this stage of the programme:

- children finding it difficult to come up with ten words and phrases with which to describe themselves

- disagreements between the child and the adults over whether certain information about the individual's personality should be included in, or excluded from, their booklet

- children being unable to conclude from the list of their traits that they are a good person overall.

Children having to list ten words or phrases to describe themselves can often prove time-consuming and challenging. Many individuals are unable to complete this activity without some structured support. Lacking theory of mind, children with autism have less of a sense of *self* and *other* (Baron-Cohen *et al.* 1985). Moreover, they may not make assumptions about themselves that seem obvious to typical people (Blackburn 2013). In addition to this, they may not have a preference for completing open-ended tasks. In this case, they are also being asked to use abstract words and concepts which they might not understand or have in their vocabulary in the first place. These cognitive and communicative differences can make it harder for individuals with autism to accurately assess who they are and describe themselves to others. There are some very intelligent individuals with autism who have vast amounts of knowledge about academic subjects they are interested in, but who appear to know very little about themselves.

Children can complete this task more easily if given a selection of the *Personal trait cards* from the electronic resources (D1) to sort through. Each card depicts a different personal trait (e.g. tidy, messy, friendly or quiet). When using them in the session, the child is told to read the words on the cards carefully, and then choose some that they think could be used to describe their own personality. It may be necessary to explain what the words on some of the cards mean and provide the child with concrete examples, since much of this vocabulary could be outside the child's experience, even though it might be commonly used by typical children in their age group. Some individuals can find making choices or being presented with too much visual information challenging and should therefore only be asked to sort a few cards at a time.

Children with limited self-knowledge ought to be identified during the pre-programme work. If time and circumstances allow, the adults supporting them can then be advised to start working on addressing these gaps in the child's self-knowledge before they participate in the programme. Copies of the *Personal trait cards* can be given to children's parents and school staff to help them do this through carrying out matching and sorting activities. Adults can also help children to develop an increased self-understanding by labelling the child's personal traits for them in the context of their daily lives. After clearing up their bedroom, for example, a child could be told that they were being a *tidy* person. After completing a chore, it could be pointed out that they were being *helpful*. Some of these instances could be recorded visually with the child in a personal traits diary. This could be presented in a similar way to the friendship diaries which are recommended for use with some children by Tony Attwood (2008). Entries in this type of diary might read like these two examples:

> 20 May 2016: I found some money in the playground this morning. Instead of keeping it, I gave it to Mr Cohen. This was an honest thing to do. When I did this I was being an honest person. It is good to be honest.
>
> 21 May 2016: I went to the supermarket with Daddy today and helped him pack the shopping at the checkout counter. When I did this I was being a helpful person. It is good to be helpful.

If, despite having access to the *Personal trait cards*, a child still experiences difficulties coming up with words to describe themselves during the session, the adults may need to use their own knowledge of the child to prompt them with relevant questions. Ricky, for example, laughed and said that he was a messy person when his mother asked him to describe the state of his bedroom. As a final resort, if the child still cannot complete this task, the adults might need to supply the remaining information themselves so that the programme can move forward. Although this involves a more deductive teaching approach, it is still possible to give the child a degree of ownership over what is written about them in their booklet. This can be done by giving the child concrete examples of when they have displayed each of the traits that the adults suggest and then asking them to decide whether they agree with what has been said about them.

Children with autism have distorted self-image (Vermeulen 2013) and, like anyone, can be upset by being presented with what appears from their perspective to be unpleasant or inaccurate information about themselves.

Consequently, adults and children have sometimes disagreed with each other over whether particular attributes should be included in the booklet. The content of the booklet needs to be truthful and provide each child with an accurate and honest description of themselves and their autism. Adults should therefore take a firm stand in ensuring that inaccurate information about a child is not included in their booklet and that essential information is recorded even if this might go against the child's wishes. When certain things must be included in the booklet in these circumstances, the disagreement should be noted in the narrative. Things can usually be resolved satisfactorily by listing any disputed attributes separately beneath an explanatory sentence which says something like 'My parents and the adults who work with me think that these words also describe my personality...'

Children often seem to find it hard to identify any sort of overall pattern in the personal traits that they list. Instead of concluding, for example, that they are a nice or a good person, children have sometimes described themselves by reciting all ten traits from their list (e.g. 'This makes me a friendly, funny, clever, hardworking, distractible, caring, kind, helpful, talkative and polite person'). Other children have responded by randomly picking out a single item from the list (e.g. 'This makes me a talkative person'). This may be because people with autism have a more fragmented view of the world around them and so have difficulty generalizing information (Frith 2003). They might also not know which of their traits might be associated with being either a good or bad person. They may never have been taught explicitly that, for example, being tidy, loving or helpful is regarded as a positive personal quality. Furthermore, it is possible that a child with autism might not be able to appreciate how these various types of behaviour can influence the way others feel about them unless they have been taught this over time. It is important therefore that when teaching children with autism about their attributes and labelling them, they are told explicitly which ones other people might look upon as either being positive or not to be encouraged.

When children experience problems with this activity, the adults could go back through the list of their traits with them and help them assess which might be positive and can be used to describe a good person before counting them up. This process could be worked through visually on notepaper as a sorting activity. The child could be shown these three headings: *good*, *okay* and *not so good*; and then be asked to say which column they think each of their own traits should be listed under. In Kim's case, this may have led to her initial list being rearranged to appear like this:

Good	Okay	Not so good
friendly	talkative	messy
funny		
clever		
hardworking		
caring		
kind		
helpful		
polite		

When their traits are sorted and presented visually in this way, it can often be much easier for children to then conclude that on the whole they are a good person. There are still going to be some children, however, who may not necessarily be able to make a similar deduction. They will just need to be told that they are a good person as a fact so that they can progress on to the next stage.

5.8 STAGE 3: EXPLORING AND IDENTIFYING THE CHILD'S AREAS OF STRENGTH

5.8.1 Introduction

This section explains how to help a child complete page 3 of the Level 2 autism template (C2) as shown in Kim's booklet (B2). By the end of this stage the child should have identified their individual and overall areas of strength. This involves working through each of the following steps:

- reading the title and first sentence on page 3 of the template

- explaining what a strength is and how everyone, including the child, has things that they are good at doing

- showing the child the partial sentences that are written next and asking them to complete each one by naming a relevant famous person

- guiding the child towards drawing up a list of ten of their own strengths to record in the template

- guiding the child towards completing the partial sentence which says, 'These are mostly things that…' so that it describes a general overall pattern in the things that they are able to do well

- reading and discussing the last sentence on page 3 of the template to affirm that the child has many strengths

- recapping on the key teaching points from the first three stages of the programme

- referring the child to their session schedule.

5.8.2 Instructions and explanation

This stage should be introduced by reading and discussing the first sentence on page 3 of the template which says, 'All people, including me, have strengths. Strengths are things that people are good at doing.' To illustrate this point, the child should then be shown the four partial sentences that are written below this (starting with 'Some people are great musicians like…') and be asked to try to complete each sentence by naming a relevant famous person. Children are usually asked to choose a renowned musician, actor, sportsperson and artist. Some children may come up with more than one example under a particular category or ask to include famous people who have achieved things in other areas they are interested in (e.g. politicians, astronauts, scientists, dancers) and this is fine as long as it does not take up too much time or cause the work to become sidetracked. In Kim's booklet (B2) these four sentences read as follows once they had been completed:

Some people are great musicians like Alicia Keys.

Some people are great actors like Rowan Atkinson and Marilyn Monroe.

Some people are great sportspeople like Mohammed Ali.

Some people are great artists like Andy Warhol.

This passage can be illustrated with passport-sized photographs of the people named by the child, taken from the internet, as shown in Kim's booklet (B2). In the interests of time and helping children stay focused on their work, it is impractical to go online to search for these photographs during the session. This is best done by the person leading the work later while they are preparing the template for the second session. Children have seldom appeared to be bothered about this, but if it does turn out to be a problem, the child can be allowed to choose their own photographs later, provided it is possible for someone to forward them to the person leading the work by email before an agreed deadline.

Having discussed the achievements of famous people, the work then focuses on exploring and affirming the child's own strengths. The child should be shown the next partial sentence which says, 'We all have strengths. Here is a list of some of the things that I am good at, or becoming good at: …' They should then be asked to think about the things that they are good at doing and try to say what they are. This is so that a list of ten of the child's strengths can be included in the child's booklet. Again, children are encouraged to supply as much of this information themselves as possible. A distinction should be made between activities that the child enjoys doing and those that they can do well when deciding what to add to this list. It can include things that the child is experiencing relative success in at school and activities that they are able to do competently elsewhere. Importantly, the child does not have to be the best person at doing any of them. Kim's booklet lists her having strengths in the following areas:

• designing clothes	• electronic gaming	• spelling
• drawing	• reading	• finding out about clothes and animals
• using a computer	• maths	
	• using an iPad	• swimming.

Table 5.1 offers real examples of areas that children participating in the programme have been described as being good at doing.

After this list has been compiled, the child should be shown the next partial sentence, which says, 'These are mostly things that…' They are then asked to try to spot an overall pattern in their areas of strength so that their reply can be used to complete it. This can be started off by going back through the items in the list with the child and then asking them a question like 'What sort of things do you think you are mostly good at doing?'

If possible, it is hoped that the child will conclude in some way that their strengths are based mainly around things like their special interests, similar academic areas (e.g. sciences), the types of objects they might prefer using (e.g. musical instruments, computers or electronic gadgets, vacuum cleaners) or activities that are less dependent upon them interacting and communicating with others. If the child provides an appropriate answer, the leading adult should complete the sentence with the child to reflect their reply, and read it back as a key point. In Kim's case, the completed sentence says, 'These are mostly things that I can do on my own without my friends or other people.'

A few more examples of how this sentence could be completed with different children are:

- 'I am mostly good at using electronic gadgets.'

- 'I am mostly good at things which do not involve working or playing with other people.'

- 'I am mostly good at working with facts and numbers.'

- 'I am mostly good at designing and making things.'

While it is important to a child's self-esteem to acknowledge their individual areas of strength, this generalized sentence is going to be valuable later. The overall pattern it describes will be instrumental in providing the child with their own personalized headline sentence to describe what having autism means during the next session.

To round things off, the child should be referred to the final prewritten sentence on page 3 of the template which says, 'I am clever and good at lots of things!' This is another key statement that needs to be reaffirmed constantly as the work progresses to protect and develop the individual's emotional well-being and self-esteem. Finally, this stage should be completed by recapping positively on the main points from the session so far, as listed below:

- All people are different on the outside and on the inside so it must be okay to be different.

- The child is a good person who is loved by the supportive people around them and they are proud of them for being who they are.

- The child is intelligent and good at doing a number of things.

- The child is particularly good at doing things which fall into the overall pattern identified during this stage (e.g. using things and objects, learning facts and figures, working with gadgets, making things or engaging in activities that can be done alone).

5.8.3 Key issues and adjustments

This subsection provides advice on how to prevent or manage the following issues which can interfere with some children's progress during this stage of the programme:

- the child's progress being delayed by them being unable to name four famous people

- the child being unable to identify ten of their own strengths

- the child appearing to have few recognizable strengths

- disagreements between the child and adults over whether certain information about their strengths should be included in, or excluded from, the booklet

- the child being unable to identify an overall pattern in their individual areas of strength.

Children are sometimes unable to come up with names to complete the partial sentences about famous people unaided. Individuals have found it hard to narrow down their choices or to come up with any in the first place. This problem can often be solved by their parents or another adult using their knowledge of the child to prompt them with more specific questions like:

- 'Who is your favourite football player?'

- 'Who sings that song you're always listening to on your iPod?'

- 'Which artist have you been learning about in class?'

- 'What is the name of the actor you liked in the film we watched together last night?'

When necessary, children can be asked to come up with fewer examples of famous people and on some occasions this task could be left out of the programme altogether if it is felt that it will be irrelevant to the child. This omission never seems to have had a negative impact on the overall outcome of the work and in any case this part of the narrative is not included in the template for children working at Level 1 in the programme.

While many children can easily think of and say what their strengths are, others can find it difficult to compose a list containing more than a few things that they think they can do well. More aloof children with autism often pay less attention to the people around them (Wing 2002) so may not be able to compare how well they do things with their peers. Besides this, most of the reasons why children can have difficulty identifying their strengths appear to be fairly similar to the self-assessment issues that cause individuals difficulty coming up with words to describe their personality, and so, as suggested below, they may respond positively to fairly similar support strategies.

The initial meeting with the child and the adult conversations that take place during the pre-programme work should provide an idea of how easily the child can identify and talk about their areas of strength. If it is anticipated that the child will have problems doing this during the sessions, the adults caring for and working with them can be advised to prepare the individual for this in the meantime by labelling their strengths for them in the context of their daily lives. For example, if a child makes a model from a construction kit, an adult might say something like 'Well done, Kim, this is a really good model; this shows that you are good at construction!'

There are various ways that the adults can prompt children who run into difficulties in listing their strengths during the session itself. For instance, they could ask the child to look through a copy of their school timetable to check if there are any lessons in which they think they might be making good progress. The adults can also refer to the back-up list of the child's strengths that they should have drawn up during the pre-programme work. Relevant questions can then be asked to prompt the child on the basis of the contents of that list or their other knowledge of the child. Ricky's mother, for example, asked him to say what he enjoyed doing on Friday evenings, to which he replied, 'Playing badminton.' After talking about this further, it was decided that this was one of the things that Ricky was learning to do well and so it was included in his list.

Another way to support children who have difficulties in identifying their strengths more independently is to turn this activity into a visual sorting task by using a relevant selection of the *Strength cards* provided in the electronic resources (D2). Each of these cards names an activity or situation in which different individuals could have strengths (e.g. mathematics, using a computer, learning facts). These are similar to the *Personal trait cards* described above and can be used in the same ways. Again, the child can be asked to look at the cards and read the words carefully before choosing those that show things they think they are good at doing or find easy. The main activities that adults know a child has strengths in will need to be included in the selection of cards, but, again, the child should only be given as many cards as they can manage at a time. These cards are not exhaustive, so blank cards have been provided for adults to add in any strengths a child has that are not included in this set. Parents and school staff can also use these cards to prepare children before the programme.

Alternatively, some of the *Challenge cards* (D3), which are designed for use during the next stage, could be mixed in with the *Strength cards* which the child might be given now. The *Challenge cards* name situations and activities that children with autism tend to find harder than typical people (e.g. making friends, being in crowds, working in groups). The child should be asked to sort the combination of cards that they have been given from both sets into three separate piles, showing things they can do well, what they find harder and things that are neither very easy nor overly challenging. The first pile of cards can then be used to help compile the list of the child's strengths. This approach may also save time and make things far less stressful when the child is asked to try to identify their areas of difficulty during Stage 4. The second pile of cards can be used then to help formulate the list of their challenges. Moreover, the child will have identified their difficulties discreetly within the context of a more positive activity (i.e. exploring the things that they are good at doing).

Occasionally, adults might need to name some of the child's strengths for them so that the programme can continue. Again, if this happens, the child's ownership of the information can still be partially maintained by offering them concrete examples of when they have done these things well and then inviting them to comment on whether they agree with what has been said. If a child is unsure about whether they have strengths in given areas, the visual *Easiness rating scale* (D4) can be used to help them to assess their ability. The child should be asked to use the scale to rate how easy they think they find each of the activities suggested by the adults, with a score of 1 being 'very easy' and 5 'lots harder'. Anything rated by the child at either 1 or 2 can be added to the list of the child's strengths.

Helping children list ten things that they can do well can be far more testing if they also have learning difficulties. Children with these needs may have fewer obvious strengths than typical children or other individuals with autism. This problem can be solved by asking them to come up with a shorter list, perhaps containing around five or six items, and by including everyday activities such as different types of household chores, looking after pets, helping with gardening or shopping and doing jobs for their teachers among the things that they are good at doing.

As with their personality traits, children and adults can disagree over whether certain things should be included in a list of an individual's strengths. Children may sometimes want to add activities that they find enjoyable and rewarding, regardless of whether they can do them well. Alternatively, some children might believe that they are good at doing things that they unknowingly find challenging. This could apply to things that they are only able to do with a considerable amount of support from others. As already stated in 3.4.1, passive children's difficulties in areas such as joining in with games or finding a partner to work with can be masked by the one-sided efforts of typical children (Wing 2002). It is important that this does not lead to the inclusion of things that are innately challenging for children with autism in a list of an individual's strengths. This would be inconsistent with the child's diagnosis and make it harder to explain autism correctly to the individual concerned. This could also mislead children into believing that they do not need support.

At the same time, the adults should try to avoid telling a child they are not very good at doing things that they gain pleasure and enjoyment from if these are unrelated to their autism (e.g. singing or drawing). If the child wrongly thinks that they can do them well, and is insistent that they should be included in the booklet, a sensible compromise might be to include these activities in an additional sentence beneath the list of their strengths which begins by saying 'I also enjoy doing these things…'.

In some instances, children may argue against areas that they are able in being recorded in their booklet. This could be because someone has previously made a disparaging remark about a particular activity or that the child does not find engaging in it pleasurable. Some less flexible individuals may not be able to accept that they have strengths in areas in which they know other children can do as well as them or better. These disputes can be managed similarly to disagreements over the inclusion of information about the child's personality traits. Things can usually be resolved by listing any attributes the child does not want to have written in the booklet separately under a heading which notes that 'The adults who know me think that I am good at doing the following things…'.

For the same reasons that many children may need help in coming up with a generalized description of their own personality, some are also likely to need support in spotting an overall pattern in their individual areas of strength. In all cases, adults leading this session should try to identify a relevant generalized pattern in the child's strengths themselves while the individual's list is being compiled and before they ask the child to try to complete the sentence about this. As stated above, this should be a pattern which can be used later to help explain the child's own manifestation of autism to them. Taking Kim's list as an example, the adults might have already concluded privately that her collection of individual strengths pointed towards her having an overall preference for activities that she can participate in without necessarily having to interact with others. A child with the strengths attributed to Kim might be helped to reach a similar conclusion by being referred back to their list of strengths and asked to say whether each activity was something they preferred to do alone or with other people. Again, this could be presented to them visually on notepaper as a sorting task. Using the same list as an example, the adult could write the following three headings:

- things I always like doing on my own

- things I like to do on my own and with other people

- things I always like doing with other people.

The child can then be asked to say which column they think each of their strengths should be classified under. This activity might have led to Kim's list being rearranged like this:

Things I always like doing alone	Things I like doing alone and with other people	Things I only like doing with other people
designing clothes	finding out about clothes and animals	swimming
drawing	electronic gaming	
using a computer		
maths		
using an iPad		
spelling		
reading		

From here it should be easier for a child with these types of attributes to conclude that, overall, they are perhaps mostly good at doing things that can be done without interacting much with others.

All children with autism are different, so the adult should look to elicit a pattern that is well matched to an individual's own strength types and how their autism will need to be described to them. For some children, the comparisons could be between abilities that they have in activities that lean towards an individual using objects (e.g. computers, gadgets and musical instruments), learning about certain groups of academic subjects (e.g. mathematics, sciences and technology), working with facts and figures, or designing and making things, as opposed to things that involve working, playing and communicating with others. It has to be accepted, however, that some children will still need to be provided with this information about themselves directly by the adults so that they can move on to the next stage of the programme.

5.9 STAGE 4: IDENTIFYING THE CHILD'S CHALLENGES

5.9.1 Introduction

This section explains how to work through page 4 of the template (C2) as illustrated in Kim's booklet (B2). The aim of this stage is to raise the child's awareness of their main individual and overall challenges while causing them as little anxiety or upset as possible. This involves working through each of the following steps:

- reminding the child of how to request help or a short break if they become anxious or upset about anything that needs to be talked about

- explaining that everyone finds some things harder to do

- guiding the child towards drawing up a list of up to six situations or activities which they can find harder than other children of their age and recording this in the template

- guiding the child towards completing the partial sentence which says, 'These are mostly things that…' so that it reflects a general pattern in the types of things that they find harder

- reading the next sentence on the page to inform the child that they can make improvements in their challenging areas

- informing the child that their challenges are reciprocal (i.e. typical people also find it harder to interact with them) and then completing the partial sentence which starts with 'Other children might need help learning…'

- recapping briefly on the main points learned during this stage

- referring the child to their schedule.

5.9.2 Instructions and explanation

Some children can find this stage more emotionally challenging. It involves talking to them about issues that could be very uncomfortable for them to discuss. Needless to say, it is essential that the adults try to appear outwardly calm, behave reassuringly and resist any temptation to rush through this stage if things start to get difficult.

If a child has behavioural challenges that impact negatively on the people around them, this is going to have to be mentioned here. It is important to the child's self-esteem and the success of the programme that the adults appear non-judgemental when doing this. They need to avoid saying things that might unwittingly make the child feel they are a bad person or that the point of this meeting is to tell them off and blame them for their past behaviour. Although it can be harder to make this into a positive discussion, it does not have to be a negative one either; rather, it should be conducted in a matter-of-fact way.

It is vital to recap on and reaffirm the child's positive qualities and strengths for them before starting to work through this more sensitive stage. If the programme has been restructured so that this stage is taught as the first activity in one of a series of shorter sessions, it is essential that the child is given a thorough recap of the main points that are meant to be emphasized at the end of Stage 3. Before moving on, the child should also be reminded about how they can ask for help or request a break. They should also be shown, on their schedule, how much they have accomplished so far and that the session has almost been completed.

To offer them some initial reassurance, children should be told that they are not the only ones who find certain things challenging. It is made clear that everyone finds some things harder to do than other people and that this is a perfectly normal part of life. Although this seems to be a fairly obvious fact, a lack of theory of mind and inattention to others may mean that there will be children who might not know that other people experience difficulties unless they have already told them this. The adults in the room could share one or two of their areas of difficulty with the child. As explained in 4.2.3, the word 'harder' is used consistently in this programme when referring to things that children find difficult. To minimize the negative impact of working through this stage on their self-esteem, children should be told that this means that it is possible for them to make some progress in the areas that they find more stressful and challenging before going on to read these sentences from page 4 of the template:

> I find some things harder.
>
> Like everyone, I find some things easy to understand and do.
>
> Everyone finds some things harder to do.
>
> Here is a list of some things that I find harder than most children of my age: …

The child should then be supported to draw up a short list of things that they think they find harder than most other children so that this can be included in their booklet. This is done by asking the child to try to think of some of the activities and situations that they find challenging or stressful and say what they are. Children should be told, however, that some of the things that they say will be included in the booklet and some might not.

Adult decisions on the types of challenges that should be recorded in the final list ought to focus on whether they relate to the child's differences in the areas of social interaction, communication, thinking and behaving flexibly, and sensory processing. Challenges that tend to be common to typical children too, such as difficulties with school work and other practical activities, need to be given less priority for inclusion in this list. Whatever is recorded needs to relate more directly to the child's autism-related differences so that they can be used to formulate an appropriate pattern for explaining their diagnosis to them later.

Wherever possible, the challenges recorded here should relate to specific situations rather than be listed as more general things such as socializing and communicating. This will help to make their areas of difficulty more tangible for the child and give them a clearer idea of their support needs and the reasons for them having it in different circumstances (Vermeulen 2013). In the example booklet, Kim's list of challenges is as follows:

- working with a partner or in a group
- playtimes and making friends
- listening to other people and talking about the right thing
- taking turns
- being in crowded or noisy places.

Further examples of things that children who have participated in this programme have found harder are listed in the bottom section of Table 5.1.

Adults should always try to keep the number of items in a child's list of challenges down to an absolute minimum. This is to maintain the child's engagement in the work as well as preserve their long-term self-esteem and expectations. In any event, this list ought to contain fewer items than the one that itemizes their strengths, and this positive imbalance should be made obvious to the child. It is vital, however, that all of the child's most pressing challenges are recorded and they are made aware of what they are. To keep this list concise therefore, the adults may need to look for opportunities to pair up or group some of the child's similar difficulties together. An example of this is shown above where Kim's challenges with making friends and finding children to play with are combined into a single item. So too are the issues with being in crowded and noisy environments.

Having completed this list, children then need to be helped to complete the sentence which starts 'These are mostly things that...' Once finished, this sentence should describe a general overall pattern in the areas that the individual finds harder. This is usually initiated by asking the child to read back through their listed challenges and then try to answer a question such as 'What sort of things do you mostly find harder?' There are no set answers to this question, but the child should be led towards reaching the conclusion that their main overall difficulties are associated with interacting with and understanding other people. In Kim's narrative, the completed sentence says:

> These are mostly things that can make it harder for me to join in and do things with other people.

Whatever is written in this sentence will also have an important bearing on the wording of the main headline sentence which the child will be given in the next session to explain what their diagnosis means. Again, this is because autism is explained to children as being a term for describing people whose overall strengths and challenges may be like their own. The child should then be shown the next sentence which is intended to offer them the reassurance that they can make progress in their areas of difficulty by saying:

> I can learn to do the things I find harder better and I might need some help.

To avoid attributing their overall challenges solely to the child, the final sentence on this page needs to be completed to raise the individual's awareness that their difficulties are reciprocal for the typical people around them. This points out that other children may also have support needs in learning to interact with the child. In Kim's booklet, for example, the completed sentence states:

> Other children might need help learning how to join in and do things with me too.

Before moving on to sum up the session as a whole, the following points from this stage should be recapped briefly:

- Like everyone else, the child finds certain things harder than other children.

- Most of the child's main challenges follow the overall pattern that was identified during this stage (i.e. they are mostly in areas that involve interacting with and understanding other people).

- With help, the child can make some improvements in the areas that they find challenging and stressful.

- The other people around the child may need support of their own in learning how to interact with the child better.

5.9.3 Key issues and adjustments

This subsection contains guidance on how to prevent or respond to the following issues that can occur while working through this stage:

- children reacting negatively to learning about and discussing some of their challenges

- children being unable to list their challenges or acknowledge having some of them

- disagreements between the child and adults over whether certain information about their challenges should be included in, or excluded from, the booklet

- the child being unable to identify an overall pattern in their areas of challenge.

Not surprisingly, some children can become anxious while having to discuss things that they find challenging. This issue seems to arise more when working with cognitively able and older children (Miller 2014), rather than with individuals who think at more literal levels, have additional learning difficulties and pay less attention to people around them. Able children who have little prior awareness about their differences before having this conversation can sometimes appear shocked or surprised when they find out about these issues (Miller 2014). To date, however, no child has ever had a serious emotional outburst which led to them refusing to take any further part in the work at this point. Those who have experienced these difficulties appeared mildly distressed or agitated and on some occasions did not want to talk about some of their difficulties or tried to deny having them.

To try to ensure that these types of situations do not escalate and get out of hand, it has already been stated that the pre-programme work should be used to discover the signs that might indicate when the child is becoming anxious and distressed. These signs can be unique to the individual and be very different to, or even the exact opposite of, those presented by typical children when they are upset. Some children may smile or laugh. Others might have blank facial expressions while at the same time doing things like tapping their feet, rubbing their hands together or rocking slightly on their chair. It is essential to find out what strategies are most effective in helping an individual to manage their arousal levels when they are becoming agitated (e.g. doing breathing exercises, counting, being given a fidget toy to hold or offered a calming break).

Children with autism can find it difficult to express their feelings verbally so the *Emotions rating scale* (D5) can be a useful tool for helping them do this. The adults can use this with the child to monitor their emotional state at various points throughout the programme by asking them to rate how they are feeling numerically. On this scale, a score of 1 would indicate that the child is feeling totally relaxed and happy, whereas a rating of 5 would communicate that they are very upset and feel in danger of having an outburst. If a child gives a rating of 3 or 4, they may need to be offered a short break from the work. A score of 5 needs to be avoided at all costs, so if a child's rating remains consistently at 4 and things do not appear to be improving, an early end to the session and a temporary suspension of the work should be seriously considered.

Although it has not happened in any of the work that I have carried out, if a child does react with extreme anger to being asked to talk about their challenges and refuses to engage with the programme any further, the rest of the work will need to be put on hold. It should be made clear to the child in the meantime that there are caring people there to support them in managing their areas of difficulty. The child should also be informed that they will be able to continue with the programme when they feel ready to find out more about themselves and the reasons why they find certain things challenging and harder to discuss.

Some children have been unable to produce a list of their challenges. This has usually been for similar reasons that individuals have found it difficult to come up with words to describe both their personal traits and their areas of strength. Similar strategies can again be applied to help these children. Children who are identified during the pre-programme work as being unaware of what their challenges are can be prepared for this session by having their challenges labelled for them gently by the adults around them. In much the same way as suggested for labelling children's other attributes, this should be done sympathetically in the context of real-life situations as they arise. Introducing children to their challenges gradually in this way may perhaps avoid the prospect of a child experiencing the shock that could occur if they find out about all their main differences at the same time and have to discuss them in an unfamiliar and potentially stressful situation such as this session. It is vital, however, that children are reminded of their positive attributes when their difficulties are being labelled and that they are also told that there are supportive people available to help them.

Adults can help children who get stuck while trying to list their challenges in the session, again by referring to the list that they drew up themselves before the programme started and using their own knowledge of the individual to prompt them with questions and comments. Children have, for instance, decided that 'being with lots of people' was harder for them after the adults reminded them that they were avoidant of certain situations such as eating in the school lunch hall, sitting in assembly or going to parties.

Children who need more visual prompting during the session can be offered a selection of the *Challenge cards* (D3) to sort. The cards given to the child should include the main situations that the individual is likely to experience difficulties in, or find distressing, because of their autism (e.g. group work, making friends, playing with other people). They should also be given some cards that do not apply to them. As suggested in the previous section, this task may be easier and perhaps more positive for the child if the same cards are used first during the previous stage when helping them to identify their strengths. By doing this, the child would already have identified their key challenges discreetly through the cards that were left over from that task.

If an individual is still unable to come up with an adequate list of their challenges, the adults may again have to provide the information themselves. Once more, it is still possible for the child to be given some ownership of this information. The adults can present the child with some concrete examples of situations that they are known to find challenging, before asking the individual to use the *Easiness rating scale* to decide whether they agree with the adults' views. Anything that the child rates at 4 or 5 would present a challenge that could be included in this list. This approach can also be applied when working with children who are too anxious to talk about their challenges and differences themselves, but are still willing to continue working.

As with their other attributes, children can sometimes argue against some of their challenges being recorded in their booklet. Like typical people, individuals with autism can find thinking about their difficulties upsetting and be unable to believe and accept that they have them in the first place. Adults need to remain firm and not backtrack just to spare the child's feelings when it comes to recording an individual's main challenges, though. It is perhaps vital to the child's future progress and acceptance of their support that they are made aware of what they find more difficult. The approach used with children who are reluctant or opposed to having some of their other attributes recorded can usually help to resolve these disputes reasonably calmly too. Challenges that children argue against being recorded should be listed in the booklet under a heading such as 'The adults who know me think I find these things harder'.

Identifying a general pattern in the completed list of their challenges is again something that some children have found difficult. Many individuals will need help with this, usually for the same reasons that children needed support in generalizing their other traits during the previous two stages. Ideally, this particular list should contain no more than five or six different items, which relate mainly to issues the child experiences when interacting with other people. As this is a shorter and more focused list, when shown it, children can find it easier to conclude that their main difficulties are associated with them joining in and doing things with other people or children. Frequent inclusion of the words 'children' or 'people' in the phrases recorded in this list is likely to help. If, for example, a child's list of challenges is 'working and playing with other people, talking to people I don't know well and being in places where there are lots of people', they could be asked to look for the words that appear most frequently. In this example, a child might more readily be helped to see that their key challenges are mainly associated with them interacting with people. If a child needs any further assistance, the adult could work through the list with them and ask them to sort each challenge according to whether it involves doing things with other people or is something that is focused around learning about particular subjects, engaging in similar kinds of activities or using certain types of objects.

5.10 SESSION SUMMARY: WHAT WE LEARNED TODAY

In the final part of the session, the key points that the child will have been taught so far are all drawn together. To avoid the inconvenience of having to refer back to several different pages in this book, these points are listed collectively below as follows:

- All people are different on the outside and on the inside, so it must be okay for the child to be different.

- The child is a good person who is loved by their family and the supportive people around them.

- The child has many strengths and theirs mostly fall into the overall pattern which was identified and recorded in their booklet during Stage 3.

- Like everyone, they have various challenges and theirs mainly follow the overall pattern which was identified and recorded in their booklet during Stage 4.

- The child can learn to do the things they find harder better and will need some help with this.

- Other people can find it harder to interact with the child and they may also need help with learning to do this better.

This recap also offers a brief opportunity for assessing how much the child is able to recall from what they were taught in this session. Children can be asked questions before being shown each of the above points again in the relevant parts of the booklet while checking their answers. The following sample questions have been used with some children when doing this:

- How many people look exactly the same on the outside (none or lots)?

- How many people have the same personality (none or lots)?

- What type of person are you (a good person or a bad person)?

- What sort of things do you find it easier to do (group activities or things that you can do by yourself/involve using gadgets, etc.)?

- What sorts of things do you find it harder to do (joining in with other people or doing things by yourself)?

These questions are only meant as rough examples. Whatever the child is asked will need to be adjusted according to their individual language skills and cognitive levels. Some children might need to be given alternative answers from which to choose a correct one, as in the bracketed alternatives written at the end of each of the above questions.

It needs to be noted again, however, that a child with autism repeating back information they were given earlier should not be taken as definite proof that they have understood, accepted or internalized what they were taught. The possibility that they are just echoing what they have been told about themselves must always be considered (Vermeulen 2013).

Children are taught a lot about themselves in this session, so there should not be an expectation that any individual will remember and understand all this straight away. This is why the booklet is an important tool for helping children to continue learning about themselves at their own pace later. If felt necessary, the child's parents, and other adults, can be provided with printouts of the work from this session to go back over what the child was taught and revise specific points with them before the next session. But care should be taken not to overload or put the child off.

Having recapped all the key points, it is advisable to set aside a few moments also to assess how the child might have responded emotionally to the work. In addition to observations made throughout the session, this can be done by asking the child to use the *Emotions rating scale* to rate their feelings again now that the session is ending. The child should also be asked to say whether there was anything in particular that they either enjoyed learning about and doing or which they found harder or upsetting.

The session should end by referring the child first to their schedule and then to the programme guide. They should be shown on their schedule that all the activities for this session have been completed and what they are going to do next when they leave the room. Finally, the child should be directed to tick or cross out Session 1 on the programme guide to show that it has finished and be reminded of the arrangements for the other two sessions.

5.11 ASSESSING THE SESSION AND DECIDING HOW TO PROCEED

This section considers what might need to be done immediately after completing the first session. If someone other than the child's parents is leading the work, they will need to try to liaise briefly with them as well as any other available adults who are significantly involved with the individual and this work. A decision will need to be reached on whether it is still thought sensible and safe to tell the child about their autism as originally planned. Although the first session of *All About Me* is meant to be the initial part of a broader programme for telling and teaching children about their autism diagnosis, it can be treated as a stand-alone or assessment session. The programme can be halted at this stage, or earlier, if a child experiences difficulties which indicate that it would be unwise at that time to go on to disclose their diagnosis.

Decisions on whether to proceed with or suspend the programme should be judged on the basis of the adults' perceptions of how well the child understood the first part of the work and their emotional response to it. Everyone concerned will need to be mindful that the final point at which sharing the child's diagnosis with them can be deferred has almost been reached. Children who do not already know about it will be told that they have autism in the second session. It goes without saying that once this has been done there can be no turning back, so the child's and their parents' readiness need to be reviewed both now and immediately before the start of the next session.

If a decision is taken to suspend the work, the adults will need to try to agree on what might have to be done next to try to get things back on track. This might include taking more time over labelling the child's attributes with them, going back over particular aspects of what was taught during this session in more detail, creating opportunities for the child to develop further familiarity with the person leading the work, or, in more extreme circumstances, allowing the child to come to terms with any negative reactions they may have had to discussing their differences. All the written work from this session could be used to produce a shorter booklet about the child and their attributes which could be used as a support tool in the meantime.

If the work is to proceed as planned, the adults will need to use what they already knew about the child, along with what was discovered about them in this session, to finalize how they will describe the child's autism to them. The explanation that each child is given is personal to them. As already mentioned, in this programme the child's headline explanation of their diagnosis is intended to present autism to them as being a word for describing a person with similar attributes to theirs. The wording of this explanation has to be framed within the context of what the child has just learned about the overall patterns in their strengths and challenges during Stages 3 and 4 of the programme. It will also need to be presented in language that is appropriate to the child's level of understanding. The person leading the programme will have to add this into the template's content by following the advice given in Chapter 6 on preparing for Session 2. Thought should be given as to whether the template's language and formatting were appropriate to the levels that the child is working at when they were used in the first session. If not, adjustments will need to be made to this so that the completed booklet will be suitable for the child's needs (for more advice on this see 7.2.2).

If a child found it difficult to engage in or understand the first part of the work, the adults will need to decide whether this calls for the programme being differentiated further. This may involve bringing in some of the additional resources and strategies described in Chapter 7. Finally, progressive adjustments will need to be made if a child did not seem to find the work challenging enough or felt that it was more suited to younger and less able children.

Chapter 6

TEACHING SESSIONS 2 AND 3: DISCLOSING AND EXPLAINING THE CHILD'S DIAGNOSIS

The programme resources for this chapter can be downloaded from www.jkp.com/voucher using the code QLspdxjP

6.1 INTRODUCTION

This chapter provides the generic instructions for guiding children through the rest of the programme. Although it is structured in a slightly different way to Chapter 5, it also contains descriptions of how different children might respond to the work, identifies the key issues that could occur and suggests ways to address them.

Session 2 involves working through Stages 5 to 10 of the programme framework, as shown in Table 4.1, while completing the remaining pages in the child's booklet template. This is when children are first told, or reminded, that they have been diagnosed with autism and are given a personalized explanation of what it means. The finished booklet is read through and discussed during Session 3 to review its contents and informally assess the child's levels of understanding and acceptance of what they have been taught across the whole programme.

Most of the key issues that can interfere with some children's progress during Session 1 occur when they are asked to provide the information needed to compile lists of their various personal attributes and then use these to draw overall conclusions about themselves. These two sessions rely more on the leading adults providing children with a manageable amount of factual information about autism and explaining what it means to them in the context of what they would have already discovered about themselves during the first session. Very little new information is sought from the children and therefore there are fewer opportunities for the work to stall.

The key issues that can occur during Sessions 2 and 3 are mainly linked to how children might react emotionally and psychologically to being told that they have autism, and them making sense of and accepting what they are told about their diagnosis. As already stated, it can take some children a long time to gain a sufficient understanding and acceptance of their autism, regardless of how their diagnosis is shared with them and who tells them about it. This means that once a child has been told about their autism, these kinds of issues could affect the outcomes of any of the remaining stages of the programme. Some children continue to experience these difficulties after all the work has been completed. This being so, and to avoid unnecessary repetition, the key issues associated with these two sessions are first identified and noted when describing the stages of the programme within which they could first occur. Advice for addressing each of these issues is then provided in a separate section (6.15) after the instructions for teaching the final session. In some cases, further work may need to be carried out later, and this is outlined in more detail in Chapter 8, which suggests some ways to follow up the programme.

The instructions for teaching these two sessions are also illustrated by the fictional booklet about Kim (B2), which was referred to in Chapter 5, and they offer guidance on how to complete the remaining sections in the blank template which was used to produce it (C2). However, there are a few slight differences in how this part of the programme needs to be taught to children with AS who are operating at similar developmental levels to Kim. These differences are pointed out when they occur and references are made to the relevant sections of the Level 2 template for children with AS (C3) and the corresponding booklet about a fictional boy called Max (B3). Again, it is advisable to have copies of these resources to hand so that they can be referred to for clarity while reading through the instructions given in this chapter.

6.2 TEACHING AND LEARNING OBJECTIVES

As already noted in Table 4.1, the main teaching and learning objectives for Session 2 are as follows:

- To tell, or remind, the child they have autism or AS in a positive and matter-of-fact way, while framing their diagnosis in the context of what they learned about their own overall attributes in Session 1.

- To make the child aware that others have autism or AS and that, like many of them, they can lead a happy and fulfilling life.

- To help the child understand that autism or AS is a term that can be used to describe a type of individual with similar overall strengths and challenges to theirs, and that it is a difference rather than a disorder.

- To provide the child with simple basic information about what autism or AS is, and is not, including a personalized 'headline' sentence to define the child's own autism or AS.

- To inform the child about the main people who are there to offer them support at home, school and elsewhere.

If Session 2 is delivered successfully, the child will learn that they have autism without becoming needlessly upset, be given an initial account of what their diagnosis means and finish writing their booklet.

All the learning objectives from Sessions 1 and 2 are reinforced while reading through and discussing the booklet during Session 3.

6.3 PREPARING FOR SESSION 2

6.3.1 Resources for Session 2

With the exception of the items noted below, all of the resources used in Session 1 (as listed in 5.3.3) are required again during the second session, for the reasons already given in Chapter 5. In addition, it is recommended that printed copies of the remaining pages of the child's booklet template are brought along for back-up purposes once they have been prepared for use.

Items which are *not* needed in Session 2:

- digital camera, batteries and leads

- *Personal trait cards*

- *Strength cards*

- *Challenge cards*

- draft lists of the child's strengths and challenges.

Details of what to itemize on a child's schedule for Session 2 are included later in the guidance on how to introduce this session (see 6.5). Certain sections of the booklet template will need to be prepared individually for the child before the session, as advised below.

6.3.2 Preparing the booklet template for use in Session 2

Session 2 involves working through and completing the remaining pages in the relevant booklet template: C2 for most children with autism and C3 for the majority of individuals who have AS. Several additions and adjustments need to be made to parts of the narrative in each template to personalize the explanation of autism so that it matches the child's own differences and reflects what they have discovered about themselves during the first session. These preparations can only be carried out after Session 1 has been taught. This should all be done before the second session to allow for the work to continue at an appropriate pace and without the child having to wait around.

The child's diagnosis is first disclosed to them on page 5 (in the Level 2 template, C2), where it says, 'I have autism.' This may need to be altered and added to if the official wording of the child's diagnosis does not include the word 'autism'. If the child has AS, then the adults should already be using a parallel template for this work (either C3 or C5) and need do nothing else. Adults working with children who have other conditions on the autism spectrum, such as pathological demand avoidance syndrome (PDA) or pervasive developmental disorder not otherwise specified, will have to tell the child about this first and then explain to them that it is a form of autism. If the child has PDA, for instance, this part of the narrative could be amended to read as follows: 'I have pathological demand avoidance syndrome or PDA for short. PDA is a type of autism.'

The adults involved in planning the work must decide on whether to continue referring to the child's condition as autism or to use the formal diagnostic label. If making the latter choice, then each instance of the word 'autism' in the template will need to be replaced by the term that is going to be used instead.

Page 5 (in the Level 2 templates) also contains these two partial sentences which are intended to help introduce the child's diagnosis:

- I am good at lots of things, such as…

- And there are some things that I find harder, like…

Both sentences need to be completed by adding one or two of the child's main attributes from the respective lists of their strengths and challenges which were drawn up in Session 1, as shown in the examples below:

- I am good at lots of things, such as using laptops and tablets.

- And there are some things that I find harder, like playing with other children.

Pages 6 to 8 (in the Level 2 templates) contain information about some famous people who may have been on the autism spectrum. Inserting pictures of these individuals from the internet would add more meaning to this section of the booklet. The templates accompanying this book only refer to individuals whose diagnosis or traits have been reported by reliable published sources. Numerous other individuals are cited on various websites as possibly having (or having had) autism. This leaves scope for those leading the work to include other people whose achievements are perhaps more relevant to a child's special interests and strengths or who they might have already heard about. When doing this, it should be stated clearly in the booklet that it is only *supposed* that those individuals have or had autism unless their diagnosis can be reliably verified (e.g. by the person concerned having publicly revealed their diagnosis themselves).

Page 10 (in the Level 2 templates) contains the partial sentence which, when completed, will be used to give the child the main headline explanation of their autism. When left blank, this sentence is set out like this:

Having autism describes someone like me who might be:
    good at…
    and
    can find it harder to…

The description of each child's autism is meant to be personal to them, and therefore there is no set way to complete either half of this very important sentence. What adults decide to write at the end of each clause should reflect the generalized patterns in the child's strengths and challenges which they were guided towards arriving at during the first session. It must also be consistent with an autism diagnosis. Not only that, it should appear separately, on its own page, to make it stand out clearly from the rest of the narrative.

Some examples of how this sentence could be written for different children are presented in Table 6.1 as guidance.

Table 6.1: How autism could be explained in a single headline sentence to different individuals

	Headline description of the child's autism
Example 1	Having autism describes someone like me who might be: good at doing certain things like acting and singing and can find it harder to understand other people.
Example 2	Having autism describes someone like me who might be: good at things like using computers and tablets and can need some help with learning how to play with other children.
Example 3	Having autism describes someone like me who might be: very talented in certain areas like maths and technology and can find it harder to make friends and find people to play with.
Example 4	Having autism describes someone like me who might be: good at doing some things that they can do on their own like computer gaming or swimming and can find it harder to get along with other people.

Some children might not be ready to accept that whatever is written in this sentence accurately describes them, particularly those who find it harder to acknowledge and discuss their challenges and differences during Session 1. It may be necessary to depersonalize the opening part of this sentence as a compromise for these children, by making it say, 'Having autism describes *someone who might be…*' rather than 'Having autism describes someone *like me who might be…*'

It is important to try to share the final wording of this sentence with all of the significant adults who feature in the child's daily life since the individual could approach any of them later with questions, comments or concerns about their autism.

Finally, page 13 of C2 (for children working at Level 2) has been intentionally left blank except for the adult guidance on how to complete it.

It was noted earlier (in 2.4.3) that parents and other adults can occasionally be concerned that a child might go on to use their autism as an excuse for not being able to do certain things or for behaving inappropriately towards others. Where this is thought possible, this space can be used to provide the child with relevant advice. If, as in most cases, this is not a concern, then this page can be deleted.

Any guidance that is included on this page needs to briefly tell the child in precise, unambiguous language that it is not appropriate for them to use their autism in these ways. Where appropriate, this should also instruct them on alternative ways to behave. Directions written for a child who it is believed might try to use their diagnosis to avoid following adult instructions could be worded similarly to this example:

- Having autism does not mean that I cannot do things that my parents and teachers ask me to do.

- If I think something is going to be hard, I should try to do it first.

- I can always ask for help if I still can't do it after that.

This type of guidance could also be written specifically to refer to things that a child already tries to get out of doing despite these being easily within their capability, as shown in the next example:

- Having autism does not mean that I cannot do things like vacuuming my bedroom, feeding my pet cat or washing the dishes.

Children who are thought liable to go on to use their autism to try to excuse angry outbursts could be told:

- Sometimes children with autism can get angry and might feel like hitting or shouting at other people.

- This is because having autism can make it harder for them to control their own feelings.

- Having autism does not make it okay for me to get cross with other people or hurt them if I am angry.

- While it is okay for everyone to feel angry, I will need to try to learn better ways to deal with my anger.

- I may need some help with this.

The programme's main purpose is to teach children about their autism rather than to directly address any challenging behaviours some of them might exhibit. This advice ought to be short and only be referred to briefly during the session. If these problems do materialize and become persistent once a child has been given their diagnosis, then they may need to be addressed more fully through the individual's behaviour support programme.

6.4 THE FINAL PRE-DISCLOSURE MEETING WITH THE CHILD'S PARENTS

Unless the child's parents are carrying out the work themselves, the person leading it should arrange to meet with them once more before the child arrives for Session 2. This is to outline exactly what the child is about to be told about their autism and how this will be done. This is the final point at which the disclosure of the child's diagnosis can be postponed, thus making it essential to check that their parents still agree to their son or daughter being told about their autism and that they are satisfied with the explanation they are going to be given. Parents can often be very anxious about how both their child and they themselves might react when the diagnosis is disclosed and therefore they are likely to need some last-minute reassurance. Furthermore, a decision by a child's parents to withdraw their consent at this late stage should always be respected.

6.5 INTRODUCING THE CHILD TO SESSION 2

6.5.1 Introducing the session in its usual one-hour format

The child should be referred back to their visual programme guide at the start of this session to remind them about what the work involves doing as a whole and how far they have progressed through this. The child should then be shown the schedule for this session to inform them as fully as possible about what they are going to have to do during this meeting. However, if the child does not already know about their diagnosis, drawing up and sharing this particular schedule can be problematic because the session mainly involves teaching children about their autism. In these circumstances, autism should be abbreviated and presented on the child's schedule as a capital 'A'; for AS it can appear as 'AS'. Using this abbreviation, a schedule for a child who has not been told that they have autism could be set out similarly to the following example:

> ## *ALL ABOUT ME* SESSION 2: MORE INFORMATION ABOUT ME AND WHY I HAVE A TEACHING ASSISTANT
>
> 1. What we learned last time
> 2. A
> 3. People like me
> 4. Information about A
> 5. People who help me
> 6. Special interests
> 7. Who am I?
>
> Back to class to do science (*around* 2.15pm).

A script that usually seems to work well when going through this schedule with children has been provided below as an example of how to tell a child what is going to happen in this session without using the word 'autism'. Again, dots have been included to indicate where the adult may need to pause to allow the child to process what has been said.

> Today we are going to finish making your booklet on the computer…
>
> I will give you the booklet to keep next time we meet…
>
> First we will talk about the things that we learned about you last time we met…
>
> Then we are going to find out something new and interesting about you… We will talk about something which begins with the letter A… I will tell you what this letter stands for then…and this will be okay…
>
> After that we are going to find out about some other people who are just like you…
>
> Next we will find out some more about this special word that begins with an A…
>
> Then we will make a list of all the people who help you at home and at school…

> When we have done that...we will talk about your special interests and the things that you really like doing...
>
> Finally, we will read the last page in your booklet... This page is called 'Who am I?' ...and we will talk about all of the good things that have been written about you in your booklet.

The child should also be told the approximate time at which the session is due to end and what they are going to do afterwards.

Following the same advice given for Session 1, each child should be referred back to their schedule during every transition to remind them of what is going to happen next and to help them track their progress towards completing the session or earning any agreed rewards. Children should also be shown the schedule if they begin to show any signs that they could be about to experience a difficult moment. Although it might be hard to reduce the number of words on the schedule that is presented above, some children might again need to have theirs augmented with symbols or pictures. It may be hard to find a symbol or a picture that represents autism so a large capital letter 'A' may need to be used instead.

Once the child has been shown their schedule, reminders will need to be given of any specific rules and procedures that are being applied during the programme sessions. This might include the management of the computer, as well as how children can request help or ask for breaks from the work.

6.5.2 Introducing the Session 2 content if it is being taught over more than one meeting

If necessary, this session can be taught across two separate meetings. The child's diagnosis would be disclosed in the first part of the initial meeting. It is therefore vital that the child does not leave the first meeting without at least having been told about other people with autism, being given their headline explanation of what having autism means and being reminded of their own positive attributes. The introduction to the second meeting would need to include a recap of everything that has come before. Taking all of this into account, the original schedule shown above could be divided into two and rearranged to appear like this:

**MORE INFORMATION ABOUT ME AND
WHY I HAVE A TEACHING ASSISTANT**

1. What we learned last time
2. A
3. People like me
4. Information about A
5. What I know about me now.

Back to class to do science (*around* 2:15pm).

MORE ABOUT MY AUTISM

1. What we have learned about me and my autism
2. More about autism
4. People who help me
5. Special interests
6. Who am I?

Back to class to do science (*around* 2.15pm).

The child would have been told about their diagnosis in the first meetings so it would not be necessary to abbreviate autism (or AS) on the second schedule.

6.6 STAGE 5: 'I HAVE AUTISM' (DISCLOSING THE DIAGNOSIS)

6.6.1 Introduction

This section advises on how to work through page 5 of the Level 2 autism template (C2) and is illustrated by the completed example which is given in Kim's booklet (B2). Those working with children who have AS are advised to refer to the same page in Max's booklet (B3) and the corresponding template (C3). The aim of this stage is to use the information gathered about the child in the first session to calmly tell, or remind, them that they have autism. This involves working through each of the following steps:

- recapping positively on the main teaching points from Session 1

- referring the child to the second item on their schedule to prepare them for being told something new about themselves

- calmly telling the child that they have autism and reassuring them that this is okay

- reading page 5 of the booklet template

- attempting to find out what the child already thinks they know about autism

- trying to gauge the child's initial responses to being given their diagnosis

- inviting the child to ask their own questions about autism

- referring the child to their session schedule.

6.6.2 Instructions and explanation

It has been stated a number of times already that the prospect of telling a child that they have autism can evoke a great deal of stress and anxiety in the adults involved in this process, particularly parents. It needs to be remembered that these anxieties can cause some to parents to delay telling their child about their autism for years (Jackson 2006) and that disclosing their diagnosis has the potential to upset and destabilize the child (Huws and Jones 2008; Punshon *et al.* 2009; Whitaker 2006). It is therefore vital that no matter how they are feeling on the inside, the adults involved must try to present an outward appearance of being calm so as to avoid transferring their own anxieties on to the child.

It is essential to create a positive and relaxed context for telling a child that they have autism. I have found that this can usually be done effectively by reminding children of the following key points about themselves from the first session:

- Everyone is different on the outside and the inside so being different must be okay.

- They are a good person who is loved by the supportive people around them.

- They have many strengths.

- Like everyone, they find some things harder to do (especially things related to interacting with and understanding other people) and, with help, they can learn to do those things better.

Going through these points positively does not only seem to help prepare children well for what they are about to told about their diagnosis; I have found that it can also seem to reduce adult tensions in the lead-up to making the disclosure. Provided it can be done without causing a child any anxiety, it can be useful to try to assess how much of the above information they are able to recall independently. This could be done by using some of the assessment questions that are suggested for use during the final part of Session 1 (see 5.10).

Having positively summarized the earlier work, the child can then be told about their diagnosis. What is said now may turn out to be life-changing for the child and their family, and therefore the person leading the work needs to prepare and rehearse a simple script for doing this in advance so that they know exactly what they are going to say at the time. The model given next has been used with many children and is intended to show how the initial disclosure ought to be clear and precise rather than lengthy and complex. After showing the child that they have now reached the activity represented by the letter A on their schedule, the lead adult should say something similar to this:

I am going to tell you something new and interesting about yourself and it will be okay…

You have autism…

It is okay to have autism…

I will tell you a little bit about what having autism means now and we will talk about it more later.

This should be followed up immediately by reading page 5 in the child's booklet. As explained earlier in this chapter, the blank spaces on this page will need to have been filled in while preparing for the session so that this passage is reflective of the child's own attributes. In Kim's booklet, the completed version of this page reads as follows:

I have autism…

- I am good at lots of things, such as using computers to design clothes and to learn about animals.

- And there are some things that I find harder, like making friends.

- There is a name for being like that. It's called having autism.

- It is okay to have autism.

Although children should generally be told little else about what having autism means at this point in the session, they ought to be asked whether they have heard the word 'autism' before and to try to say what they think it means. This could inform the adults of any misunderstandings or negative views that the child might already have developed through hearing about autism elsewhere. It could also alert them to any immediate conclusions the child might have just drawn about autism based on false beliefs they had developed about themselves while they were waiting for an accurate explanation for their differences (e.g. having autism means that they are badly behaved, weird, stupid or mentally ill). Such issues can then be attended to as the session progresses. Observing the child's initial outward reactions to being told that they have autism and asking them to say or rate how it makes them feel can also help the adults to judge how best to approach the rest of the session. Again, it is important to know beforehand what signs indicate when the child is becoming anxious and upset as these could vary significantly from those presented by typical children.

Before moving on, the child should be invited to ask their own questions about autism so that, if they do have any, these can either be answered straight away or returned to later during a more relevant part of the work. This stage should be completed by briefly recapping calmly on the points listed below:

- The child has autism.

- It is okay to have autism.

- 'Autism' is a word for describing a special type of person with similar patterns of strengths and challenges to the child.

- The child is a good person who is loved by the supportive people around them.

6.6.3 How children could respond when they are first told about their diagnosis

How each individual child might react to being told that they have autism in this way can only be known once it has happened. Experience has shown that this can differ significantly from one individual to another. However, some patterns seem to have emerged over time, which might help others using this approach to predict roughly how things might turn out in various cases.

Experience of working with a large group of children has suggested that cognitively able and older individuals seem more likely to appear negatively destabilized when they first find out about their diagnosis, even if they are uncertain about what it means. This also seems to apply to individuals who previously encountered less positive information about autism before they learned that they had it themselves. Able children who were previously unaware that they had any issues with social understanding also appeared to react more anxiously and experience a slight sense of shock. Those operating at more literal levels and with more obvious learning difficulties have usually reacted indifferently. Children who were aware of their differences and had expressed concerns about them have often expressed a sense of relief and, in some cases, celebrated being given their diagnosis. This brought its own problems for a boy called Hugh who was so delighted that he then wanted to go around sharing his good news indiscriminately with other people.

Overall, the majority of children seem to have accepted their diagnosis well when it was given to them through the methods used in this programme (Miller 2014, 2015). Although it has never happened in instances of my own work, given its sensitivity, it would be wrong to completely rule out the possibility that a child could become too shocked, upset or angry to carry on with the rest of this programme.

On the basis of what is written above, there appear to be two key issues with which some children may need to be supported after being given their diagnosis. These are as follows:

- children becoming emotionally upset after being told about their diagnosis and not accepting that it is okay to have autism

- individuals wanting to tell other people about their diagnosis.

6.7 STAGE 6: OTHER PEOPLE WITH AUTISM

6.7.1 Introduction

This stage involves reading through and discussing the information about other people with autism, which is contained in pages 6–8 of the template (C2 or C3), while working through the following steps:

- telling the child that they are not alone in having autism

- reading and discussing the first three bullet points about other people with autism (on page 6 of the template)

- telling the child that some individuals with autism have made exceptional achievements

- reading the rest of page 6

- showing the child the selection of famous people who are thought to have, or have had, autism, featured on pages 7 and 8 in the booklet template, and providing a small amount of information about each person

- emphasizing the point that although not everyone with autism is going to be rich and famous, they can all lead fulfilling lives, and so can the child

- recapping on the main points covered so far in this session

- referring the child to their session schedule.

6.7.2 Instructions and explanation

There are two main reasons why this stage is included in the programme. The first is to offer reassurance to children who might feel isolated by their differences by letting them know that they are not alone and that there are lots of other people just like them. Its second purpose is to offer children positive encouragement by informing them about the notable achievements of some individuals who could be on the autism spectrum. The title and first three points on page 6 should be read through and discussed after first telling the child that they are not the only person with autism. This section of the narrative says:

OTHER PEOPLE HAVE AUTISM

- I am not the only person with autism. Most people don't have autism but thousands of people in this country do have autism.

- In every country in the world thousands of people have autism so there must be several million people like me spread across the world.

- There are other children and young people that I know who have autism. Those who know that they have autism will tell me if they want me to know!

'Thousands' and 'millions' can be difficult concepts for some children to comprehend or for them to tell apart, and so those two words may need to be written numerically on the notepad for them to see that they both represent very large amounts and that one is much bigger than the other.

If the child knows any other children or adults who are on the autism spectrum, their names could be added to this page, provided appropriate consent for sharing this information is obtained first from any individuals concerned or their parents. Either way, the child should then be told about the achievements of notable figures from the past and present who have been diagnosed as having autism, or who it has been widely speculated would have been if they had undergone an assessment. The rest of page 6 contains the following information related to this topic, which should be read through and discussed with the child:

Some people think that Albert Einstein might have had autism and he was one of the most intelligent people to have ever lived (Elder 2006)!

Daniel Tammet has autism and is a mathematical genius who can also speak ten different languages (Tammet 2007).

Susan Boyle has got autism and she is a world-famous singer who appeared on television in *Britain's Got Talent* (Schocker 2013).

The next two pages contain lists of other famous people living today who have autism and famous people from the past who it has been said may have had autism. Individuals whose areas of achievement happen to coincide with the child's own special interests and strengths should be highlighted. If time allows, the child should be provided with a small amount of information about each person who is listed on these pages (e.g. 'Stephen Wiltshire is a gifted artist with autism who draws pictures of buildings and cities'). Children who want to find out more about any of these people can be told that they will be able to research this information themselves later. This is something that their parents or school staff could offer to help them with when they are following up the programme.

Unless told otherwise, some children can falsely conclude from reading and discussing this section in their booklet that having autism means they will automatically become rich and famous themselves. It should be explained sensitively to all children that this is not the case, while still trying to give them the hope of having a happy and meaningful life. This should be done by drawing the child's attention to the last two sentences on page 8 of the template, which have been included for this purpose: 'Most people with autism do not become rich and famous (this is true for all people). They can all go on to live happy lives and so can I.'

Before completing this stage, it is advisable to recap positively on the main teaching points which will have been covered so far in this session. These are as follows:

- The child is a good person who is loved by the supportive people around them for being who they are.

- The child has autism and that is okay.

- The child is not on their own as there are lots of other people like them.

- The child and other people with autism have strengths.

- Some people with autism have become famous for their achievements.

- The child and other people with autism can lead happy and fulfilling lives.

6.7.3 How children might respond to this stage of the work

The majority of children have reported in their feedback that finding out about other people like them was their favourite or most helpful part of this work. Furthermore, children usually seem to behave more attentively and calmly during this particular stage than at any other time in the programme.

This is often noticeable among children who are more easily distracted and those who exhibit stereotypical behaviours. Although children may not always know who any of the famous people are, they usually appear to be fascinated by being presented with an array of pictures of people who they are told might be the same as them.

Children's positive responses during this stage led to the initial programme framework being reordered. This stage used to be carried out towards the end of this session, after children had been provided with the main explanation of their autism, which now takes place during Stage 7. This stage now occurs straight after the initial disclosure, or reminder, of the child's diagnosis but before they are given any further details about autism. This change came about because some children often appeared disinterested or restless when they were being taught about what having autism means. It became apparent that they needed to do something immediately after receiving their diagnosis which would help them to positively identify with it and thus encourage them to want to find out more.

This change to the programme framework has been successful. Children have become more receptive to finding out about their autism. Individuals who seemed anxious when they were first told about their diagnosis have appeared to become more relaxed and positive about it by the time they reached the end of this stage. Despite his initial sense of shock, a boy called Phil, for example, was delighted to learn that the creator of one of his favourite video games might also be on the autism spectrum. This seemed to help reduce his anxieties and allow him to continue working calmly. Perhaps unsurprisingly, children have not appeared to have had any significant problems during this part of the programme.

6.8 STAGE 7: EXPLAINING AUTISM TO THE CHILD

6.8.1 Introduction

This section explains how to work through and complete pages 9–13 of the Level 2 templates (C2 and C3) and this is illustrated by the contents of pages 9–12 in Kim's and Max's booklets (B2 and B3). During this stage, children are given their own personalized account of what their diagnosis means. This involves working through the steps listed below:

- reading the title and first two bullet points on page 9 of the template to explain the origin of the word 'autism' (or the term 'Asperger syndrome' for individuals with that diagnosis)

- reading the remaining bullet points on page 9 containing short facts about what autism does and does not mean

- explaining that autism (or AS) is a term for describing a type of person with similar patterns of strengths and challenges to the child

- reading and discussing the personalized headline sentence about the child's diagnosis, on page 10

- reading and discussing the information about *people sense* on page 11

- identifying any support the child is given for developing social skills and then completing the partial sentence about this in the fourth bullet point on page 11

- guiding the child towards completing the partial sentences on page 12 about coping with changes and sensory sensitivities

- reading through any additional guidance about behaviour written for the child on page 13 (if relevant)

- assessing the child's understanding of what they have been taught about autism so far and how this makes them feel

- recapping on the key points about the child

- referring the child to the session schedule.

6.8.2 Instructions and explanation

This is the longest stage in the programme and it often turns out to be the hardest part for children to understand. Furthermore, this stage needs to be approached sensitively because it necessitates going back over the child's key challenges and then informing them that autism is a lifelong condition. Therefore, this seems to be an appropriate point to ask the child to rate how they are feeling and to remind them of how they can request help or a short break from the work if things start to get too difficult.

Although this stage involves talking about issues that can be uncomfortable for the child, it can still be made into a positive experience for them. To do this, the adults need to try to outweigh the more negative aspects of having autism by stressing how the child's positive attributes are also associated with their diagnosis.

The following points on page 9 of the template explain how the word 'autism' originated and should be read to introduce this stage:

Why is it called autism?

- *Autos* is the Greek word for self.

- People with autism can find it harder to play, work or talk with other people. They might find it easier being by themselves.

The parallel page in the Level 2 template for children with AS (C3) offers them this alternative explanation of how their condition came to be named:

Why is it called Asperger syndrome?

- A 'syndrome' means a pattern or collection of things.

- And it is called 'Asperger syndrome' because a man named Hans Asperger first saw a particular pattern of strengths and differences like mine in some children and young people (Welton 2004a). He did this in the 1940s in Austria.

After reading this, the child should be referred to the remaining bullet points on page 9. Despite being written under the subtitle 'What does having autism mean?' these facts are included to provide children with further reassurance that it is okay to have autism by pointing out some of the things that it does *not* mean. This information is presented as follows:

- It is okay to have autism.

- Having autism does *not* mean that I am sick or unhealthy.

- I am a fit, healthy and intelligent person.

- It does not mean that someone is a bad person.

- I am a good person.

- It means that my brain works in a different way to most people's brains.

- People with autism think in a special and different way to most people.

It has already been explained in Chapter 4 how the description of each child's diagnosis is supported primarily by the personalized headline sentence which presents their autism tangibly as being a way of describing someone with similar sets of strengths and challenges to their own. This should have been added to the content of the booklet while preparing the template for this session, by following the advice given above in 6.3.2, so that it can be read and discussed next. In Kim's booklet, this sentence says:

> Having autism describes someone like me who might be good at working by themselves with *things and objects* like computers…and can find it harder to make friends and join in with other people.

The child's views on how accurately they feel this sentence applies to them should be sought so that appropriate alterations can be made to its final wording. It should be pointed out that they can refer back to this page in their booklet whenever they need reminding what having autism means for them. Other adults who live and work with the child will also need to be aware of this sentence and its overall importance.

Before continuing, it should be made clear to the child that each person's manifestation of autism is unique to them. It needs to be explained that although they all share certain similarities, like the famous people listed in the previous section of the booklet, individuals with autism do not all have the exact same individual areas of strengths and challenges.

After being given this headline sentence, most children are then provided with further details about their autism as they work through the next few pages in the booklet as described below. In individual cases where it is felt that the child may not be ready to learn any more about their autism now, the adults can decide to move straight to Stage 8 at this point, after deleting any information that is not going to be taught now. In any case, this stage usually ends here for children who are using the Level 1 template, and advice on how to increase these children's knowledge about their autism as they become ready later is given in 8.2.1.

Page 11 in the template is meant to explain the child's differences in developing *people sense* (or *social sense*, as described in Welton 2004b). This involves telling the child that their challenges with interacting with others are due to them having innate differences in understanding how other people are thinking, feeling or behaving, and that this is because of the way in which their brains work differently to most other people. It must be stressed again that it is okay to be different. This discussion should be based around reading these points from page 11:

> - Most children who *don't* have autism can tell what other people are feeling, even if the other person doesn't say so. This is called 'people sense' and it comes naturally to most people.
>
> - People sense helps children know how to join in playing, working and talking together easily without having to think about it.
>
> - Children with autism, including me, find it harder to understand other people – so knowing what other people are feeling or thinking or meaning or expecting is harder.
>
> - Children with autism need some help learning the people things that most children know without having to learn.

The partial sentence which comes next ('This is why...') can be completed to help the child recognize the point behind any support they receive for helping them to develop social skills. In Kim's booklet, for instance, it tells her, 'This is why Mr Cohen helps me to find children to spend my playtimes with.'

The final two points on page 11 are intended to inform children that the challenges they face when trying to interact with others are reciprocal and, as such, are not just down to them having difficulties. Applying a social model towards explaining autism they tell the child that:

> - Children who *don't* have autism can find it harder to understand children who *do* have autism.
>
> - Other children may need some help learning how to talk, play and work with me.

Once all of the spaces on page 12 have been completed, the narrative should offer the child a short explanation of any issues they may have with trying to cope with changes and their responses to certain types of sensory stimuli.

The child should be encouraged to identify their own differences in these areas. The adults can help the child to become involved in a discussion about their reactions to unexpected changes by reminding them about how they might have felt and behaved when certain situations arose such as last-minute timetable changes, teachers being absent, buses being late or them finding that their property has been rearranged. The partial sentence in the second point about changes ('This is why…') should then be completed to make a link between the child's desire for sameness and any support they might be given to help them manage this. The following extract from Kim's booklet gives an example of how this sentence could be used to clarify the point behind a child needing to have a visual timetable:

- People who have autism can be upset if there is a change of plan or if something unexpected happens.

- This is why I have my own visual timetable. It can be altered so that I will know what is going to happen if things need to change.

After this, the child should be asked to try to identify any types of sensory input that they find unpleasant or upsetting so that this information can be used to complete the next series of partial sentences. Adults can again use knowledge of the child to prompt them with relevant questions about their own everyday experiences. Children have found questions like these useful:

What makes you put your hands over your ears sometimes?

What don't you like about eating with the other children in the lunch hall?

How does it make you feel when other people touch you?

What is that smell that you said makes you feel sick?

Besides including an explanation for the child's differences in sensory processing, there is also scope for providing clarification for any differences in the way that the child is treated to support them with these issues. In Kim's booklet, for example, the rest of page 12 has been completed to read as follows:

- Some people with autism don't like loud noises or bright light, as well as certain smells and tastes or being touched.

- I don't like it when the other children in my class are all talking – this gives me a headache.

- Some smells make me feel sick too.

- This is because I have super powers of hearing and smell, just like a superhero. This is why I am the only child in my class who uses ear defenders.

- As I grow older, I will still have autism. It is a part of being me.

- With help, I will continue to learn to understand people things more easily as I get older, bit by bit.

- I will continue to learn to cope with changes, noises and smells better too.

The last three of these points also introduce the child to the fact that autism is lifelong. Being told that they will always have autism can be upsetting for individuals who are working at a cognitive level that would enable them to understand the implications of this. When reading this with them, it should be stressed calmly and in a matter-of-fact way that the reason they will always have autism is because it is a part of being who they are as a person. It is vital to remind the child at the same time that they are a good person and that they are loved by the supportive people around them for being who they are. Children ought to be offered further reassurances that while they may always find certain aspects of their autism challenging or upsetting, they can make progress and learn to cope better with its less pleasant aspects as they get older.

Parents and other adults have often positively reinforced this by making supportive comments about how things such as the child's behaviour and their communication skills have already improved over recent years. A few children have said similar things about themselves too. These types of positive contributions should always be recorded in the individual's booklet as encouragement. This remark was added to the narrative of one child's booklet: 'When I was in Year 2, I would get upset and cross easily, particularly when my routines changed. Now I am in Year 5; I don't do this any more.'

The main explanation of most children's autism ends here. Page 13 in the template has been left blank so that specific advice can be written there for children who might try to use their autism to excuse avoidant or inappropriate behaviours. Where needed, this guidance should already have been written beforehand by following the instructions given earlier (in 6.3.2), so that it can be read and discussed briefly at this point in the session.

At the end of this stage, a further attempt should be made to assess the child's understanding of what they have been told about their autism and how they are feeling about their diagnosis now. This can be done by asking the child to try to answer a short series of questions in their own words, similar to these:

- What types of things can people with autism do well?

- What types of things can people with autism find harder than other people?

- What do you think having autism means?

- How do you feel about having autism?

The child's replies to the first three questions can be checked and corrected if necessary by referring them back to page 10 to read the personalized headline sentence about their autism. The *Emotions rating scale* could be used again to aid children who are unable to easily express their feelings in words. As the child will have just discussed some potentially upsetting issues, it is recommended that the following positive points are reinforced before moving on to the next stage:

- The child has many positive personal attributes and strengths.

- It is okay to have autism.

- People with autism can make progress in areas that they find challenging and can learn to tolerate its less pleasant aspects better.

- Some people with autism can achieve highly.

- The child can go on to lead a happy and fulfilling life.

- The child is a good person who is loved by their family and the supportive people around them for being who they are.

6.8.3 How children might respond to this stage of the work

Although this stage involves discussing sensitive issues which some children could find distressing, they usually manage to remain calm enough to sit through the entire explanation of what their diagnosis means without having to take any unscheduled breaks. Moreover, every child who has reached this point in the programme has subsequently gone on to complete the rest of the work.

As already suggested, preparing children for this stage by telling them about the achievements of other people with autism appears to help calm individuals who initially appear to be uneasy or anxious after being told about their diagnosis. Beginning this stage by reassuring children that having autism does not make them into a bad person and that it is not some type of physical or mental illness also seems to help. So too does placing a strong emphasis on each child's own strengths and positive qualities throughout the explanation of their diagnosis.

Some children have said that this explanation of their diagnosis was useful since it helped them make sense of things that had happened to them before and enabled them to understand why they found it more difficult to manage in situations where they had to interact and communicate with others. Children like Hugh expressed relief when they were told what having autism did *not* mean. He was delighted to discover that he was not a bad person and did not have any form of brain damage, to which he had wrongly attributed his differences up until then. Although Hugh was unable to give an accurate description of what having autism meant at the end of the programme, finding out what it did not mean was perhaps of far greater importance to him at that time (Miller 2014).

Despite this, not all children appear readily to believe that having autism is okay or feel relaxed about discussing it by the time they reach the end of the programme. Although children do not tend to behave disruptively during this stage of the work, some individuals can become more passive or withdrawn, and there can be a few anxious and tearful moments. Some children will need ongoing support in learning to internalize and accept the validity of their diagnosis too, especially those individuals who were previously unaware of their main challenges. For example, although a boy called Alexis said on several occasions that having autism meant that he had difficulties with social understanding, he qualified this each time by adding 'so I have been told' (Miller 2014).

The level to which children understand the explanation they are given for their diagnosis can differ considerably from one individual to another. It can also be hard to judge how much children who are operating at more literal levels have understood about their autism because of their communication difficulties. It is possible that they may learn more than they are able to express verbally. At the same time, more articulate children with autism who can describe their diagnosis accurately could just be repeating back what they have been told without reflecting upon its meaning or how it applies to them (Vermeulen 2013). Although each child is provided with a short personalized headline sentence in an attempt to explain their autism in simple and tangible terms, experience has shown that some individuals will need ongoing help after the programme with learning what this and the rest of the explanation of their diagnosis means and how to express this to others.

Once a child has been told about their diagnosis, their parents and other adults working with them need to be aware that the individual could approach them with questions about it at any time. Adults can find some of these questions awkward or difficult to answer appropriately, but they might be important to the child in making sense of what they have been told about their diagnosis. Moreover, they could be symbolic of the diagnosis having had destabilizing effects on their personal identity, hence this issue is given further consideration in 6.15.4.

In conclusion, the following additional issues can arise from this stage of the programme:

- the child not having a clear understanding of what they are told about autism or not being able to express this to others

- the child not accepting what they are told about their diagnosis and continuing to have difficulty believing that it is okay to have autism

- children raising questions about autism that adults might find awkward or difficult to answer.

6.9 STAGE 8: INFORMING THE CHILD ABOUT THEIR SUPPORT NETWORK

6.9.1 Introduction

This section describes how to work through and complete page 14 in a Level 2 template (C2 or C3). This should provide the child with details about the people who make up their support network and positively explain why they are there to help them. The corresponding pages in Kim's and Max's booklets (page 13 in B2 and B3) offer examples of how this information might be presented. This stage involves working through the following steps:

- telling, or reminding, the child that various people are available to support them in developing their strengths and making progress in areas that they find challenging

- guiding the child towards identifying the main people who offer them support at home, school and elsewhere, and those whom they can approach with questions about autism

- using the information gained from the child to complete page 14 in the template

- reading back page 14

- referring the child to the session schedule.

6.9.2 Instructions and explanation

While introducing this stage, the child should be offered the assurance that there are numerous people available to offer them support both with developing their strengths and in helping them to learn to address the challenges they face in having autism. The child should be asked to think about who these people might be and then say who they are. To make this easier, the child can be prompted to think separately about specific times, places and situations when various people might be around to work with or care for them. For instance, this could be when they are at home, while they are travelling to and from school, during certain lessons, when they are taking part in individual or group programmes and when they are in the playground or the lunch hall. Besides their parents and school staff, this list could include outside professionals, such as therapists, who regularly meet with the child as well as anyone providing child care. Their names should then be written into the relevant spaces on page 14 of the template before reading it back. Fictional names were used to complete the following example in Kim's booklet:

PEOPLE HELP ME

- At home: my mum and dad know about my autism, and love me very much! So do my grandparents.

- They will continue helping me to develop my strengths, help me to cope with things that I find harder and help me learn to understand other people more.

- All the adults that work with me at West Street Primary School know that I have autism.

- Like my family, the adults at my school will carry on helping me to develop my people sense more, so that I can feel more relaxed in school.

- They will help me with my school work too so that I can have a more successful life in the future.

- This is why Mrs Corker helps me in some of my lessons.

- If I want to ask any questions about autism, I can ask my mum or dad, Miss Smith, Mrs Corker or Mr Cohen.

There should be an emphasis on the positive benefits of the child accepting their support. It needs to be made clear that these people are not only available to assist the individual with the things they find harder and stressful but are also there to help them to succeed further in their areas of strength (Gray 1996).

This activity should take no more than a few minutes and therefore children will not usually need to be reminded about what came earlier in the session before they move on to the next stage.

6.9.3 How children might respond to this stage of the work

Significant issues seldom arise while children are being helped to list the members of their support network. If they do miss out any important members of this group, the adults can remind them of who they are. Many children positively accept having support, but individuals can sometimes express doubts about needing or wanting the help on offer to them. This conversation can occasionally prompt children to comment about feeling uncomfortable with having additional adult support during lessons and say that it makes them stand out as being different. Furthermore, children can sometimes be surprised to learn that the group of adults around them already knew about their autism. Children could question why these people had been told about it before they had and why none of them had ever shared this information with them.

In summary, any of the following three issues may sometimes need to be addressed later:

- the child not accepting that they need support

- the child expressing concerns about additional adult support making them stand out

- the child querying why the people in their support network were informed about their diagnosis before they were and then kept this information from them.

6.10 STAGE 9: AUTISM AND SPECIAL INTERESTS

6.10.1 Introduction

This section explains how to complete page 15 in the Level 2 templates (C2 and C3) as illustrated on page 14 in Kim's and Max's booklets (B2 and B3). This stage is intended to draw a positive link between the child's diagnosis and their special interests or preferred activities, by working through the following steps:

- reading through and discussing the text on page 15 of the template, 'The good things about autism: Special interests'

- asking the child to say what their own special interests are

- adding a list of two or three of the child's main interests beneath the prewritten text

- referring the child to their session schedule.

6.10.2 Instructions and explanation

This stage focuses further on raising the child's awareness of the positive aspects of their diagnosis by relating their autism to the enjoyment that they might gain from pursuing their special interests and engaging in their preferred activities. It should begin by reading all of the text on page 15 of the template with the child which says:

THE GOOD THINGS ABOUT AUTISM

Special interests

- While autism makes some things harder for me (especially people things), there are good things about having autism.

- People with autism often have special things that they are really interested in.

- They can really enjoy finding out about and doing these things.

- They can spend lots of time on them and learn to do them very well.

These are my special interests and favourite activities: …

The child should then be asked to say what they particularly enjoy spending their own time on, finding out about or doing, so that this information can be added at the foot of the page to complete the final sentence. Children with autism tend to have narrow ranges of interests so it does not matter if this is a short list. Kim only listed two things which were 'clothes' and 'animals'. The interests that children have listed here have varied broadly to include things like cartoon and movie characters, using computers, playing video games, learning about their favourite school subjects, types of transport, sports statistics, playing with construction toys, designing and making things, drawing, playing musical instruments, collecting things, counting, cookery and gardening.

The booklet can be made more engaging and personal for the child by illustrating this page with images related to their interests, taken from the internet. Because of time constraints, however, this will usually need to be done later by the adult leading the work. However, children have never seemed to have had a problem with adults choosing the pictures related to their interests.

The next stage summarizes all the main points about the child and their autism, so it is not necessary to recap on the earlier work any further before then.

6.10.3 How children might respond to this stage of the work

Rory Hoy (2007) and Wen Lawson (2011) have both described how important the special interests of individuals with autism are to them. It is unsurprising therefore that children usually appear to enjoy this part of the work and concentrate on it fully. Feedback from children suggests that this is the second most popular part of the programme (after finding out about other people who may have autism). Consequently, this stage of the programme does not raise any significant issues. The only problems that might occur are minor and can be easily addressed at the time.

Children with autism can find it difficult to switch the topic of conversation away from talking about their special interests. There are individuals for whom this can be a persistent problem throughout the three sessions, so more structured ways of managing this are considered in Chapter 7. In most cases, though, it usually works well to say that this conversation has to end now but can be returned to at the end of the session, especially if the child's schedule is altered to show them that this is going to happen.

6.11 STAGE 10: 'WHO AM I?'

6.11.1 Introduction

This section explains how to read through and discuss the final page in the child's booklet (B2 or B3) and conclude the session by carrying out the following steps:

- reading the text on the last page of the template, 'Who am I?'

- asking the child to say in their own words what they now think having autism means and attempting to assess how this makes them feel

- referring the child to the programme guide and session schedule to show them that Session 2 has finished and what is going to happen in the final meeting.

6.11.2 Instructions and explanation

The child should be asked to read the final page in the booklet. In Kim's booklet, this says:

WHO AM I?

I am good at lots of things.

I am fit and healthy.

I have autism and find some people things harder.

I can learn to do those things better and might need some help.

Lots of other people have autism and some of them are famous for their achievements.

I can have a happy life.

> Most importantly…
>   I am a good person called Kim.
>   My family love me and they are very proud of me!

This page is included in every child's booklet to summarize what they have learned about themselves and to conclude the narrative on a positive note. A few minutes should then be spent on trying to reassess the individual's understanding of what they have been told about their diagnosis and how they might be feeling about having autism. The questions and prompts suggested in 6.8.2 for assessing the initial outcome of Stage 7 can be used again. The child's responses might help the adults identify specific areas that will need to be focused on more when all the work is being reviewed in Session 3. They may also be useful in determining how to approach the subject of autism with the child in the meantime.

When ending this session, the child should be referred first to their schedule and then to the programme guide to show them that they have completed all of their work and what the arrangements are for the next session. The child should be praised for having completed their booklet on the computer and be told that they will receive a hard copy of it to keep at the start of the final meeting.

6.11.3 How children might respond to this stage of the work

Most children seem happy to read the last page of their booklet. Doing this is unlikely to raise any new issues since it only summarizes what the child has already been taught and uses positive and comforting language. The extent to which children now appear able to understand, accept and express their diagnosis to others will continue to vary from one individual to another in similar ways to those highlighted in the earlier sections in this chapter.

6.12 MONITORING AND SUPPORTING THE CHILD BETWEEN SESSIONS 2 AND 3

Adults who are likely to come into contact with the child before Session 3 need to consider how they will approach discussing autism with the individual during this time. This ought to be determined by the child's responses to being told about their diagnosis during Session 2. If the child did not appear bothered, it should be okay for adults to talk to them about what they have learned so far about autism. If, on the other hand, the child seemed upset or unsettled, it is perhaps best to allow the individual some time to absorb their diagnosis by not mentioning the subject unless they raise it themselves. Adults should try to ensure that any conversations that do take place focus as much as possible on the positive aspects of the child and their autism.

Some children may be confused and need extra support with learning to understand and express what their diagnosis means. The headline sentence about the child's autism can be used for doing this. A printed copy of the sentence could be given to the child's parents or one of their key workers to read through with them a few times before Session 3, as long as the child is happy to do this. A further copy of this sentence could be placed in a prominent position in the child's home to act as a visual reminder.

Adults should monitor the child closely after they have been given their diagnosis and share their observations with the others involved in the programme before the start of the final session. The person leading the work will need to know about anything the child has said or asked about their autism, as well as noticeable changes in their behaviour and moods. This information will help them to determine the level of sensitivity that may be required during Session 3 as well as identify specific issues that the child might want to have explained further or be given answers to.

6.13 MAKING THE BOOKLET IN PREPARATION FOR SESSION 3

Extra care needs to be taken when editing and proofreading the completed template. Because of their strong attention to detail, some children can find it difficult to tolerate having any minor errors and imperfections in their booklet. To minimize confusion, the page breaks need to be in the places indicated in the original templates so that each stage of the work is presented separately, and all of the adult guidance notes should be deleted.

Once any additional photographs have been added and the template is ready to be made into a booklet, copies will need to be printed, laminated and bound for the child to keep at home and, maybe, at school. If the person leading the work is able to meet with the child between Sessions 2 and 3, they could include them in the process of assembling the booklet. However, I have found that, despite their desire for predictability, virtually every child has appeared to enjoy the sense of surprise they got from seeing the finished booklet for the first time at the beginning of the final session.

The following equipment and resources will be needed for making the booklet:

- a computer

- a printer

- A4 printer paper

- a laminator and laminating pouches – recommended (for making the front and back covers more durable)

- a comb-binding machine and combs (for binding the booklet).

Parents carrying out this work themselves at home are unlikely to have binding and laminating machines. Purchasing them just to make the booklet would not be economical but most schools have this equipment and staff who are trained in how to use it may be able to offer support in producing the booklet.

6.14 SESSION 3: REVISION AND ASSESSMENT SESSION

6.14.1 Introduction

The purpose of this session is to revise everything that the child was taught while they were producing the booklet about themselves in the first two sessions. This should also be seen as an opportunity to informally assess the child's understanding and acceptance of their diagnosis so that appropriate follow-up work can be planned. This can all be accomplished by doing the following:

- introducing the session to tell the child what will happen

- giving the child their booklet and allowing them a few minutes to browse through its contents

- reading and discussing the booklet while emphasizing the main teaching points at the end of each section and assessing how well the child has understood and accepted them

- referring the child to the programme guide and session schedule to show them that the session has finished

- praising the child for having completed the whole programme.

6.14.2 Instructions and explanation

This is usually the easiest session to prepare for and teach. It only involves reading through and discussing the finished booklet and therefore there is no new learning to plan for. Along with an appropriate number of copies of the booklet to share between the people attending this session, all the resources that were used to support the child in Session 2 will be needed again, apart from the computer. Similarly to introducing the other two sessions, the child will need to be referred to the programme guide to show them how far they have progressed through it, and the session schedule so that they are aware of what they are going to do this time. The schedule for this session only needs to include one activity, as shown in this example:

ALL ABOUT ME SESSION 3: MY BOOKLET

Reading and talking about my booklet

Back to class to do science (*around* 2.15pm).

Since this schedule only contains one item, it may be harder for some children to work out how much longer the session is going to last for, even if they can tell the time from a clock face. It should be made clear to children that the session will finish a few minutes after they have read and discussed the last page in the booklet so that its page numbers can be referred to as an alternative visual schedule.

Reading the sections that list the child's challenges and describe some of the less positive aspects of their autism may still prove to be upsetting for some children and therefore they will need to be reminded about how to request help or breaks. This should especially apply to individuals who have already experienced some difficult moments when these issues were being discussed in the previous sessions. Children's anxieties seem to have been reduced in this session, however, by making a point of recapping verbally on the child's positive attributes both before and after reading each of these more sensitive parts of the booklet.

After being given their copy of the booklet, children are usually allowed a few minutes to browse through it by themselves. It is then read and discussed as a group activity. While doing this, the adults can continue to assess the child's progress in accepting and understanding what they have been taught about themselves and their autism. This also provides further opportunities to reiterate all of the programme's main teaching points. Both these things can be done by asking the child to try to reply to questions that are similar to those used in the earlier sessions when they reach the end of each stage of their booklet. The child's attention can be drawn to the key sentences at the end of the relevant pages to check their answers and highlight the main teaching points. Children should also be encouraged to ask their own questions throughout the session.

When everything has been done, the child should be referred to their schedule and programme guide to inform them that they have reached the end of the programme before praising them on completing *All About Me*.

6.14.3 How children might respond to Session 3

No fresh issues tend to arise in this session since it involves revising and evaluating all the previous work. Children have almost invariably appeared pleased or excited when they were given their copies of the booklet, including some of those who were still unhappy about their differences and were less accepting of certain aspects of their diagnosis. Children have often turned excitedly straight to the pages about other people with autism and their special interests. In many cases, children have said that they would treasure their booklet and keep it in a secure or special place. A few children, like Hugh, added that they would read it whenever they were 'a bit upset or in a tricky situation' (Miller 2014).

Most children seem to accept their autism well by the end of this session, which is the programme's main aim. Even those who have found it harder to accept their diagnosis were prepared to read through the booklet with the adults. Nevertheless, many of the potential problems that could occur earlier in the programme when discussing the child's challenges and their autism can crop up or persist in this session. Even so, children who previously found parts of the work upsetting usually seemed much calmer and more willing to discuss their autism at this stage. This may be because they are not being presented with any new and unexpected information about themselves and they have had time to start becoming accustomed to what they have already been told. It could also be because they felt more motivated to participate in the work after being given their booklet at the start of the session.

However, some children can still find it difficult to understand, accept or express what they are told about their diagnosis. Given their needs and the complexity of autism, expecting otherwise from any short programme would be unrealistic and this is reflected in the programme's other main aims. These are to provide the child with a personalized account of their autism which will start them off on the lengthier processes of learning more about what it means and how to live with its challenges. Parents have usually said that they were relieved that their child had been told about their diagnosis without it causing them upset and that they would now be able to discuss autism openly with them. Most have said that they thought that the booklet would be a useful tool for helping them to continue developing their child's understanding and acceptance of their diagnosis.

6.15 ADDRESSING KEY ISSUES THAT CAN OCCUR AND PERSIST ACROSS SESSIONS 2 AND 3

6.15.1 Introduction

This section examines the key issues that were highlighted in the descriptions of how children might respond to the various stages of the work carried out in Sessions 2 and 3. Advice is given on adjustments that might help address some of these problems if they occur during a session. Further work that might need to be carried out to help resolve some of the more complicated matters over time is also suggested.

6.15.2 Supporting children who might react negatively to being told about their diagnosis (Stage 5 of the programme onwards)

There is very little that can be done to adjust the initial disclosure of a child's diagnosis since it involves communicating a fact in only three words – 'You have autism'. Therefore, the generic advice already given on how to lead up to and say this in a calm and matter-of-fact way needs to be applied in all cases. There is no way of predicting for certain how a child is going react to being told this and therefore any adjustments will need to be made immediately afterwards and on the basis of how they do respond. This should not involve backtracking or trying to reach any compromises if the child becomes angry about their diagnosis or refuses to accept and engage with it. Upset or angry children should not be told something different and more ambiguous such as 'Other people think you have autism.' Although this could possibly calm things slightly and might spare the child's feelings at the time, this sort of ambiguity will only confuse the child and make it much harder for them to accept that they have autism in the long term.

Adults need to continuously monitor the child's emotional state throughout the programme after sharing the diagnosis with them and offer them the option of a break if they appear to be having too much difficulty managing to stay calm. Should it become apparent that a child has reached a stage at which they are too upset to continue any further, the session this occurs in would need to be curtailed while trying to make this appear to be on the adults' terms. An attempt should then be made to resume the work about a week later so that the child can go on to complete the programme if things have calmed down sufficiently. Although it has not happened in instances of my own work, should a child still be too angry or anxious to carry on discussing their autism altogether, it is recommended that they are provided with a much longer and more open-ended cooling-off period. The child would need to be informed in the meantime that the offer to explain their diagnosis remains open for them to take up whenever they feel ready to continue.

A child seeming happy to engage in this work should not always be taken as absolute proof of them having reached a reasonable level of acceptance of their diagnosis. As able children, two boys called Phil and Alexis, for example, were eager to find out about their autism, but both made comments at the end of the programme that suggested they felt disappointed by its challenging aspects and perhaps still regarded it as being something bad. It should also be remembered that not all children will be able to voice such feelings easily. This programme sets out to try to help children see that it is okay to have autism. However, it will be difficult for a child with autism to believe this if they are constantly confronted with the negative aspects of their diagnosis (Vermeulen 2013), especially if they know that these are going to be lifelong (Lawson 2006). Therefore, in addition to monitoring the child for signs of distress, it is essential that the adults around them make a deliberate point of offering them explicit ongoing proof that having autism can be okay, as advised in 8.7.

6.15.3 Supporting children who are unable to understand, internalize or express what they have been told about autism (Stage 7 of the programme onwards)

It should not be expected that all children will be able to recall and recite everything that they are taught about their diagnosis by the time they reach the end of the third session. Chapter 8 therefore contains advice on how parents and professionals can continue using the booklet and other resources to expand a child's knowledge of what having autism means after they have completed the programme. The headline sentence it contains about the child's own autism is the main starting point for helping each individual to understand what it means and then become able to explain this to others as appropriate.

Children who are judged able to learn either more or less about their autism than those operating within the programme's generic developmental levels should be using a template with appropriately differentiated content (as advised in Chapter 7). However, if it becomes obvious during Session 2 that a child working through the programme at this level is experiencing unforeseen difficulties with understanding parts of the explanation of their diagnosis, it may be necessary to reduce or backtrack on the amount of information they are given during Stage 7. Nevertheless, it is essential that the short factual statements about what autism does and does not mean (on page 9), and the headline sentence describing the individual's own diagnosis (on page 10) are both worked through and kept in the booklet. This is because these form the programme's baseline explanation of autism. The remaining information about autism (on pages 11–13) is less vital when first introducing children to their diagnosis, therefore, some or all of this can be removed from the final copy of the booklet. If it is saved elsewhere, the deleted content can be used to revise the booklet at a later stage once the child has grasped the most basic facts about what their diagnosis means and they become ready to learn more about it, as described in 8.2.1.

While being able to clearly express what their diagnosis means, some children may nevertheless struggle to recognize how it applies to them. These individuals may need to be given tangible proof of this over a lengthy period. Adults can help them with this by positively labelling the child's differences and challenges for them in the context of situations that arise in their everyday lives and by relating this back to how the individual's autism is described in their booklet.

6.15.4 Answering children's questions about their autism (Stage 5 onwards)

Telling a child about their diagnosis opens up the possibility that they will ask all sorts of questions about autism, including some that adults might find awkward or difficult to answer. However, finding time to reply to children's questions honestly is vital. These questions could be asked at any time after the child has been told that they have autism, thus meaning again that the three-session programme can only be the start of the process of explaining autism and helping children to learn to live with it. Parents and other adults will need to be prepared to continue with these conversations. They can return to the booklet when doing this and should update it to include the answers to any questions that are not already covered by its existing content (as advised in 8.2.1).

The most frequently asked questions have perhaps been about why children were not told about their autism sooner and why other people knew about it before they did. If a satisfactory response is not given, this could strain a child's relationships with the people on whom they rely for support and reassurance. These particular questions have usually been answered acceptably by explaining to the child that the adults were waiting until the individual was old enough to understand what having autism meant. However, this answer is likely to be less credible the longer a child is kept waiting for their diagnosis, thus adding weight to the case for disclosing as early as possible.

Children might ask their parents whether other members of their family have autism. A boy called Phil was confused by his mother's reply that he was the only person in his immediate family who had autism, because he knew that 'parents have babies like themselves' (Miller 2014, 2015). Finding out about their diagnosis can cause some children to feel destabilized and query their self-identity (Punshon *et al.* 2009) and a child asking this type of question shows how disclosing an autism diagnosis could potentially lead towards an individual feeling alienated from their family and even querying their parentage. This emphasizes the importance of regularly reminding children of the positive statements that were written about them in their booklet and stressing that they are loved by their family for being who they are. In situations like Phil's, parents might also consider showing their child family photographs taken at around the time of their birth. Some of these photographs could be included in an appendix at the end of the child's booklet.

A few individuals have asked whether they would still have autism when they grew up. As it is already anticipated that some children will ask this question, a reply to this is already given in the booklet. Even so, children may still ask this question again later, or be concerned about the answer that they have already been given, thus emphasizing the need to offer children proof that it is okay to have autism, as advised in 8.7.

6.15.5 Children wanting to tell others (Stage 5 of the programme onwards)

Some children may ask whether they can tell other people about their autism. If the child wants to tell a close friend or small group of trustworthy peers, it could be arranged for an appropriate adult to meet with those children and the child to share their booklet together. The child's parents would need to consent to this and there would have to be a conversation with those children first about the confidential nature of what they are going to be told.

If the child wants to tell a whole range of random people, it should be explained to them that although having autism is not a bad thing, other people might not understand what it means and could mistakenly view it as being something negative. Children are helped to identify the members of their support network during Stage 8 of the programme. The child could be told that these are the people with whom it is safe to talk about their autism. A sentence explaining this can be added to the page where they are listed in the booklet.

If a child is impulsive and determined to tell others about their diagnosis, there is very little that any of the adults can do to guarantee this not happening. Risks of potential negative consequences of a child's classmates finding out about their autism have often been avoided when adults took control of the situation themselves by arranging for them to be told about it in an autism awareness lesson. Because of its sensitive nature, this is work that would require parental consent as well as careful consideration and detailed planning. This being so, this topic is discussed more fully in Chapter 8 together with guidance on how to plan for and teach this kind of lesson.

6.15.6 Children saying that they do not need support and expressing concerns that it makes them stand out (Stage 8 of the programme)

My own conversations with children on the autism spectrum have led me to conclude that there are three main reasons why some of individuals can be reluctant to accept having support. First, this can be because they are unaware of or unable to accept that they have their underlying challenges. Second, they may not see the point behind having their support in the context of how it may influence their future life chances. Finally, they may be anxious that their support makes them seem to stand out as being different from their peers. Not all children will have reached a reasonable enough level of acceptance of their autism or their challenges, or see themselves as needing to be treated differently by the end of this programme. It is important that any concerns children raise when they are talking about their support network in these two sessions are seen as opportunities for engaging them later in discussions about how to maximize its benefits.

The booklet can be used to remind children about the challenges they face because of their autism and which people are there to support them in those areas. However, this may not be enough to engage some children with their classroom support since the booklet usually contains very little information about how having autism can affect their ability to do academic work. The child may need to be provided with a separate written list of the people who support them which details their specific roles and says exactly why the child needs each one's help. Advice is also given in 8.3.4 on how to implement a follow-up programme called *My Future*. This initiative is intended to support able children who, after being told about their diagnosis, continue having difficulties in seeing that they have a vested interest in engaging with their support.

Despite being told throughout the programme and in their booklet that it is okay to be different, not all children will feel comfortable with being treated as such. Concerns that children raised during the programme about their support making them stand out ought to lead to the child being included in discussions with school staff aimed at exploring ways to make it appear less obvious and more acceptable to the child.

6.16 SUMMARY

Chapters 5 and 6 set out to achieve the following:

- provide generic step-by-step instructions for teaching the whole programme

- explain the rationale behind the teaching instructions

- identify key issues that could arise at, or affect, various stages of the programme

- offer guidance on various adjustments that can be carried out to prevent or ameliorate the effects of these issues before, during and after the programme's completion.

Readers should now have an understanding of how this programme can be used to tell most children that they have autism and provide them with a personalized explanation of what their diagnosis means. This chapter highlighted some issues around children's understanding and acceptance of their challenges, differences and diagnosis. It would be unrealistic to expect to fully resolve these issues over the course of a programme like *All About Me*. However, they are returned to in Chapter 8 where guidance is given on how to follow up the programme and continue the ongoing process of teaching children about their autism. Before that, Chapter 7 advises on broader adjustments that can be made to cater for children whose individual differences in behaviour, communication and learning might present significant barriers to them being able to participate in *All About Me*. This also includes suggestions on how to differentiate the programme and its teaching resources for children who might not regard the work as being appropriate to their age and ability.

Chapter 7

DIFFERENTIATING *ALL ABOUT ME* TO MAKE IT ACCESSIBLE TO MORE CHILDREN

The programme resources for this chapter can be downloaded from www.jkp.com/voucher using the code QLspdxjP

7.1 INTRODUCTION

This chapter provides guidance on how to differentiate various aspects of the programme's overarching generic methods, structure, delivery style and resources. The intention is to broaden the range of children who can be included in the programme in the first place as well as help individuals with varying learning preferences and behavioural differences gain more from their participation.

There are two main sections in this chapter. The first section advises on how to allow for differences in children's learning preferences and is meant to apply especially to supporting individuals falling into either of these two groups:

- children whose learning preferences and the developmental stages at which they are operating might prevent them from understanding or fully participating in the generic version of the programme

- more able individuals who could be put off by being asked to complete work that they feel is not suitably challenging for them and appears to be intended for younger or less able children.

The second section considers how to modify the work to support children who exhibit behaviours which place them in the following group:

- learners who are perhaps cognitively able enough to understand the work but usually find it harder to concentrate, remain calm and follow adult-led agendas for sufficient amounts of time.

Both main sections explore some of the possible reasons why certain children might not be able to be included in the generic programme. They then suggest ways that aspects of its overall structure, resources and adult delivery style can be altered to help some individuals overcome those barriers.

It should be stressed that the advice given in this chapter is not intended to provide long-term solutions for children's behavioural and learning difficulties. Its purpose is to offer more immediate ways of working around some individuals' current needs so that they present fewer obstacles to them participating in this programme. Nevertheless, the measures described below are all grounded in recognized good practice for teaching children with autism. It should be possible therefore to generalize at least some of this advice to other day-to-day learning situations. It must be accepted, however, that the adjustments suggested in this chapter will not enable every single child on the autism spectrum to access this type of programme. No matter what support they are given, some individuals will still be unable to meet the programme's inclusion criteria because of the extent and severity of their needs.

7.2 MEETING INDIVIDUAL CHILDREN'S COGNITIVE, COMMUNICATION AND LITERACY NEEDS

7.2.1 Introduction

This section examines some of the adjustments that can be made to help include children of all ages who are operating outside of the programme's generic developmental levels in cognition, communication and literacy. Autism is arguably a difference in development (Jordan 2005), so teaching programmes for children on the autism spectrum should be matched to the levels at which its participants are functioning in the above areas, rather than their chronological ages. Moreover, children with autism have widely varying differences in how they process sensory stimuli (Bogdashina 2003; Laurie 2013). This will also need to be taken into account both when thinking about how to set up a suitable working environment and while trying to design appropriate learning materials.

The *All About Me* booklet template is the most important tool for working through this programme and the completed booklet is essential for consolidating and following up the work with children afterwards; ways of making these materials more accessible to different children are therefore examined first. This programme also relies heavily upon children and adults exchanging and discussing information orally, so this section also suggests possible ways of supporting this vital two-way communication.

7.2.2 Differentiating the template and the booklet

Children who are operating at earlier levels in language and literacy are likely to find at least one of the following key reading skills more challenging: acquiring sight vocabulary; decoding words; and comprehending texts (Hannah 2014). Adults planning this work also need to be aware that some children with autism who, at first glance, appear to be very able readers may have hyperlexia. This can be deceptive since individuals who are hyperlexic can accurately read words and texts at levels well in advance of those expected for children of their age, while at the same time gaining little or no understanding of what they mean (Boucher 2009; Jordan 2005). In any case, children with autism generally interpret what they are able to read and hear literally to varying degrees (Wing 2002). Furthermore, they do not always interpret things according to their intended contexts (Vermeulen 2013). Therefore, not all children will be able to read, understand or correctly interpret the types of abstract language and vocabulary that are used in generic versions of the completed *All About Me* booklets.

More cognitively able and older children can be demotivated from participating in this work if they are presented with teaching and learning materials that look as if they have been designed for younger children or individuals who have learning difficulties. They can respond similarly if they regard the language in their booklet as being too simplistic. It should also be recognized, however, that some older children may actually prefer to read books designed for younger children.

Unless addressed, each of the issues described above can present significant barriers to children being able to work through and complete the template in the sessions and then use the finished booklet as a viable learning resource later. Hence, additional templates have been included in the electronic resources (Section C) for use with children who are working at levels prior to or beyond the generic Level 2 booklet templates described in the previous two chapters. However, the complexity of how autism manifests across the spectrum means that, despite having common areas of difference, every child's learning preferences are unique to them (Jones 2002). They cannot easily be assigned to specific groups. Since individual children with autism also have uneven learning profiles within themselves (AET 2012;

Boucher 2009; Wing 2002), there may be children who need to have some aspects of their booklet matched to earlier developmental levels and others to later ones. This means that there are a vast number of ways in which the visual formatting, content and language used in different children's booklets might need to be adjusted to cater for this diversity in their individual learning preferences and needs. Within my own work, no two children's completed booklets have ever appeared exactly alike.

For practical reasons, however, the booklet templates accompanying this book have only been produced for children operating within three very broad and approximate developmental levels. All these templates are generic to their given levels, so it is improbable that, in their current form, any of them will exactly match a certain individual's learning profile. Anyone carrying out this work will need to choose one of these templates first, as advised below, and then make their own adaptations to its various features according to what they know about the child's strengths, differences and needs.

The templates supplied in Section C are intended to be adaptable for use with individuals who are operating at development levels loosely in line with typical children in the following age ranges:

- Level 1: seven years and below (C1)

- Level 2: 8–13 years (C2 and C3)

- Level 3: 13 years onwards (C4 and C5).

These templates were used to produce the booklets included in Section B as practical examples of how this work might turn out when it is completed at each of the above levels. The Level 1 template was used to produce Roger's booklet (B1); those for Kim and Max (B2 and B3) were created from Level 2 templates, while Janet's and Sara's (B4 and B5) were made using Level 3 templates. When trying to decide which level template to use with a child, it is recommended that adults compare the language and formatting in these booklets with those in the types of books the individual usually prefers reading, regardless of their chronological age. They should also take into account the types of oral and written language that the child normally uses to express themselves and usually responds to best.

Assuming it is possible to find a reasonable match, various aspects of that template, and the booklet that will be produced from it, can then be differentiated further on a computer to make it more accessible for the child for whom it is intended. Table 7.1 offers guidance for anyone trying to do this. It suggests various ways in which the language, content and page layout in an *All About Me* booklet can be altered to suit children in any discrete areas where their learning preferences might differ and where they appear to be operating at either earlier or later developmental levels than those that the template is intended for. When making these alterations, individual features could also be borrowed from some of the other booklets in Section B and from the child's usual preferred reading matter.

Table 7.1: Possible ways to adjust *All About Me* booklets for children who are operating at different developmental levels

Booklet feature	Possible adjustments for children working at earlier developmental levels	Possible adjustments for children working at later developmental levels
Page layout	To minimize confusion/address the child's perceptual differences: • fewer sentences per page • larger font sizes and more bold typeface • more blank spaces between lines of text and elsewhere on pages. To make the booklet more attractive to the child and illustrate points made in the text visually: • more images • larger images.	To make the booklet appear more appropriate to the child's age and/or cognitive level: • smaller font sizes and less bold typeface • fewer bullet points and lists • more sentences per page • less space between lines of text • grouping more sentences into paragraphs • fewer images • smaller images.
Complexity of written language	To help the child read and understand the booklet more independently: • shorter, more precise sentences, reduced as much as possible to main meaning-carrying words • starting all sentences on a new line • more lists and bullet points • simpler and more concrete language, using more high-frequency words and language that is known to be within the child's existing vocabulary • augmenting the text with symbols and/or pictures.	To satisfy the learning preferences of children with AS or high-functioning autism who have acquired more advanced language and literacy skills: • use of longer and more complex sentences • fewer bullet points and more paragraphs • use of more abstract and mature vocabulary (e.g. use of words and phrases such as 'socializing' rather than 'playing and working with others', and 'communicating' instead of 'talking').

Booklet feature	Possible adjustments for children working at earlier developmental levels	Possible adjustments for children working at later developmental levels
Amount of information about the child and their autism	To avoid overloading children with information about autism and help them to more easily understand what it means: • fewer sentences in each section • fewer ideas/themes per page • ask the child to identify and record fewer personal traits, areas of strength and challenges • pages containing pictures of and information about other people with autism can be omitted from the booklet and given to the child as a separate handout for parallel use • provide a shorter and more precise explanation of what having autism means – perhaps reduced to just the main headline sentence • not including additional pages containing guidance related to the child's behaviour.	To meet the needs of children who are able to learn more about autism: • more sentences in each section to add detail to what is being taught • include additional information about autism (e.g. a list of the four key areas of difference; see page 10 of Janet's booklet (B4), or details about neurological differences).

Regardless of the developmental levels children are operating at, their individual differences in visual processing also need to be considered carefully when deciding how to format the text and set out the pages in their booklets. For example, children can be distracted or confused if pages appear overly cluttered and too colourful as well as by varying amounts of detail in the illustrations. Some children may need to have everything presented in black and white. Laurie (2013) recommended using buff-coloured pages, rather than white paper, to help reduce the amount of glare in learning resources that are made for individuals who can be more easily overwhelmed by visual stimulation.

The majority of children with autism have strong preferences towards thinking and learning visually (Mesibov *et al.* 2004). Again, this is why the programme's main delivery method is the production of a booklet on a computer. Augmenting the booklet's narrative and support aids such as schedules with symbols or pictures has helped include a number of children who found understanding texts challenging as well as those who had limited word-decoding skills and restricted sight vocabularies. Pictures and symbols provided them with visual cues to help them make sense of what individual words said and meant. Some of these individuals particularly benefited from this because symbols were already being used regularly to support their functional communication at home, school and elsewhere. There are a few issues, however, that need to be thought through before deciding whether to augment the text in a child's booklet with symbols and what might be the best way to do it.

Anyone planning to include symbolic support in a child's booklet will need access to specialized symbol-processing software, such as InPrint 3 (Widgit 2016) and have the necessary computing skills to work with it. This program would also need to be installed on to the computer that will be used with the child in the first two sessions. The booklet template would then have to be imported into a file that is compatible with the symbol-processing program. This can take time as, depending on which software is being used, the template might need to be retyped or copied into the new document at a rate of a few sentences at a time. Once this has been done, the text may also have to be resized and reformatted.

In my experience, children can sometimes have problems with reading back and making sense of the text written beneath the symbols. Adults will need to check that the child is aware of the correct words and meanings represented by all the symbols in their completed booklet and teach them any they are uncertain of. It is especially important that this is done with symbols that are being used to augment unfamiliar or more abstract words, as well as those depicting homonyms. Otherwise, children might come up with their own inaccurate meanings for words. For example, the symbol for 'loving' which was used in Ricky's booklet was a pink heart shape beside an exclamation mark, and this was exactly what he said when he came to that word while reading the narrative aloud (i.e. 'I am a pink heart exclamation mark person'). Because of the levels that Ricky was working at in understanding and using language, he never questioned whether or not this made any sense.

As already stated, children with autism can be confused by the presence of too much visual information and clutter on pages. Augmenting every single word with a picture or symbol could therefore prove perplexing for some individuals and make accessing their booklet much harder still. It is perhaps best therefore to consider minimizing the number of symbols or pictures on each page, so that they are only used to augment a few key words about the child and any that they might have particular difficulty understanding. Adults can always help children with any sight words that they get stuck on when they are reading the booklet together later. Some individuals may even be able to memorize and recite the entire narrative in their booklet without having to look at the text after it has been read through with them a few times. However, because of their autism, the extent to which such children would understand the narrative may be doubtful, so it is advisable to check this by asking them suitable questions. In any case, a child's readiness to participate in this programme may need to be questioned if it is felt that they would not be able understand the majority of the words in a Level 1 booklet without being given symbols or pictures to refer to.

7.2.3 Supporting two-way communication

Given the programme's delivery methods and inclusion criteria, its overall success will always be reliant upon children being able to use and understand language to do the following things:

- answer questions and provide information about themselves

- listen to and understand what they are taught about their autism

- engage in discussions about the work with the adults.

All participating children will have some degree of difficulty with these things. However, it is not surprising that children operating at earlier developmental levels in communication and learning will by far need the most support. This will perhaps be mainly because they have more significant difficulties with processing auditory information, narrower vocabularies and a stronger tendency to interpret all types of language at far more literal levels. These kinds of difficulties are compounded in cases where children are more easily distracted from listening and frequently digress or go off topic when speaking. The level of their expressive language development can make it harder for these individuals to find the right words to respond to adult questioning and coherently explain much of what they had been told about their diagnosis. It is far more difficult to assess with any accuracy how much they actually learn about their autism and how they feel about having it (Miller 2014, 2015).

Given their differences in communication and the transactional nature of autism, adults will need to adjust their own speech and language to help all children understand the types of oral questioning and information that they could be presented with if they are considered able enough to participate in this programme. Adults will also need to provide individualized structured support to enable children to express themselves better during the sessions. However, children's levels and preferred methods of communication can differ widely from one individual to another across the autism spectrum.

This may range anywhere between a child using and understanding little or no verbal language at all to those who understand and use complex language in relation to things they find interesting. Children with autism also have uneven learning profiles, and therefore they can operate at different levels within individual areas of their own communication (Wing 2002). This complicated diversity limits the extent to which this book can offer specific advice on how to adjust the overall programme to meet individual children's differing communication needs.

Adults planning this work will need to use their own knowledge of the child's preferred communication methods and the support strategies that seem to work best for them in learning situations. If the child is receiving support from a speech and language therapist, they should be able to advise on the various levels at which the child is working in speaking and listening and the kinds of personalized adaptations that might help them access this work better.

In general, adults should try to adapt their own speech to help children understand what they are saying in similar ways to those suggested in Table 7.1 for differentiating the written language in children's booklets. At the same time, the programme methods require that the template and the finished booklet are used as communication aids throughout the three sessions to visually record and augment everything that is taught and discussed orally with the child.

For children working at more literal levels and who find it harder to understand and respond appropriately to spoken language, it is advised that adults make the following generic adaptations to their own verbal communication:

- start each verbal interaction by cuing the child in by saying their name, and then waiting silently until it is clear that the child is paying attention

- reduce the amount of words they use

- use more concrete vocabulary and literal language

- speak more slowly

- allow the child sufficient processing time before saying anything else or repeating questions and instructions that have already been put to them

- augment key words visually in ways the child will be able to understand (e.g. with gestures, sign language, drawings, written words).

Overall, adults should try to use short and precise sentences while placing greater emphasis on the most essential meaning-carrying words.

Whenever possible, adults should try to use words that the child is likely to be familiar with and will already have some understanding of. However, it is probable that many of the words used in this programme will be new to some children. This is why it was suggested earlier (in Chapter 5) that adults should always check if children have fully understood any language with which they choose to describe themselves by asking them to try to explain what it means in their own words. This strategy can be applied across the programme in general when trying to assess children's understanding of other key teaching points (e.g. saying to the child 'Tell me some things that people with autism can be good at doing'). If it is then found that the child has not understood something, adults can provide them with a more concrete explanation and perhaps use a notepad to illustrate this for them visually. Similarly, children who find it harder to explain themselves verbally can be asked to write or draw what they are trying to say, if they have sufficient literacy and fine motor skills.

Some parents and school staff have been supplied with copies of the attribute cards that are used in the first session (D1, D2 and D3) so that they could prepare children for using them before they started the programme. This has proved to be a useful way of pre-teaching and familiarizing children with some of the programme's core vocabulary. Doing this meant that this vocabulary was no longer new to those children when it was used with them during the sessions. These cards could also be augmented with symbols or pictures to make the words on them more meaningful for children with stronger preferences for having information presented to them in more concrete and visual ways.

More abstract and complex oral language can be used at a regular spoken rate in discussions and conversations with the most cognitively able children, as long as it is fairly certain that they will be able to accurately understand and follow most of what is being said. Adults will need to be just as cautious and consistent in checking these children's comprehension. There are individuals who, despite appearing to have more advanced expressive language skills, have significant auditory processing difficulties and are working at earlier levels in understanding language. Children with more sophisticated vocabularies can still find simple everyday words confusing and, like all children with autism, tend to interpret much of what they hear literally in any case. This does not only apply to metaphorical language (Frith 2003, Jordan 2005; Wing 2002). Cognitively able children have, for instance, replied to questions like 'Can you explain what that means to me?' by simply saying 'yes' (i.e. they could) or by trying to define what 'that' meant. Potential misunderstandings like this require adults to try to be as precise and unambiguous as possible in everything they say to all children with autism. In the example cited above, it would have perhaps been more appropriate to have presented this request as an instruction rather than in the form of a question, and to have specified exactly what the individual had to explain (i.e. 'Say what you think the word "socializing" means').

Children are asked to draw up lists of words to describe their own personal characteristics, strengths and challenges during the first session. Generic strategies for helping children overcome difficulties in coming up with enough words to complete these three tasks have already been suggested. This included providing children with attribute cards to sort. These activities have then been made easier for children working at earlier levels by:

- showing the child just two cards at a time to represent opposite attributes (e.g. 'tidy' and 'messy'; 'lazy' and 'hardworking'; 'quiet' and 'loud')

- asking the child a closed question to go with each pair of cards

- providing two possible answers for the child to choose from – for example, 'Kim, are you a hardworking person or a lazy person?'

Similar closed questioning techniques can be used more generally throughout the programme to support children with more significant expressive language difficulties and who find it harder to make choices. If necessary, the alternative answers could be written down for the child to choose between visually.

Partial sentences are used at specific points in the booklet template to help children supply information that is needed to complete some of the gaps in the narrative. This approach can also be used more generally with children who find it harder to answer questions so that they can contribute more to verbal discussions and tell the adults what they might have learned. If necessary, adults can write partial sentences on notepaper to visually support children while they try to formulate answers to oral questions. For example, when checking whether a child knows which people make up their support network, they could be given the following sentence to complete: 'The people I can ask for help at home are…' The child would need to read what was written and then add some words of their own to complete the sentence; again, this can be done either verbally or in writing.

Some children's participation in the programme can be significantly affected by constantly thinking and talking about their special interests or being easily distracted by things in the surrounding environment. Besides not listening appropriately, this can lead to children interrupting what adults are saying and trying to change the topic of conversation. The next section includes advice on how to restructure the sessions for children who have more extreme difficulties with this kind of behaviour. In most cases, however, it is possible to help children refocus themselves quickly by referring them back to their session schedule and asking them to state what they should have been thinking and talking about instead. When children still insist that they want to talk about something of importance to them, adding that subject to the end of their schedule will often help move matters forward. The child can then see that they will be able to return to their preferred conversation later, on the condition that everything else has been said and done first.

Finally, there are some children with autism who have good vocabularies but say very little (Wing 2002). Children like this should not be discounted from participating in this programme if they meet its inclusion criteria and have learned to express themselves effectively by using an alternative communication system that the adults involved are able to make sense of. This could involve the use of sign language, picture cards, computerized voice output communication aids or children simply writing what they want to say on paper.

7.3 STRATEGIES FOR INCLUDING CHILDREN WITH BEHAVIOURAL ISSUES

7.3.1 Introduction

This section suggests possible ways to support children who may be able enough to understand the programme but exhibit challenging behaviours that could prevent them from focusing on the work and completing each stage. Attention is given to working with individuals who have more substantial difficulties with staying calm, working to adult-led agendas and ignoring distractions for more than a few minutes at a time. Preventing and managing these kinds of challenging behaviours requires an understanding of their underlying causes (Whitaker 2001), and therefore a few of the possible reasons why children might experience these difficulties are suggested below.

7.3.2 Some possible reasons why children's behaviour might prevent them from participating in adult-directed work activities

As described in Chapter 3, differences in sensory processing can make regular environments overly arousing, unpredictable and difficult for individuals with autism to make sense of, thus causing them to become more easily anxious and confused in everyday learning situations. Children with hypersensitivities to certain types of sensory stimuli can be constantly distracted or made anxious by this – for example, through hearing what others are saying and doing elsewhere or by repetitive sounds like clocks ticking. These kinds of sensitivities cause some children to become increasingly agitated and aroused by various kinds of stimuli that typical people would not notice or be bothered by. This can cause a build-up of stress in children who do not have the communication and coping skills needed to tell others when they are starting to feel distressed and anxious. Without appropriate support, such children can resort to extreme and unpredictable negative behaviours as a means of communicating that they are not managing well and need to escape from an overwhelming environment (Clements 2005).

Although some children can behave as *sensory avoiders*, as described in the previous paragraph, others can be *sensory seekers*. These children constantly require certain kinds of environmental stimulation in order to self-regulate (Laurie 2013). Unless they are given managed access to their preferred stimuli, it can be challenging for them to sit still, remain calm and concentrate on work-related activities for as little as a few minutes at a time.

Providing sensory-seeking children with the kinds of fidget toys and alternative seating recommended in Corinna Laurie's book *Sensory Strategies* (2013) can help satisfy some of these children's needs while they are trying to work. However, there are individuals whose needs are significant enough for them to have to stop working at various points in their lessons to engage in a programme of scheduled movement breaks or other activities they find stimulating such as messy play. Often done on the advice of an occupational therapist, this is meant to provide children with appropriately managed ways of accessing their preferred sensations, so that they do not have to resort to negative behaviours instead to obtain them. When children with these sensory processing issues are denied regular access to this input, they can quickly become aroused and may try to run away (Laurie 2013), thus making it difficult to include them in this programme, because of the length of the sessions. Moreover, while taking frequent breaks for sensory stimulation might help these children remain calmer during their work periods, interrupting sessions in this way could also create practical barriers to them participating in this work.

People with autism have difficulties channelling their attention towards more than one thing at a time or switching their thoughts from one subject to another. At the same time, children with autism can find it just as hard to attend to subjects outside of their own limited ranges of interest (Lawson

2011). Consequently, children can be continuously distracted from their work by being preoccupied with their interests and find it very hard to avoid being drawn back into doing this. As mentioned earlier, a boy called Hugh described how he was upset by having intrusive thoughts about his favourite cartoon characters. He said that this was because of the adverse effects they were having on his school work (Miller 2014, 2015). Similarly, children's thoughts can fixate intently on interesting objects in the environment and things they can see or hear happening around them. Some children may want to keep talking about these things or might be tempted to go over to something that they find fascinating, instead of working. Furthermore, children can become distracted and increasingly distressed by being similarly preoccupied by things that are causing them to worry (e.g. not having finished a homework task that is due to be handed in later that day).

Having such an intense focus on their own special interests and preferred activities no doubt makes it harder for all children with autism to work to adult-led agendas. In my experience, children's differences in developing social understanding and awareness seem to make it unlikely that individuals exhibiting more rigid behaviour patterns will compromise on this to please others. As mentioned in the previous section, children can make continued attempts to steer conversations away from their work and towards their favourite interests instead of attending to adult attempts to refocus their attention. Less flexible children can become more distressed and angry and behave non-compliantly if they are denied access to their preferred activities and are required to complete less interesting adult-directed tasks.

The next part of this section looks briefly again at how to set up a calm and focused environment for this work to take place in. This is followed by a description of how the programme's structure and scheduling could be adjusted to motivate and engage some children whose behaviour might otherwise prevent them from being able to work for long enough to complete the required activities.

7.3.3 Some general strategies for helping to keep things calm and focused

Having access to an appropriate low-arousal, distraction-free and predictable learning environment is fundamental to children with autism being able to remain calm and focused on their work for lengthier periods (AET 2012; Mesibov *et al.* 2004). That said, it must be noted again that each child's sensory processing profile is different and that their individual needs can vary broadly in nature and severity (Bogdashina 2003). It is essential therefore that each individual's specific differences in these areas are identified as fully as possible during the pre-programme work so that the adults will have a clearer idea of the kind of environment the child might work best in. This information then needs to be applied to finding and setting up a workroom which is personalized to the individual's differences as advised in 3.8.

Participating adults need to be mindful that they form a crucial part of the learning environment and adapt their own behaviour during the programme accordingly. They will need to try to monitor and adjust their arousal levels in order to avoid inadvertently causing things to escalate if anything does start to go wrong (Whitaker 2001). This should include speaking one at a time and quietly and calmly while trying not to overload the individual with too much auditory input. By doing this consistently, the probability of the child becoming confused and aroused in the first place can thus be reduced.

As recommended in Chapter 3, time needs to be taken before starting the programme to discuss the child's most recent behaviour programme. This should help participating adults identify which areas are challenging for the child as well as the strategies and resources that are already being used successfully to prevent or manage instances of negative behaviour. These should then be incorporated into the programme's delivery methods. In particular, adults ought to have become aware, from the pre-programme work, of the signs that indicate when the child is starting to become anxious and what steps usually need to be taken in these circumstances. To make the environment and the work itself predictable, it is strongly advised that all children are given visual work schedules to follow throughout all three sessions. Although most children taking part in this work will probably be at the stage at which they are able to understand a schedule formatted as a written list, individuals who find it more difficult to process and understand written communication may not make much sense of the generic examples given in Chapters 5 and 6, especially if their stress levels are raised. The schedule is meant to be used as a calming tool and, as such, children should be referred to it during each transition between activities and at the first sign that they could be about to experience a difficult moment. These children will therefore need their schedules to be adjusted so that they contain fewer written words and are augmented visually with symbols or pictures when necessary. Ideally, children's work schedules should follow the same format as those with which they are familiar through their regular use at school and elsewhere.

This work is sensitive and some parts of it have the potential for upsetting children, and it is therefore also important to ensure that children have access to other tools that might already be used to support them with staying calm while working. As mentioned above, this might include fidget toys and specialist seating for children who find it more difficult to regulate themselves in less stimulating environments as well as alternative means of communicating their needs when they are feeling stressed, agitated, anxious or overwhelmed (such as the *Emotions rating scale* and the help and break card systems described in 5.3.2). Some children may also need to be given managed access to their preferred objects and activities as described below.

7.3.4 Restructuring the programme to support children who can only work for more limited time periods

There are children whose needs are severe enough to prevent them from being able to sit and focus on adult-directed work activities lasting for as little as one or two minutes, despite having high levels of support and access to specialized learning environments. This programme would not be suitable for those children and it is unlikely that they might find what is taught relevant to them.

As explained in Chapters 5 and 6, each of the first two sessions can be split and delivered across a series of shorter meetings lasting for no more than 30 minutes if this is as much as the child can manage. Some children with autism may not even be able to work for that long; at the same time, spreading the work over numerous sessions could affect the continuity of the programme. However, although all three sessions are designed to last for around an hour each, it is possible to adapt the structure and scheduling within them to make the whole programme accessible to children who are at a stage where they can work calmly to an adult-led agenda for a minimum of 20 minutes at a time when offered suitably motivating rewards.

As described below, it is possible to incorporate scheduled reward breaks into the structure of each session to encourage these children to carry out at least 30 minutes of adult-directed work in a single meeting or even go on to complete all the activities intended to take place in a regular one-hour session. Similarly, appropriate activities can also be included into the sessions to help children with sensory-seeking behaviours by providing them with timetabled breaks for accessing the stimuli they need to help them stay calm and focused on their work.

Their special interests are among the most important things in the life of a child with autism (Hoy 2007). As such, they can create some of the distractions that might prevent children from being able to engage in this work in the first place. On the other hand, guaranteeing managed access to their special interests, favourite activities or preferred objects and sensory stimuli can prove successful in motivating children to complete a series of short and specific amounts of adult-directed work. While being taught in single meetings, the content of each session can be divided into several smaller and more manageable chunks of work that are punctuated by structured breaks for rewards or sensory stimulating activities. This needs to be communicated to the children through their work schedule so that they can see when the reward breaks are due to take place and what they must do first in order to earn each of them. The following example shows one way in which this adjustment could be presented on a child's schedule if this approach were to be applied in Session 1 with a child whose preferred activity is building models with LEGO® bricks:

ALL ABOUT ME SESSION 1: FINDING OUT ABOUT MYSELF

1. A photograph of me on the outside
2. Reward: 5 minutes LEGO
3. My personality: me on the inside
4. Reward: 5 minutes LEGO
5. The things I am good at doing
6. Reward: 5 minutes LEGO
7. Some things that I find harder to do
8. Reward: 5 minutes LEGO
9. What I have learned today
10. Reward: 5 minutes LEGO.

Back to class to do science (*around* 2.35pm).

The number of breaks and the set amount of work that would need to be completed in between them can be set flexibly according to what the child can realistically manage to achieve. Some children may be able to complete two or more stages of the programme between breaks whereas others might need to have additional breaks halfway through some of the activities during the lengthier stages (e.g. after listing five of their ten strengths). It is vital, however, that the amount of time a child is required to work for is set comfortably within the minimum of what the individual usually manages in other learning situations before things start going wrong. As a guide, the longest stages of this programme usually take around 20 minutes to complete. Once a limit has been set with the child on the amount of work that needs to be done before each scheduled break, it is essential that the adults stay within it. They should always resist any temptation to continue working for longer, even if things appear to be going very well at the time.

A few practical problems can arise from using this approach, but these can usually be solved fairly easily. First, there is usually only one main activity on the schedule for the final session (i.e. reading the booklet) so this cannot be broken down further on a visual schedule to show the child when the reward breaks are going to occur. This issue can be resolved by attaching Post-it notes to the pages in the booklet that the child has to reach in order to earn each reward break. These can be shown at the beginning of the session so that the child knows how much needs to be read and discussed before each break.

There can be difficulties around choosing appropriate rewards. To be effective, rewards must not only be meaningful to children, but they should also be practical to administer in the context of a session and the workroom environment. The child needs to be motivated by the chosen rewards, so ideally they should be consulted about what they would like to do beforehand. The rewards must be things that can be done in short periods of time (ideally 3–5 minutes) and without them having to leave the room. If the child cannot decide upon a reward or asks to do something that would be impractical (such as going outside to play football), broader knowledge of the individual's interests should be used to present them with an adult-controlled choice of two or three activities which they might still find interesting and motivating. Before starting each block of work, the child can be asked to choose which one they want to work for and this should be written on to their schedule as a reminder. The types of rewards that different children have chosen have included playing with favourite toys, holding preferred objects, completing puzzles, building parts of LEGO® models, drawing, blowing bubbles and looking through books about their special interests.

It is possible that children could try to engage in the rewarding activities before they have completed the set amount of work, and therefore it is essential that the lead adult keeps motivating items firmly under their control, preferably out of sight and reach, when the child is meant to be working. Furthermore, if a child does try to demand their reward too early, they should be referred back to their schedule and firmly reminded of what needs to be done first.

Having earned a reward, some children can be resistant towards handing it back and continuing with their work at the end of the allotted time. Situations like this are mostly pre-empted by using a visual timer along with the child's schedule so that they can see the precise duration of the reward, how much time is remaining as it is being administered and when they will be able to have access to it again later. Children should be told when they have approximately one minute left to prepare them for the time running out and the subsequent transition to the next block of work. At the end of the time, children can be helped through this transition by being given a five-seconds countdown and shown straight away when the next reward break is due to take place. Carrying out this last step before retrieving the reward item from the child may be vital towards preventing possible outbursts, especially if a child is in the middle of doing something that they are anxious to complete, such a puzzle, a drawing, reading a book or building a model.

If adults are concerned that the above strategies will not work for their child, or that taking time out for rewarding activities might be too time-consuming and distracting for them, the individual could be encouraged to work for instant rewards instead. This would involve giving a child a small inexpensive item to keep before moving directly on to the next task. For many children with autism, typical token rewards, such as stickers and certificates, are ineffective as they have little tangible meaning for them. However, many individuals will try to concentrate on completing their work if offered homemade picture cards featuring their special interests (e.g. photographs of animals, cars, trains and aircraft). These cards can be made cheaply and easily by printing and laminating images copied from the internet. Children are asked to choose which card they would like to earn before starting each scheduled activity and are given it on completion of the required amount of work.

The need for some sensory-seeking children taking regular timetabled breaks from their work can be met by scheduling the breaks into the sessions in the same way described above for incorporating reward breaks. In some cases, it may be possible to carry out the relevant activities quickly and easily in the area where the child is working – for example, where the activities involve using hand-held toys that light up, vibrate or make noises; carrying out movement exercises which require no equipment and little space; or having access to a tray containing materials for messy play or other tactile activities.

However, some children's calming activities might require using specialized equipment kept in other areas of the building such as a sensory room or completing movement and balance exercises that require a lot of space or having to go outdoors. Being away from the work for too long and entering and leaving the room are likely to have a detrimental effect on the continuity of each session. Issues like this need to be factored in when trying to determine the most convenient location and ideal size for the workroom. An occupational therapist supporting a child may be able to advise on alternative activities which would be more appropriate within the given confines of the work space and still be suitable for the child's needs. Alternatively, Corinna Laurie's book (referred to earlier in this section) contains lots of ideas and instructions for short activities for helping children with autism with various sensory needs that parents, school staff and other professionals might generally find useful.

Breaking down the work into more manageable parts, as described above, could mean that the work activities from a one-hour session will take at least 20 minutes longer to complete (i.e. the meeting will last for around 80 minutes in total including breaks). Even so, this approach and the other adjustments suggested in this section can help a number of individuals with various behavioural issues manage to participate successfully in the whole programme. None of this means that children with less severe behavioural needs should not be rewarded for completing the work.

7.4 CONCLUSION

This chapter concludes all the guidance on how to prepare for and teach *All About Me*. Differentiating the generic work in some of the ways described above can enable very different children to complete this programme successfully at their own level and gain more from doing so. It must be accepted, however, that no matter how children are first told about their autism, it can take some of them a long time to reach a reasonable understanding and acceptance of their diagnosis. This programme aims to give all children a short, simple, personalized and positive introduction to what having autism means. In this context, Chapter 8 explores some ways for helping children to continue on their autism learning journey after the programme has been completed.

Chapter 8

WHAT NEXT?

The programme resources for this chapter can be downloaded from
www.jkp.com/voucher using the code QLspdxjP

8.1 INTRODUCTION

Throughout this book it has been advised that *All About Me* should only be regarded as the first step in what could prove to be a lengthy journey for a child in learning to understand, internalize and accept their diagnosis. Autism's complexity and its inherent cognitive differences make it difficult to explain fully to children on the spectrum during a short introductory programme like *All About Me*. Taking this into account, the programme sets out to disclose the diagnosis positively and then provide children with a small amount of manageable information about autism that is relevant to their current circumstances. Much more is left for later learning, particularly because children's challenges and differences evolve as they get older (Wing 2002). Importantly, however, parents and other adults should be in a position to talk more openly with children about autism at the end of the programme.

This chapter has been written to bring together a range of ideas, initiatives and resources that parents and professionals might call upon when continuing with this work as an individual progresses further through childhood towards adult life. Possible ways of teaching children more about their diagnosis and how to live with it are suggested in the first part of this chapter. Advice is then given on how to help children benefit from knowing about their autism through developing more of a vested interest in their school work, utilizing their support much better and becoming more involved in planning for their future lives. How well children with autism do learn to manage their challenges can be significantly affected by the responses of the typical people around them (Mesibov *et al.* 2004). Therefore, thought is also given to which other people close to the child may need to be told about their diagnosis, how this sensitive information can be disseminated among them safely and how the child could be supported in having a role in this.

Throughout *All About Me*, children are repeatedly offered reassurance that it is okay to have autism. However, this will be hard for a child to believe if they are constantly confronted with the negative consequences of their diagnosis. Therefore, the final section in this chapter reflects on how the typical people involved with an individual can help them to feel happier and more positive about their lives.

All the ideas, resources and initiatives described in this chapter could be incorporated into some children's post-disclosure programmes, but it should be emphasized that not all of them will be appropriate for every child. Parents and professionals are advised to examine each one for themselves before deciding on its suitability and how it might best be used. Decisions like this ought to be based on knowledge of the child's situation including the developmental levels at which they are operating in communication and cognition, their individual preferences and how well they have responded to being told about their diagnosis.

8.2 CONTINUING THE PROCESSES OF TEACHING CHILDREN ABOUT THEIR AUTISM AND HELPING THEM LEARN TO UNDERSTAND AND LIVE WITH THEIR DIAGNOSIS

8.2.1 Using the booklet

At the end of the programme, each child is given a copy of their *All About Me* booklet to take home as a permanent reference. This can then be used by the child and their parents to continue the work together. It is recommended that a copy is kept at school too and that the child is made aware of whom they should approach when they want to look at it. Care should be taken to ensure that copies in schools or elsewhere are stored securely so that other children and adults who do not know about the child's diagnosis cannot come across them. If a child wants to read their booklet while they are at school, they should be offered a suitably private space in which to do this.

There are no set ways for using the booklet once a child has completed the programme. Nor are there any prescribed reasons and frequencies for referring them to it. All children's needs are different, as will be their understanding and acceptance of their autism. Some children may want to look at their booklet from time to time simply for enjoyment. Others may have very little to do with it unless prompted by adults.

There will be children who will not initially understand or accept the validity of parts of the programme content. The finished booklet can be used by adults to help children with this by taking them back through and discussing sections that they have not understood and those that they want to know more about. Adult decisions on when and how regularly to refer children back to the booklet will need to be judged individually. Children who are resistant to either reading their booklet or using any other autism-related resources should not be coaxed or coerced unduly into complying. Information about a sensitive issue like autism should not be forced on to children and trying to do so is only likely to make matters worse. To prevent a child from rejecting their diagnosis out of hand, it may be best in these circumstances simply to say that the booklet is there for them to read when they are ready to look at it. The booklet can then be left in a place where the child can find it. Having a backed-up electronic copy means that no real harm can be done if the child destroys their booklet in a moment of rage. It would be wise, as an extra precaution, to store the booklet on a computer or memory card that the child cannot access.

For some children, a good time to reach for the booklet might be when they are feeling anxious and upset or shortly after they have had a negative experience. Of course, there are children who could find this even more distressing, especially if they have attached the blame for all of the negative aspects of their life to their autism, but some individuals might find it comforting to take themselves off into a quiet and private space to read their booklet after difficult moments. As mentioned in Chapter 6, a child can be referred to appropriate pages in their booklet when answering questions they might raise about their autism and why certain things happen to them.

The booklet only provides a limited snapshot of the child at a single point in time so should never be looked upon as being a finished product. It needs to be treated as a dynamic resource. Sections of the booklet might need updating occasionally with fresh information in response to new questions posed by the child or changes in their personal situation that are not covered by the initial content. This can be done easily on a computer if the original electronic file is kept. It is recommended that the whole programme is revisited if possible every year or so, to produce a new or updated edition of the booklet with the child. This would allow an individual to note progress in their behaviour and challenges, as well as record newly developed strengths and changes in their special interests. Alterations and additions can also be made to the description of their autism. The language and appearance of the booklet could also be adjusted to reflect the child's current developmental levels and ensure that they still find it attractive. This may require the use of one of the other templates.

As well as helping children to continue developing their own understanding of autism, the booklet can be used, in the ways described later in this chapter, as a tool for sharing their diagnosis with the people around them and thus giving the individual more of a voice in explaining themselves to others.

The booklet is meant to provide children with a positive explanation of what having autism means, but is somewhat restricted by the amount of practical advice that it offers them for learning to live with and overcome the challenges it describes. Autism workbooks have been designed for that purpose and Social Stories™ (as described in Gray 2015) can also be effective resources for helping children develop important life skills and come up with their own coping strategies.

8.2.2 Autism workbooks and Social Stories™

Asperger's... What Does It Mean to Me? by Catherine Faherty (2006) and *The ASD Workbook* by Penny Kershaw (2011) each contain a wealth of information about autism. Either of these workbooks could be used over time to help consolidate and add more detail to what some children learn about their autism through participating in a shorter bespoke programme like *All About Me*. Both books also offer extensive practical problem-solving advice that, with adult support, is intended to steer children towards developing their own strategies for coping with everyday difficulties and managing in situations that they might find challenging at various stages in their lives.

Because they are generic resources and autism is a hugely diverse condition, workbooks inevitably cover some issues that, while being very important for certain individuals, are not applicable to all children. For instance, Faherty advises on how to deal with problems with eating, self-harming and oppositional behaviours. Also, some sections may repeat things that children have already learned during *All About Me* or from other sources since then. This might help to consolidate, clarify or reinforce children's understanding and acceptance of what they were taught earlier, but individuals who are less flexible could be put off by repetition. These difficulties can be addressed easily in many instances, however, by working through a book selectively, missing out certain pages or worksheets along the way.

Individual workbooks will not be suitable for all children with autism as they have their target audiences and may require an individual to have attained a certain level of literacy and understanding. Kershaw's book is aimed at children aged ten years and above, whereas Faherty's has been written for children with high-functioning autism and AS who will therefore be functioning at more advanced stages in cognition and communication than other children on the spectrum. Adults will need to use their own judgement as to whether a child has reached a stage at which they will be able to understand a workbook's text and the concepts it covers. They will also need to think about whether the child would find it engaging and be able to manage the volume of information provided.

The main disadvantage of printed workbooks is that their content, language and formatting cannot be altered to suit each reader's individual needs and preferences. However, their authors are highly experienced practitioners and the ideas and advice contained in these workbooks are grounded in successful work with large groups of children. Even if it is decided not to use them directly with particular individuals, adults could still find these workbooks extremely valuable as guides for planning more personalized work of their own.

Another option is the use of Social Stories™. They can offer an effective way of helping children to understand and cope better with different aspects of their autism. *The New Social Story™ Book* by Carol Gray (2015) offers guidance on how to write and use Social Stories™ to teach everyday social skills to individual children on the autism spectrum. The book also provides more than 180 editable stories which can be personalized for use with children of all ages or act as examples for adults writing different stories relevant to individual children. After participating in *All About Me*, a child would know about their diagnosis. This means autism could be discussed openly in the content of any Social Stories™ that are made for them. Furthermore, specific stories could be written to support children in working through some of their own challenges listed in their booklets.

8.2.3 Other useful books and resources

Besides the workbooks described above, numerous resources have been produced across other autism genres that could be used selectively and creatively to supplement a child's understanding of their diagnosis and help them view it more positively (Fletcher 2013). There is a constantly growing array of information books, accounts of people with autism, self-help books and novels featuring characters with autism. There are far too many of these resources to list in full here or offer advice on how to use them. Nevertheless, Table 8.1 offers a starting point by briefly describing a small selection of books and films which could be considered for use with children of various ages and abilities. These resources are all fully referenced at the end of this book.

Table 8.1: A selection of published resources that could be used in post-disclosure work with children and young people on the autism spectrum

Title and author(s)	Description
Autism: Receiving and Understanding a Diagnosis produced by the AET (2011)	A DVD containing a series of short films in which teenagers and successful young adults with autism talk about living with their diagnosis.
Been There. Done That. Try This! An Aspie's Guide to Life on Earth edited by Tony Attwood, Craig Evans and Anita Lesko (2014)	This self-help book identifies and explores 17 issues that appear to cause individuals with high-functioning autism the most stress. It passes on the insights of a group of notable and successful Aspie mentors in coping with those issues. By describing how they have personally dealt with a range of well-being and practical difficulties, Aspie mentors offer guidance for readers who want to draw up their own coping strategies. This book may be suitable for able older teenagers and adults.
My Autism Book: A Child's Guide to Their Autism Spectrum Diagnosis by Gloria Dura-Vila and Tamar Levi (2014)	A short illustrated book with a simple text that positively explores the strengths and differences of people with autism. It has been written for children aged five and above.
Different Like Me: My Book of Autism Heroes by Jennifer Elder (2006)	Written from the viewpoint of a boy with autism, this book describes the achievements of famous and historical figures who may have been on the autism spectrum. It is intended for children aged 8–12.
Finding out about Asperger Syndrome, High-Functioning Autism and PDD by Gunilla Gerland (2000)	This short book has been written to explain their differences to children and young people who, like the author, have been diagnosed with AS or high-functioning autism.
The Curious Incident of the Dog in the Night-Time by Mark Haddon (2003)	A bestselling novel written from the viewpoint of the main character who is a 15-year-old boy who presents as possibly having AS.
Blue Bottle Mystery: An Asperger Adventure by Kathy Hoopmann (2000 as a novel and 2016 as a graphic novel)	Written first as a novel and then, for readers with more visual preferences, as a graphic novel. The story's main character is a boy called Ben who has AS. Instances throughout the book provide matter-of-fact examples of how Ben behaves and sees things differently to the typical characters, while also highlighting his strengths and how these include areas that others find challenging. Two further novels have been written in this series by the same author (Hoopmann 2001, 2002).

Autism and Me by Rory Hoy (2007)	A DVD containing a short film written and presented by Rory Hoy (when he was an 18-year-old with autism). Rory positively describes his differences and the progress he made as he became older. This film can be used with able older primary school children as well as teenagers and adults.
Freaks, Geeks and Asperger Syndrome: A User Guide to Adolescence by Luke Jackson (2002)	An autobiographical account written by Luke Jackson when he was 12 which may appeal to more able adolescents and some adults.
Can I Tell You about Asperger Syndrome? A Guide for Friends and Family by Jude Welton (2004b)	This book is written from the perspective of a fictional boy with AS called Adam. He describes what everyday life might be like for a child with high-functioning autism and why he behaves differently, and suggests things that other people might do to help. This book is aimed at children aged 7–15 years as well as the typical people in their lives.
Can I Tell You about Autism? *A Guide for Friends, Family and Professionals* by Jude Welton (2014)	This book is written from the perspective of a fictional boy with autism called Tom. He describes what everyday life might be like for children with autism and why he behaves differently. Tom also suggests things that others can do to help him. This book is intended for children aged seven and upwards as well as the typical people in their lives.
How to Be Yourself in a World That's Different: An Asperger Syndrome Study Guide for Adolescents by Yoko Yoshida (2007)	A self-help book for able teenagers and young adults on the autism spectrum. It provides readers with a detailed explanation of AS and its underlying neurology before offering practical advice on how to deal with specific problems they might experience in everyday life. The author recommends that children read this book with a support person who can help them decide which parts of the book are relevant and with learning to apply strategies.

When using any of these resources with children, it needs to be made explicit to them that everyone's autism is different and that not everything an individual is going to see, hear or read about it will apply exactly to them or anyone else on the spectrum. This is vital because literal interpretations could cause confusion. There is always the possibility that children might conclude that their own diagnosis is incorrect if they observe features in others that they do not recognize in themselves. This is something that children who are finding it harder to accept their diagnosis could latch on to as being proof that they do not have autism after all.

8.3 DEVELOPING A CHILD'S ENGAGEMENT WITH THEIR SCHOOL WORK, SUPPORT, AND PLANNING FOR THE FUTURE

8.3.1 Introduction

This section provides guidance for parents and professionals who are living and working with able mainstream children who, despite knowing about their diagnosis and its associated challenges, still have difficulties in any of the following areas:

- accepting support

- engaging with all their school work

- becoming actively involved in planning for their future.

8.3.2 Why children might experience difficulties in these areas

One intention of *All About Me* is to help children see the point behind accepting their support and participating more fully in all aspects of their education. It is also hoped that by informing children about their diagnosis they might then become more actively involved in making decisions affecting their future lives. Nonetheless, as also observed by Duprey (2011), I have discovered that providing children with information about their autism is often not enough in itself to prompt them to do this spontaneously. People with autism may not readily reach conclusions that are obvious to others (Blackburn 2013). This means that links between what children are taught about their strengths and challenges, the purpose and advantages of accepting support and them needing to do things differently to achieve well in the future may have to be made totally explicit to them.

A tendency towards having single fixed attention makes it harder for a child with autism to switch their thoughts away from their own narrow range of interests and on to things that other people, such as their teachers and support workers, want them to think about and do. They need to find adult-directed activities rewarding or at least be able to see that there is a clear point behind doing them (Lawson 2011). Therefore, because of their autism, children may not readily want to complete important but *less interesting* school work unless it is made obvious to them that they have a highly vested interest in it.

To engage children more in work that they find uninteresting or irrelevant, it is often necessary to look for ways to incorporate their special interests into curriculum activities or to motivate them by offering regular extrinsic rewards related to their preferred activities and objects. However, these strategies may not always be practical or time-efficient, particularly for able children in mainstream education who might be following an increasingly rigid and demanding curriculum. This all suggests that some children will need to be taught to understand how participating in their learning as fully as possible and accepting their support can be profitable for them in the future. However, doing this requires that they develop an adequate concept of time and have future aspirations that they would like to work towards.

Children with autism can have problems understanding the passage of time and may not be able to grasp the idea that the future will one day become the present (Wing 2002). They might not be able to imagine themselves ever becoming adults either, because Boucher (2009, p.246) suggests that 'mental time travel' like this is more difficult for people with autism. Children with whom I have worked have often appeared to give very little attention to their hopes for the future and seemed much more focused on the here and now instead. This is perhaps not surprising since trying to consider their own future involves an individual seeing themselves very differently which requires both flexibility of thought and the acceptance of major changes.

On the other hand, some of the children who have been able to talk to me about their future ambitions expressed unrealistic career aspirations and life goals. These included things that were unlikely to be achieved either because of the child's academic ability or because they would be reliant upon a great deal of good fortune (e.g. winning a lottery or becoming famous celebrities). Adults need to try to guide children like this towards developing more realistic, less specific and potentially more attainable aspirations.

Assuming a child has developed a realistic concept of what they would like to achieve and do in the future, they may then require guidance around what they might need to do differently or additionally in the meantime to increase their chances of succeeding. This could include them trying to engage more with school work and classroom support as well as in learning to manage challenging aspects of their autism or develop new skills. However, children with autism may have a reduced sense of agency (Jordan 1999). This implies that there could be individuals who will need to be taught that they can have an active influence over what happens to them in the future through their own actions and behaviour, as opposed to them just being passive bystanders in events that are going happen to them anyway.

8.3.3 Steps that may need to be worked through to support children's engagement

The issues described so far in this section seem to imply that some children may not be able to readily apply what they have learned about their autism to accepting support, engaging with their education or participating in planning for their future lives. For these children, some of the following steps may need to be worked through first:

- teaching the child about the passage of time between the past, present and future in relation to their own life

- helping the child to identify a short list of broad and realistic life goals

- explaining the reasons for their support in relation to how it can be used to help address some of their autism-related challenges and increase their chances of realizing their future aspirations

- explaining the purpose behind their education and its potential future value for them

- helping the child identify a few overall areas of behaviour that they might need to try to alter over time, while explaining how doing these things differently could also increase their chances of achieving their future goals.

8.3.4 *My Future*

The rest of this section describes how to teach an initiative called *My Future*. This has been used with able children in mainstream education, aged around ten and upwards, who already knew about their diagnosis but still appeared to have difficulty recognizing that they had a vested interest in accepting support and participating fully in their school work. It has provided a framework for guiding children through the steps outlined above by completing a template to create another personalized booklet. This initiative can also be used with children who need guidance on identifying their own support needs and future aspirations so that they can become more fully involved in making important decisions affecting their lives.

This piece of work could be carried out by the person who told the child about their diagnosis, their parents or a suitably skilled professional who knows enough about the individual and their autism.

Although *My Future* will not be needed by every child who participates in *All About Me*, a fictional copy of a *My Future* booklet has been included in the electronic resources as an illustrative example (E1). This five-page booklet, about Kim's future, is based on work carried out with around 50 children and offers a practical model for parents and professionals to work from. It is advisable to refer to a copy of this while reading the brief description of how to teach this initiative, given below.

A blank template (E2), with embedded guidance for producing similar booklets, has also been supplied. This template can be adapted for use in work with other children who have autism and AS. The template is short and precise, so adults with reasonable computing skills and knowledge of a child should be able to adjust its wording and formatting to levels matching those in their *All About Me* booklet.

Page 1 in the template contains a blank timeline for an adult supporter to print off, discuss and fill in by hand with the child, while guiding them through a mental and visual time-travelling exercise about their own life. This is intended to help the child gain a visual overview of their life so far and think more about what they would like to achieve in the future. The part from the child's birth to the present day is usually completed first to remind the individual of the main events in their life up until that point and to contextualize the present. This should include things like the child's date of birth, when they started school and a few other significant milestones they have reached so far. Having done this, the far end of the timeline should be filled in next, to record things that the child might want to go on to achieve and do as an adult. This can be initiated by asking a series of questions about the child's special interests and what types of career they might find interesting, as well as where they think they might want to live and what sorts of things they might want to own as an adult. These may all be questions that the child has never previously asked themselves, so adults may need to offer some examples to think about.

Some children will need to be guided towards developing aspirations that are realistic and potentially attainable. For instance, if a child said they wanted to be the head keeper at a zoo or a vet, a sensible compromise might be to agree to note something like 'I want to have a job that I enjoy – perhaps working with animals.'

Having recorded what the child might want to do as an adult, the next step is to back-fill the remaining space on the timeline between then and the present to show what it is hoped might happen over that period as well as the steps the child might need to work through and try to accomplish along the way. This should include possible changes in their educational placements and important examinations they may have to sit. Before leaving this page, adults must remember to draw the child's attention to the arrow that points past the age of 25 and reassure them that the timeline is only intended to represent the first part of the individual's life. The completed timeline will need to be scanned and pasted into the template to replace the blank copy on page 1 before the finished booklet is printed.

The script on page 2 only needs to be read and discussed with the child. This explains how time passes between the past, present and future, and tries to make it clear that the child has a vital role as an agent in shaping what will happen to them.

The completed timeline will need to be referred to again when working through page 3. This is where the child is steered towards drawing up a list of four or five broad and realistic future life goals. This list should start, like Kim's, with the more immediate goals that are intended to facilitate the chances of the others being met subsequently – such as the child wanting to do well at their present school and gain reasonable grades in examinations – before perhaps moving on to what they would like to achieve in a college or higher education setting and, lastly, on to their long-term aspirations for adult life. To try to avoid misunderstandings that could arise from a child being over-literal and lacking flexibility of thought, the final two sentences on this page have been written to emphasize that the child will not be bound rigidly by the goals that they set themselves here and, like everyone else, they are free to revise their ambitions whenever they wish.

Page 4 aims to teach children about their own vested interests in accepting support, engaging fully with their education and trying to work on their main challenges. This is done by explicitly stating that, through doing all of this, they will increase their chances of having the type of future life they would like. Once completed, this page should contain a list of four or five general behaviours that the child agrees they need to begin learning to change over the long term. In Kim's example, two of these areas are associated with challenges around social interaction and communication which could both have been taken from a real child's *All About Me* booklet. The other two areas focus on her trying to concentrate on less motivating school work and cooperate further with support workers. However, in the interests of being honest with a child, it needs to be made clear that adhering to all of the changes that they have agreed to will not guarantee them achieving all their stated goals and that they may face disappointments in life.

Page 5 ends the booklet by naming the people who make up the child's extended support team. The booklet ends with the clear message that their shared purpose is to work with the child towards maximizing their chances of future success.

The completed booklet can then be used for the following purposes:

- providing the child with visual reminders of what they are aiming for and the agreed ways forward

- helping the child evaluate their progress and revise their goals when appropriate

- as a tool for supporting the child's participation in discussions about their support needs and in making realistic decisions about their future academic and career options

- to provide a framework for setting more specific short- and medium-term targets in the child's individual education plan.

8.4 SHARING THE DIAGNOSIS WITH SIBLINGS, OTHER FAMILY MEMBERS AND FRIENDS

This is the first of three sections focusing upon sharing the child's diagnosis with the people around them, starting with their siblings, other family members and friends. Each of these sections explores in turn why the groups of people who are likely to spend most time with the child or have most responsibility for looking after them might also need to be told about their autism, what issues this could create and how the diagnosis could be disclosed to them safely. Because of their autism, many children will find it difficult to explain what they are taught about it to others (Jones 2001), and therefore thought is also given to how they can be supported to have a role in explaining themselves to these people.

Even if siblings are not told about their brother or sister's autism, they will more than likely notice differences in their behaviour and how their parents treat them (Jones 2001). Autism is a hidden condition, so without having these things properly explained, siblings may wonder about things like why their brother or sister exhibits certain behaviours and seems able to get away with doing things that they would get into trouble for or why their parents might devote far more time and attention to their sibling (Yoshida 2012). Any resentment this might create could be intensified by siblings being subjected to ridicule or bullying because of the way the child behaves at school and in the neighbourhood.

If they are kept in the dark about the diagnosis and what it means, siblings and other family members may come up with inaccurate and negative reasons of their own to explain the child's differences. This could seriously damage family members' relationships with the child (Jones 2001), especially if the individual's behaviour is having harmful, disruptive and restrictive effects on everyone else's daily lives and they come to believe that this might be deliberate.

It should not be forgotten either that once a child has been told about their own diagnosis, there is no overall guarantee that they will not disclose it to their siblings and other family members themselves. Siblings could find out accidentally in other ways too, such as by overhearing parents' conversations or finding copies of professionals' reports and other paperwork about the child's autism that has been sent to their home. Parents not sharing the diagnosis could lead to siblings forming the opinion that autism must be something too shameful to talk about when they eventually do find out.

Besides possibly addressing some of the difficulties described above, sharing and explaining the child's diagnosis across a family unit could benefit the child by increasing the number of people with the insight needed to become actively involved in their support network. Other family members might then be able to help the child with learning how to live with the challenges presented by their autism and through advocating for them at home, at school and in the community. There seems to be a consensus among experts on autism that positive changes in an individual's behaviour are more likely to occur when the typical people close to them adjust the things they do (e.g. Clements 2005; Jordan 2005; Whitaker 2001). Family members understanding the underlying causes of a child's behaviour and learning how to respond to it more appropriately could therefore have a positive impact on life for the whole family.

Parents will need to make their own judgements on when siblings are ready to be told and the amount of information they will need to be given. It is advisable not to delay beginning this process unduly, however, since they could come across negative information about autism in the meantime which would make it harder to present their brother or sister's diagnosis to them positively. Some siblings may find news of the diagnosis upsetting and difficult to accept, especially when they are told that the condition and the challenges for the family are going to be lifelong. Despite this, they live with the child and have no choice in the matter, so it is my view that siblings have a right to be given this information at the earliest appropriate time and be gradually shown how they can become more involved in helping to improve the child's life.

Deciding which other relatives and people to tell, such as grandparents, aunts, uncles, cousins, family friends, neighbours and frequent visitors to the home, may need be given careful forethought. As with society in general, some of them could hold negative views on autism and disability. Disclosing the diagnosis to other adults can have its advantages, but has an added risk of complicating matters further if they experience their own difficulties with accepting the validity of the diagnosis and possibly being devastated or ashamed by it.

Although responses like these are probably rare, where any of this is thought possible, decisions on whether to tell certain individuals perhaps need to be based on what is already known about a person's existing views on conditions such as autism, how close they are to the child and the extent to which them knowing about the diagnosis is likely to help improve the child's daily life. However, it needs to be remembered again that the possibility of them finding out accidentally or coming up with the diagnosis themselves cannot be ignored. Once the child knows, they could just tell them anyway. The potential consequences of relatives discovering the diagnosis later and reacting angrily to having had important information about a loved one withheld from them also needs to be factored into this decision.

Having decided whom to tell, the next step is to decide on how to go about doing it sensitively and safely. The easiest way would probably be to simply explain the child's diagnosis to people at various times on a need-to-know basis. However, giving this type of news in isolation without planning how to explain it properly is unlikely to be sufficient. It could be upsetting for people who have an emotional attachment to the child or prove confusing. Autism is something that cannot easily be explained in a single conversation to anyone and nor should it be (Vermeulen 2013).

A good way to start explaining things further, which might also open up opportunities for the child to express their own voice in this process, could be through sharing the individual's *All About Me* booklet with different family members and close friends. This would offer everyone concerned a positive and personalized account of the child's autism in the context of them being the person whom they already love and are proud of. Moreover, if the child is able to participate in doing this, it would provide them with further opportunities to use their booklet to revise what they have already been taught about their autism and to enhance their self-esteem and confidence.

For family members and friends who want to find out more about autism, there are numerous resources which they could be referred to. Again, there are far too many to list in full in this book but some of the resources listed in Table 8.1, for use with the child, may be suitable. The two books referred to there by Jude Welton (2004b, 2014) are also targeted at explaining autism and AS to children's typical family members and friends aged seven and upwards. Rory Hoy's short film, *Autism and Me* (2007), in which he described his own experiences of growing up with autism, might make positive and informative family viewing. It should be stressed again, however, that there may be information and portrayals of autism in these resources that family members and friends will not recognize in their child and this may need to be explained to them first.

8.5 INFORMING SCHOOL STAFF AND OTHER PROFESSIONALS ABOUT A CHILD'S DIAGNOSIS

Any school staff who are likely to encounter an individual with autism need to be told who that child is, what their main needs are and how best to support them in the context of their own work. Not having this information makes it harder for staff to support the child's educational, social, communication and emotional needs effectively. This can also make it more difficult for them to know how to treat the child fairly. Not having an adequate understanding of both what school is like from the individual's perspective and why they might behave differently in certain situations could lead to some staff mistakenly assuming that the child is intentionally awkward, aggressive or rude, and then reacting to them accordingly. Furthermore, staff not knowing how to spot signs that the child is becoming emotionally aroused or what calming strategies to apply in those circumstances can lead to minor situations unnecessarily escalating out of control into fully blown conflicts and meltdowns (Whitaker 2001).

Many mainstream staff have attended training that at least offered them some sort of basic understanding of the main characteristics of autism and an overview of generic strategies for supporting children in educational environments. By itself, this may prove insufficient because of the broad diversity among children with autism and the consequent need for individualized approaches to supporting children. Staff will need more precise information about each individual's unique form of autism and what things work best for them.

While it is hoped that children who participate in *All About Me* will eventually develop the necessary communication skills and enough knowledge about their autism to be able to explain themselves to others, not all of them will be ready to do this straight away when they complete the programme (Miller 2014, 2015). Besides, children with autism can often lose the ability to express themselves clearly in stressful situations (Jones 2002). Nevertheless, this does not mean that they cannot be given a voice in informing staff at their schools about their autism.

As a starting point, the child could be invited to share their *All About Me* booklet with a select group of familiar staff with whom they have regular contact. Given their needs, however, this may have to be restricted in some cases to the child sharing the booklet with no more than one or two people at a time. The booklet could be circulated electronically to other staff members, but it needs to be remembered that its primary purpose is to explain the child's diagnosis to them, rather than to provide support guidance for others. Bearing this in mind, a *personal communication passport*, similar to those described by Millar (2003), could offer a more suitable method of sharing essential support information efficiently across a large staff group. Furthermore, a child could be helped to make a significant contribution to its production. Written in the first person, from the individual's viewpoint, a document like this might contain the following:

- a photograph of the child

- a brief description of autism

- a list of their preferred activities and interests

- a list of their main strengths

- a summary of their main challenges

- some key teaching and communication strategies

- the names of staff members who can be contacted for further advice or for assistance during an urgent situation.

In certain cases, the child could also retain a copy of the passport and be taught how to present it discreetly to substitute classroom staff or any other unfamiliar adults that they could meet around the school and need to explain themselves to. However, the risk of the child losing their passport or it falling into the wrong hands by other means will need to be considered. Keeping the passport short and precise is vital to its effective use by staff, especially when last-minute changes occur or if the child is experiencing a difficult moment. This is also a resource that should be regularly reviewed and updated to reflect changes in the child's circumstances.

Many mainstream schools are already using passports successfully, and special needs staff in some of them have also filmed children talking about themselves and their autism and presented this at staff meetings. Films like this can be made to include the types of information that might be included in a passport.

In conclusion, it needs to be remembered that although it might be important for all staff to have an adequate understanding of the child's autism, a large number of people knowing about and discussing the diagnosis increases the chances of it being disclosed accidentally to other children around the school. The child's peers could overhear adult conversations or come across copies of children's booklets and passports if they are left lying around unattended.

8.6 SHARING A CHILD'S DIAGNOSIS WITH THEIR CLASSMATES

8.6.1 Introduction

Parents and professionals who work with children who go to mainstream schools will need to consider whether the individual's classmates should be told about the diagnosis. In my experience, the outcomes of providing typical peers with accurate and honest information about a child's autism have almost invariably turned out to be positive for everyone concerned. However, this work requires careful planning and skilful delivery, since it could create additional problems for the child when it is not done well (Jones 2001). Because of this, professionals should never disclose an individual's diagnosis to other children without the child's parents' consent. It is desirable wherever possible to gain agreement from the child too.

This section has been written to help parents and professionals reach joint decisions on whether to tell children's classmates about their autism and to offer guidance that might enable them to do this more safely. It explores the pros and cons of sharing the diagnosis with peers and then describes a method for using the content of a child's *All About Me* booklet to plan and teach an introductory class lesson about their autism.

8.6.2 Why might classmates need to be told about a child's diagnosis?

As with a child's siblings, it is to be expected that their typical classmates will start to notice an individual's differences from an early age. Although they might not always question these things out loud, it is likely that they too will want to know why a child behaves in certain ways and sometimes appears to be treated differently. Being puzzled by aspects of the child's behaviour, they might not know how to respond to it positively. They could find it unusual, upsetting or even frightening and believe that a child's negative behaviours are deliberately intended to upset or harm others. Arguably, the other children need to be given honest answers to their questions and have any concerns they might have explained before they come up with their own reasons for them.

It may be possible to provide a child's classmates with some of the information they need through teaching them about neurodiversity in general and how everyone learns and behaves differently, without mentioning the term 'autism'. However, not providing peers with the proper word to describe a child's differences may backfire in some circumstances, since typical children can be very good at coming up with and applying their own, not so pleasant, descriptive labels to individuals with autism (Sainsbury 2000).

Another alternative to direct disclosure might be to educate peers about autism in general without relating anything that they are told directly to individual children at their school. This can be done through assemblies or class lessons about autism, part of which might involve viewing a film like Rory Hoy's *Autism and Me* (2007). Some secondary schools have included books like Mark Haddon's *The Curious Incident of the Dog in the Night-Time* (2003) in their literacy curriculum. Although this approach is welcomed, it could have its own drawbacks for a child on the autism spectrum. If this is done by itself, it is possible that members of a child's peer group could diagnose the individual themselves later, on the back of the information they were given, without having an accurate enough understanding of how autism affects that particular individual or how they could respond supportively to their needs. They may even try to talk to the child about it.

In any case, there is a good chance that a deliberate attempt to hold back a child's diagnosis from the rest of their class will fail sooner or later as the group gets older. As with the child themselves and their family members, there are numerous unplanned ways that peers can find out about an individual's diagnosis. Accidental disclosure can occur, for example through peers overhearing adult conversations, the child announcing their diagnosis themselves or their peers coming across written information about the individual. As has already been suggested above, peers may even diagnose a child themselves after being given generalized information about autism. They could also do this on the basis of media portrayals of autism or after meeting similar children and being told that they had autism. Moreover, this type of disclosure could possibly occur without school staff necessarily being aware of it until it is too late to prevent the child from any harm. In these circumstances, adults will not be in a position of being able to manage the flow of information children might need in order to develop a positive and accurate initial understanding of what having autism means.

Often, while I have been delivering peer work lessons, at least one or two children have said that they had already been told, found out or guessed that the child we were talking about had autism. In my own experience, children finding out about an individual's diagnosis without having then been given much in the way of follow-up explanation are unlikely to have gained a sufficient understanding of what having autism means from elsewhere. Although some may then conclude that autism is something the child needs help with and could act empathetically towards them, without this information it is possible that some peers could develop their own inaccurate and negative views about a child and behave towards them as such.

Through my own work with peers, I have seen how teaching classmates about a child's autism can have many practical and safeguarding benefits for both the individual and the group as a whole, some of which may be unexpected. Peer lessons have been used to explain the underlying causes of children's different or inappropriate behaviour, their social isolation and difficulties in managing their emotional responses. This has helped improve and repair some very difficult situations where children with autism were isolated from or excluded by the rest of the group, as well as in instances where there was a lengthy history of the child feeling that they were bullied or there being reciprocal hostility between them and other class members.

Overall, I have found that teaching peers about a child's autism can broaden an individual's support network by recruiting them into it as active members. Given the right training, supportive and understanding peers can come up with their own valuable ways of contributing towards a child becoming more included in the group, learning to behave more appropriately, becoming more independent, remaining calmer in lessons and staying safe. Furthermore, peer group initiatives have led to classmates taking on some of the responsibility for looking out for children with autism around their school site and stepping in to support them with problems. Their protective support has made some individuals less vulnerable to unwanted attention from other children. Help like this can even come from classmates who had previously acted unkindly towards the child.

8.6.3 Potential risks of sharing a child's diagnosis with their classmates

This type of work calls upon a group's better nature and so there is always the possibility that some class members could decide to use a child's diagnosis to tease or bully them. There is also a chance that individuals who are given information about a child's autism could then tell other children outside of the group about their diagnosis and that could in turn make the child susceptible to unwanted negative attention from members of the broader school population. Furthermore, disclosure opens the possibility of the diagnosis being used prejudicially against any of the child's siblings who attend the same school.

8.6.4 Further issues to consider before and during peer work

A number of other practical and safeguarding issues need to be taken into account before reaching a final decision on whether to tell a child's classmates about their autism. These are all to protect the child from the potential risks described above and to maximize the positive value any work might have for the child's well-being.

Peer work I have carried out has almost invariably had positive results. This success can probably be put down largely to the careful group screening that has always taken place beforehand. It is important that adult decisions about whether to carry out this work are influenced by knowledge of the child's class. Work like this should not be carried out with classes that have any significant behavioural management issues that could prevent them from focusing adequately on the lesson and taking what is discussed seriously. It would not be sensible either to share a diagnosis with a group that is going through an extensive period of major disruption to their education (such as being taught by a series of temporary teachers) until things have settled back down again. A judgement on whether it is likely to be safe to share the diagnosis with a class should take group dynamics into account by considering things like how well the individuals in the class get along with each other, their level of trustworthiness and their overall past attitudes and behaviour towards children who are vulnerable and different. If it is felt unsafe to share the diagnosis with the whole class, the work could still be carried out with a selected group of more supportive children.

Two extra safeguarding procedures have been built into the autism awareness lessons that I have delivered to peers. The first is always to start the lesson by stressing both the sensitive nature of what the group is about to be told and the strict need for confidentiality on their part. Children are then given the option of withdrawing from the lesson if they think that they will not be able either to keep what is said private and within the group or use the information about the child positively. Second, as soon as the child's diagnosis has been revealed, older classes are told explicitly that treating people badly or unfairly because of their autism is illegal and can have serious consequences. Younger classes are reminded of their school's anti-bullying policy.

Thought also needs to go into who will lead the lesson and which other staff will be present to support them. The person teaching the lesson does not necessarily need to be an autism specialist but would ideally be an experienced qualified teacher, psychologist or therapist with a good understanding of the child, their needs and how best to support them. This person would have to feel confident in their own ability to answer children's questions about autism accurately and in a positive, matter-of-fact way, as well as handle any negative remarks that could be made about the child. They would need to be aware of the possible consequences for the child if things go wrong.

It is also important that key school staff, such as the child's class teacher (or form tutor), the SENCo and preferably a member of the senior leadership are present to support and give status to the lesson if they are not leading it. Class teachers in particular will have a central role in following up the lesson in school safely over time, as well as in monitoring that the group respects the sensitive and confidential nature of what they are taught.

The child concerned should not be present for the initial lesson in which their diagnosis will be disclosed. This is to safeguard individuals from hearing children say things that they could find upsetting or which might potentially damage their relationships with members of the group. The other children will also need to feel free to ask personal questions about the child's differences and express their own views openly. For similar reasons, it is best that the child's parents and other family members are asked not to attend that lesson either. Time should be set aside afterwards for the person teaching the lesson to give feedback to the child and their parents. None of this means the child cannot have an active role or a voice in telling other children about their autism. The person teaching the introductory lesson could involve them in planning and preparing the presentation that will be used to disclose their diagnosis. After the lesson has taken place, the child could be asked if they would like to share their *All About Me* booklet with some of the other children. Those who are able enough and want to do so could also be helped to write and deliver their own follow-up presentation or make a short film about their autism for their class.

8.6.5 *All About Me for Peers*

I have used the initiative described below, called *All About Me for Peers*, in work with more than 60 primary and secondary school classes. In the clear majority of instances, the outcomes were positive and similar to those described earlier in this section. This work involves delivering a one-hour interactive presentation to a child's class to introduce them to the individual's diagnosis. This is intended to initiate future ongoing discussions among the group and their class teacher about how they can contribute towards supporting the individual with some of their challenges at school and in becoming more included in the group. The principal aims of the lesson are as follows:

- to positively disclose the child's diagnosis to their classmates in the context of their personal attributes, strengths and differences

- to provide the group with a short explanation of what having autism does and does not mean

- to help the class understand why the child might behave and be treated differently to them

- for the group to become more accepting of the child's differences and view having autism as being okay

- to initiate an ongoing dialogue within the group which results in them behaving more positively towards the child and becoming more actively involved in supporting them at school.

Some children with autism, and their parents, have commented afterwards that this lesson had significantly improved the individual child's life at school and that this had made them happier in general. Importantly, no instances have been reported, so far, by children, parents or schools regarding information from the lesson being used against a child or of it being passed on to members of other classes. There appears to have been no obvious negative comeback from this initiative for children's siblings either.

The presentation about the child is intended to be personalized so follows a similar framework to *All About Me*, to disclose and provide an initial explanation of the child's diagnosis in the context of their overall personal attributes, strengths and differences. To do this, key information about the child is copied from an electronic version of the individual's *All About Me* booklet into the relevant places in one of the presentation templates provided in the electronic resources (E5 for children with autism and E6 for those with AS).

Copies of presentations that were written for fictional children with autism and AS are provided in the electronic resources (E3 and E4 respectively). These examples are intended to show what this type of lesson entails and to illustrate the brief description of the work given here.

The templates have been provided so that suitably qualified, skilled and knowledgeable professionals can create their own peer presentations on behalf of different children with autism and AS. Each template is generic but it has been possible to adjust them both for use with classes of mainstream children aged 7–16 years. Professionals using the templates will need to make alterations to the format and language according to the ages and overall abilities of the classes they are meant for. At the same time, the amount of information about autism may need to be reduced in some cases. For the youngest classes, this may need to be limited to little more than the main headline description of the child's autism that is inserted into slide 21 of both templates. Class teachers may sometimes need to be consulted when decisions are made about how to adjust the templates.

It should not be too difficult for experienced and knowledgeable teachers to follow the embedded instructions, written in red, in either template for importing the relevant information from the child's booklet. Once this has been done, the subsequent presentation will most likely contain nearly all the information that will be needed to proceed with the lesson.

The completed presentation should provide an ordered and self-explanatory script for whoever delivers the lesson to work through with the child's class. It includes questions that can be asked at various points to encourage children to contribute to the lesson by sharing their own observations about the child (see E3/E4, slides 3, 5 and 7). Importantly, it contains questions that need to be posed either side of the individual's diagnosis being disclosed. These are to help whoever is teaching the lesson evaluate whether members of the group hold any skewed or false beliefs about either the child or autism that will need to be dispelled before moving on.

The first of these questions asks why they think the child has their profile of strengths and challenges. This is asked immediately before telling the class that the child has autism (see E3/E4, slide 9). Although a few children have said that they thought that the child might have autism or AS, others have occasionally concluded that the child's differences were caused by things like parenting issues, or the child being naughty or having mental health problems. Similar answers have sometimes been given to the second question that follows the disclosure by asking what the children think having autism means (see E3/E4, slide 11). Therefore, to counter views like these, children are next given a series of precise facts about what autism is and is not before they are shown some examples of notable people who may have had autism or AS (see E3/E4, slides 12–18). After then explaining various aspects of the child's autism, and relating them to their support, the presentation returns to the list of the child's main challenges before the final slide invites the group to suggest ways they might be able to support the individual in those areas.

As mentioned above, this presentation is meant to be only the beginning of a class's autism learning journey and the starting point for discussions about how they can go on to be more supportive of their classmate. To help with this process, each child can complete the lesson evaluation form contained in the electronic resources (E7). This asks them to complete a sentence to describe what they have learned about autism and then write down one or two things that they think the group could do to help their classmate. Their written responses can then be used by the class teacher to identify children who need further support in understanding what they were taught in the lesson. The children's ideas can also be collated by their teacher so that these can be used to form the basis of a peer group support plan which can be devised and implemented by the class later.

Again, some of the resources shown in Table 8.1 could be used to follow up the initial work with the child's class. I have found that Rory Hoy's film *Autism and Me* (2007) is usually received positively by typical children and can be a very effective anti-bullying resource if it is presented in the right context.

8.7 PROVING TO THE CHILD THAT IT IS OKAY TO HAVE AUTISM

All About Me repeatedly tries to reassure children that having autism is okay. However, no matter how often they are told this or read it in their booklet, it will be difficult for a child to believe this if they are constantly confronted with negative aspects of their autism, feel overwhelmed by their challenges (Vermeulen 2013) or are treated prejudicially by other people, especially if they are able enough to grasp that their diagnosis and their differences will be lifelong (Lawson 2006).

It has already been said that it can be hard to detect when a child with autism is feeling unhappy or depressed. In some cases, a child's facial expressions and outward behaviour can appear to communicate the exact opposite. Furthermore, having less theory of mind, they may not recognize the need to verbalize their worries and concerns to others (Baron-Cohen *et al.* 1985). It is essential therefore that those supporting a child are always proactive and alert in monitoring the individual's behaviour for signs of unease. They should regularly ask the child to say how they are feeling or to rate their emotional state numerically. Parents, other adults, siblings and peers who have been told about a child's diagnosis can all contribute to supporting the individual's emotional well-being through searching for ways to adapt their own communication, behaviour and arousal levels, as well as trying to help them learn to cope in places and situations that they find stressful.

Beyond all of this, it is essential that the people involved with a child offer them ongoing concrete proof and reassurance that having autism can be okay by giving them positive feedback, helpful information about their diagnosis and opportunities to meet or learn about other people like them. Perhaps most importantly, though, like all children, those with autism should be able to experience frequent success in their areas of strength while also having enough time to relax, be themselves and do the things that they find most interesting, pleasurable and fun.

Chapter 9

A BRIEF GUIDE TO THE ELECTRONIC RESOURCES

9.1 INTRODUCTION

This is the final chapter and it is intended to bring together all of the accompanying electronic resources referred to in this book. Advice on the purpose of these resources and how to use them to support the programme either is provided in the relevant sections below, or, to avoid repetition, is signposted to where this has been done in earlier chapters. As already stated in Chapter 1, these resources are organized into the five sections which are described below and can be accessed at www.jkp.com/voucher using the code QLspdxjP.

9.2 SECTION A: PRE-PROGRAMME INFORMATION-GATHERING AND RECORDING FORMS

Section A contains the following resources used to gather key information about the child during the pre-programme work:

- A1. Pre-programme questionnaire for children

- A2. Pre-programme questionnaire for parents and professionals.

Chapter 3 highlighted the various things that the adults might need to find out about a child before deciding whether and how to take this work forward. It was noted that the pre-programme work often involves having to collect substantial amounts of information from both the child and the adults who know them. Questionnaires A1 and A2 were devised therefore to structure the pre-programme meetings with children and adults, which are described in 3.6.3, while maximizing the amount of relevant information that can be gathered in the time available. Neither questionnaire is meant to be administered rigidly or as a written exercise. Each one contains a series of exploratory questions that should be posed verbally to initiate conversations around the following themes:

- the child's awareness of their differences and their feelings towards having them

- the child's main strengths and challenges

- their special interests, preferred activities and favourite objects

- the child's sensory and perceptual processing differences

- the child's learning preferences

- how the individual uses and responds to verbal and written language

- any issues with the child's behaviour

- what strategies and resources are already being used to support the child.

These question schedules are intended as aide-memoires for the person leading the work and as tools for keeping the meetings focused on these topics and for recording the information outlined above.

It is not always practical to ask every question or to stick to the exact wording on each pro forma. The answers to later questions can often come out incidentally in conversations around earlier ones. Supplementary questions may have to be asked if a conversation dries up before an area has been fully explored. Additional questions may also be needed to clarify children's initial responses. This is vital to avoiding the types of misunderstandings that can frequently arise when trying to interpret comments made by children with autism from a typical person's viewpoint.

The questions in the child questionnaire (A1) will need to be adjusted according to the level of the individual's receptive and expressive language skills. Children with autism can find formulating responses to open-ended questions challenging so may need to be posed with a series of closed questions instead. Furthermore, children ought to be given the option of writing or drawing what they want to say as a means of working around expressive language barriers.

Form A1 has additional space for noting any observations made in meetings with children. This includes aspects of the individual's behaviour as a speaker and listener, such as them frequently going off topic, having word-finding difficulties, being overly literal, displaying little appreciation for the needs of listeners or requiring additional auditory processing time. Space has also been provided for recording the extent to which an individual appears to be aware of being different and their willingness to discuss this with others.

Both these forms were created for use in my own work as a member of an external service. As such, they were designed to support someone who might be unfamiliar with a child. Nevertheless, parents and other adults who know a child well, and are considering carrying out the work themselves, might still find these tools useful for identifying what else they might need to find out before proceeding.

9.3 SECTION B: EXAMPLE *ALL ABOUT ME* BOOKLETS

Section B contains the following selection of fictional examples of *All About Me* booklets:

- B1. Roger's booklet (Level 1 autism)

- B2. Kim's booklet (Level 2 autism)

- B3. Max's booklet (Level 2 Asperger syndrome)

- B4. Janet's booklet (Level 3 autism)

- B5. Sara's booklet (Level 3 Asperger syndrome).

These booklets are intended to illustrate how this programme can be carried out with very different children across the autism spectrum and to exemplify good practice. These booklets have been created from each of the corresponding blank templates which are contained in Section C. Although all children described in the booklets are fictitious, each booklet is based on real work with sizeable groups of similar individuals who were operating roughly within one of these developmental levels:

- Level 1: eight years and below

- Level 2: 9–13 years

- Level 3: 13 years onwards.

As noted in Chapter 2, sharing the sample booklets in the pre-programme meetings has made it easier to provide parents and other adults with an overview of what the programme entails and how it can be adjusted for different children. This has also helped adults to decide whether the work would be suitable for individual children and, if so, what level it would need to be delivered at.

This selection of booklets has also been supplied to illustrate the teaching instructions given in Chapters 5 and 6. Those instructions are generic and so explain how to complete a Level 2 autism or AS template (C2 or C3) to create a booklet which is comparable to either Kim's (B2) or Max's (B3). If it is judged that a Level 1 or 3 template would be more suitable for a child's needs, it is advisable to have a copy of the corresponding booklet to hand for comparison.

This folder does not contain a Level 1 booklet about a child with AS. Until now, the work has not needed to be differentiated at that level for any children with this diagnosis. The small group of younger participants who had AS were all able to access the Level 2 resources. This may be because children with AS do not exhibit noticeable delays in their language and cognitive development (Frith 2003) and the younger individuals with whom I worked were developmentally ahead of many of their typically developing peers in those areas.

9.4 SECTION C: *ALL ABOUT ME* BOOKLET TEMPLATES

Section C contains the following blank templates which can be adapted for use with different children to produce their booklet while working through Sessions 1 and 2:

- C1. Level 1 autism booklet template

- C2. Level 2 autism booklet template

- C3. Level 2 Asperger syndrome booklet template

- C4. Level 3 autism booklet template

- C5. Level 3 Asperger syndrome booklet template.

The booklet template is the most important tool for guiding children through *All About Me*. As such, the overall success of the programme depends on the child being able to access both the template they are provided with and the booklet created from it. In their current format, the five templates supplied with this book do have limitations. They are targeted at groups of children with autism or AS who are judged to be working within the broad developmental levels outlined in the previous section. However, as noted in Chapter 7, individuals referred for this work are seldom likely to fit neatly into one of these groups. Children with autism have uneven learning profiles (Boucher 2009), while their learning preferences and needs also tend to differ broadly from one individual to another. Moreover, the manifestation of every child's autism is unique to them (Jones 2002) and so needs to be described as such in each child's booklet.

This set of templates has been designed to help address the problems described above by making them computer-based and therefore fairly easy to reformat for use with very different children without the inconvenience of having to rewrite an entire document. Chapter 7 provides guidance on how to select the most appropriate template for individual children. It also advises on how adults can adjust whichever template they choose, to align its content, language and visual appearance more closely with the child's personal requirements.

This folder does not contain a Level 1 template for children with AS. Again, as explained above, this is because the programme has not needed to be differentiated at this level for children with AS. If necessary, however, occurrences of the word 'autism' in the Level 1 autism template (C1) can be replaced with 'Asperger syndrome' or 'AS'.

Each template is embedded with written guidance for adults. This offers advice on things such as how to fill in the gaps in the narrative, inserting images and where page breaks should be maintained to ensure that each section of the booklet remains separate and self-contained. As pointed out in Chapter 1, instructions that need to be carried out before or after a session takes place are printed in red, and everything that should be completed while working with the child is in blue. All the coloured guidance notes should be deleted from the template before the child starts working with it.

A number of notable individuals who are suggested as having (or having had) autism or AS are named in the section of the narrative called 'Other people have autism (or AS)'. The sources used to verify this information are referenced in green print in the text and again in a bibliography at the end of each template. Children's booklets are for personal and private use so these references can also be deleted from the template.

Detailed practical instructions for preparing and using the templates with children are provided across Chapters 5 and 6. Although those chapters explain how to complete the Level 2 templates, it should not be too difficult to apply this guidance to working through a template for Level 1 or 3. In either case, this involves following a differentiated version of the same framework.

9.5 SECTION D: TEACHING AND LEARNING PROMPTS

Section D contains the following support tools:

- D1. Personal trait cards

- D2. Strength cards

- D3. Challenge cards

- D4. Easiness rating scale

- D5. Emotions rating scale.

These resources were created to help overcome some common barriers that could prevent some children from being able express themselves effectively and actively participate in various parts of the programme. Chapter 5 provides detailed guidance on when and how to use all these resources both before and during the programme.

9.6 SECTION E: RESOURCES FOR FOLLOW-UP INITIATIVES

Section E contains some resources that can be used to support two of the follow-up initiatives for the child and their peers that are suggested in Chapter 8. These are listed below:

- E1. Example *My Future* booklet (for Kim)

- E2. *My Future* booklet template

- E3. Example autism peer awareness presentation (for Kim's class)

- E4. Example AS peer awareness presentation (for Max's class)

- E5. Autism peer awareness presentation template

- E6. Asperger syndrome peer awareness presentation template

- E7. Peer awareness lesson feedback form.

As explained in Chapter 8, *My Future* is a short programme to help able children, who know about their autism, to engage more actively with their school work, become more accepting of their support and participate in making decisions that will affect their future lives. This involves producing another booklet with the child. A fictional copy of a *My Future* booklet about Kim (E1) has been included in this folder to provide a model for others to work from. This booklet is also accompanied by a blank template (E2) which can be used for making similar booklets with children.

All About Me for Peers is an initiative for sharing a child's diagnosis with their classmates. This work involves delivering a presentation about autism to the child's class which is similar to that described in 8.6.5. While the two sample presentations in this folder describe fictional children with autism (E3) and AS (E4), they follow a tried and tested framework that has been used successfully with more than 50 mainstream children's classes. They are meant to provide generalized examples of what this work entails and how it should be undertaken. The accompanying templates (E5 and E6) can be used by suitably qualified professionals to create and deliver similar presentations about children they are working with, after having carefully considered the issues raised in Chapter 8 and gained consent from their parents.

The final resource in this folder is the written feedback form (E7) which the typical children in a child's class can be asked to complete at the end of a peer group presentation. As explained in Chapter 8, this pro forma can be used for assessing children's understanding of what they are taught about their classmate's autism and for them to contribute their own ideas on how the class can become more actively involved in supporting the individual concerned.

All the templates in Section E will need to be adjusted and altered according to the ages and developmental levels of the children and groups that they are intended for. Adult guidance for preparing and completing the templates for the *My Future* booklets and the peer work presentations has been embedded similarly to that in the *All About Me* booklet templates. The same colour coding is used – red for things that need to be done before or after working with the children and blue where there is anything that needs to be done while they are present.

References

American Psychiatric Association (2013) *Diagnostic and Statistical Manual of Mental Disorders, 5th Edition*. Washington, DC: American Psychiatric Association.

Asperger, H. (1991) 'Autistic Psychopathy in Childhood.' First published 1944. Translated in U. Frith (ed.) *Autism and Asperger Syndrome*. Cambridge: Cambridge University Press.

Aston, G. (2000) 'Through the eyes of autism.' *Good Autism Practice 1*, 2, 57–61.

Attwood, T. (2006) 'Diagnosis in Adults.' In D. Murray (ed.) *Coming Out Asperger: Diagnosis, Disclosure and Self-Confidence*. London: Jessica Kingsley Publishers.

Attwood, T. (2008) *The Complete Guide to Asperger Syndrome*. London: Jessica Kingsley Publishers.

Attwood, T., Evans, C. and Lesko, A. (eds) (2014) *Been There. Done That. Try This! An Aspie's Guide to Life on Earth*. London: Jessica Kingsley Publishers.

Autism Education Trust (2011) *Autism: Receiving and Understanding a Diagnosis* (DVD). London: Autism Education Trust.

Autism Education Trust (2012) *Autism Education Trust National Autism Standards for Schools and Educational Settings*. London: Autism Education Trust.

Barnes, E. and McCabe, H. (2012) 'Should we welcome a cure for autism? A survey of the arguments.' *Medicine, Health Care and Philosophy 15*, 3, 255–269.

Baron-Cohen, S., Leslie, A. and Frith, U. (1985) 'Does the autistic child have theory of mind?' *Cognition 21*, 1, 37–47.

Beadle, D. (2011) In Autism Education Trust, *Autism: Receiving and Understanding a Diagnosis* (DVD). London: Autism Education Trust.

Blackburn, R. (2013) 'Logically Illogical: Information and Insight into Autism.' Presented at the University of Birmingham, School of Education, Autism Residential Study Weekend, Birmingham, 14 September 2013.

Bogdashina, O. (2003) *Sensory Perceptual Issues in Autism and Asperger Syndrome: Different Sensory Experiences, Different Perceptual Worlds*. London: Jessica Kingsley Publishers.

Boucher, J. (2009) *The Autistic Spectrum: Characteristics, Causes and Practical Issues*. London: Sage.

Brett (2011) 'Brett's Film.' In Autism Education Trust, *Autism: Receiving and Understanding a Diagnosis* (DVD). London: Autism Education Trust.

Buron, K. and Curtis, M. (2008) *The Incredible 5-Point Scale: Assisting Students with Autistic Spectrum Disorders in Understanding Social Interactions and Controlling Their Emotional Responses*. London: National Autistic Society.

Cassidy, S. (2015) 'Suicidality in Autism: Risk and Prevention.' Presented at the National Autistic Society Mental Health Conference, London, May 2015.

Clements, J. (2005) *People with Autism Behaving Badly: Helping People with ASD Move on from Behavioural and Emotional Challenges*. London: Jessica Kingsley Publishers.

Dale, E., Jahoda, A. and Knott, F. (2006) 'Mothers' attributions following their child's diagnosis of autistic spectrum disorder: Exploring links with maternal levels of stress, depression and expectations about their child's future.' *Autism 10*, 5, 463–479.

Department for Children, Schools and Families (2009) *Inclusion Development Programme: Supporting Pupils on the Autism Spectrum*. London: DCSF.

Department for Education (2014) *Statistical First Release: Special Educational Needs in England: January 2014*. London: DfE.

Department for Education and Department of Health (2014) *Special Educational Needs and Disability Code of Practice: 0–25 Years, Statutory Guidance for Organizations Which Work with and Support Children and Young People with Special Educational Needs or Disabilities*. London: DfE and DoH.

Doherty, K., McNally, P. and Sherrard, E. (2011) *I Have Autism… What's That?* Belfast: South Eastern Health and Social Skills Trust.

Duprey, J. (2011) 'Exploration of the Process Parents Go through in Deciding to Disclose Their Child's Diagnosis of an Autism Spectrum Condition to Their Child.' Unpublished doctoral thesis, University of Essex.

Dura-Vila, G. and Levi, T. (2014) *My Autism Book: A Child's Guide to Their Autism Diagnosis*. London: Jessica Kingsley Publishers.

Elder, J. (2006) *Different Like Me: My Book of Autism Heroes*. London: Jessica Kingsley Publishers.

Faherty, C. (2006) *Asperger's… What Does It Mean to Me? A Workbook Explaining Self-Awareness and Life Lessons to the Child or Youth with High Functioning Autism or Asperger's*. Arlington, TX: Future Horizons.

Fidler, R. (2004) 'Talking to Children and Young People about Their Autism.' Presented at the Nottingham Regional Society for Children and Adults with Autism Conference, Nottingham, March 2004.

Fletcher, I. (2013) 'Exploring the diagnosis of Asperger syndrome with a primary-aged pupil: Resources, issues and strategies.' *Good Autism Practice 14*, 2, 8–15.

Frith, U. (2003) *Autism: Explaining the Enigma, 2nd Edition*. Oxford: Blackwell.

Gallo, A., Angst, D., Knafl, K., Hadley, E. and Smith, C. (2005) 'Parents sharing information with their children about genetic conditions.' *Journal of Pediatric Health Care 19*, 5, 267–275.

Gerland, G. (1997) *A Real Person: Life on the Outside*. London: Souvenir Press.

Gerland, G. (2000) *Finding out about Asperger Syndrome, High-Functioning Autism and PDD*. London: Jessica Kingsley Publishers.

Grandin, T. (1997) *Thinking in Pictures and Other Reports about My Life with Autism*. New York, NY: Vintage Books.

Gray, C. (1996) 'Pictures of Me: Introducing Students with Asperger's Syndrome to Their Talents, Personality and Diagnosis.' In *The Morning News*, Fall 1996 edition. Michigan: Jenison Public Schools.

Gray, C. (2015) *The New Social Story™ Book, 15th Anniversary Edition*. Arlington, TX: Future Horizons.

Haddon, M. (2003) *The Curious Incident of the Dog in the Night-Time*. London: Vintage.

Hannah, L. (2014) *Helping Young People with Autism to Learn: A Practical Guide for Parents and Staff in Mainstream Schools and Nurseries*. London: National Autistic Society.

Heeren, G. (2011) 'Changing methods of disclosure: Literature review of disclosure to children with terminal illnesses, including HIV.' *Innovation – the European Journal of Social Science Research 24*, 1–2, 199–208.

Helen (2011) 'Helen's Film.' In Autism Education Trust, *Autism: Receiving and Understanding a Diagnosis* (DVD). London: Autism Education Trust.

Hood, S. (2012) 'The Ugly Duckling.' In J. Santomauro (ed.) *Autism All-Stars: How We Use Our Autism and Asperger Traits to Shine in Life*. London: Jessica Kingsley Publishers.

Hoopmann, K. (2000) *Blue Bottle Mystery: An Asperger Adventure*. London: Jessica Kingsley Publishers.

Hoopmann, K. (2001) *Of Mice and Aliens: An Asperger Adventure*. London: Jessica Kingsley Publishers.

Hoopmann, K. (2002) *Lisa and the Lace Maker: An Asperger Adventure*. London: Jessica Kingsley Publishers.

Hoopmann, K. (2016) *Blue Bottle Mystery: An Asperger Adventure* (Graphic Novel). London: Jessica Kingsley Publishers.

Hoy, R. (2007) *Autism and Me* (DVD). London: Jessica Kingsley Publishers.

Huws, J. and Jones, R. (2008) 'Diagnosis, disclosure and having autism: An interpretative phenomenological analysis of the perceptions of young people with autism.' *Journal of Intellectual and Developmental Disability 33*, 2, 99–107.

Jackson, J. (2006) 'Disclosure: A Parent's Perspective.' In D. Murray (ed.) *Coming Out Asperger: Diagnosis, Disclosure and Self-Confidence.* London: Jessica Kingsley Publishers.

Jackson, L. (2002) *Freaks, Geeks and Asperger Syndrome: A User Guide to Adolescence.* London: Jessica Kingsley Publishers.

Jones, G. (2001) 'Giving the diagnosis to the young person with Asperger syndrome or high functioning autism: Issues and strategies.' *Good Autism Practice 2*, 2, 65–74.

Jones, G. (2002) *Educational Provision for Children with Autism and Asperger Syndrome.* Abingdon: David Fulton.

Jones, G., English, A., Guldberg, K., Jordan, R., Richardson, P. and Waltz, M. (2008) *Educational Provision for Children and Young People on the Autistic Spectrum Living in England: A Review of Current Practice Issues and Challenges.* London: Autism Education Trust.

Jordan, R. (1999) *Autistic Spectrum Disorders: An Introductory Handbook for Practitioners.* London: David Fulton Publishers.

Jordan, R. (2001) *Autism with Severe Learning Difficulties.* London: Souvenir Press.

Jordan, R. (2005) 'Autistic Spectrum Disorders.' In A. Lewis and B. Norwich (eds) *Special Teaching for Special Children? Pedagogies for Inclusion.* Maidenhead: Open University Press (Inclusive Education Series).

Kanner, L. (1973) 'Autistic Disturbances of Affective Contact.' First published 1943. Reprinted in L. Kanner (ed.) *Childhood Psychosis: Initial Studies and New Insights.* Washington, DC: V.H. Winston.

Kershaw, P. (2011) *The ASD Workbook: Understanding Your Autism Spectrum Disorder.* London: Jessica Kingsley Publishers.

Laurie, C. (2013) *Sensory Strategies: Practical Ways to Help Children and Young People with Autism Learn and Achieve.* London: National Autistic Society.

Lawrence, C. (2010) *Successful School Change and Transition for the Child with Asperger Syndrome.* London: Jessica Kingsley Publishers.

Lawson, W. (2006) 'Coming Out, Various.' In D. Murray (ed.) *Coming Out Asperger: Diagnosis, Disclosure and Self-Confidence.* London: Jessica Kingsley Publishers.

Lawson, W. (2011) *The Passionate Mind: How People with Autism Learn.* London: Jessica Kingsley Publishers.

MacLeod, A. and Johnston, P. (2007) 'Standing out and fitting in: A report on a support group for individuals with Asperger syndrome using a personal account.' *British Journal of Special Education 34*, 83–88.

Mesibov, G. and Howley, M. (2003) *Accessing the Curriculum for Pupils with Autistic Spectrum Disorders: Using the TEACCH Programme to Help Inclusion.* London: David Fulton.

Mesibov, G., Shea, V. and Schopler, E. (2004) *The TEACCH Approach to Autism Spectrum Disorders.* New York, NY: Springer.

Millar, S. (2003) *Personal Communication Passports: Guidelines for Good Practice.* Edinburgh: University of Edinburgh CALL Centre.

Miller, A. (2014) 'Finding out All About Me: Identifying Key Issues and Good Practice for Disclosing and Explaining Their Diagnosis to Children on the Autism Spectrum through a Retrospective Study of a Flexible Psycho-Education Programme.' Unpublished MEd dissertation, University of Birmingham.

Miller, A. (2015) 'The All About Me programme: A framework for sharing the autism diagnosis with children and young people.' *Good Autism Practice 16*, 1, 79–92.

Ministries of Health and Education (2008) *New Zealand Autism Spectrum Disorder Guideline.* Wellington: Ministry of Health.

Moyes, R. (2003) 'Settling into the Diagnosis.' In L. Willey (ed.) *Asperger Syndrome in Adolescence: Living with the Ups, the Downs and Things in Between.* London: Jessica Kingsley Publishers.

Murray, D. (2006) 'Introduction.' In D. Murray (ed.) *Coming Out Asperger: Diagnosis, Disclosure and Self-Confidence*. London: Jessica Kingsley Publishers.

National Initiative for Autism: Screening and Assessment (2003) *The National Autism Plan for Children (NAPC): Plan for the Identification, Assessment, Diagnosis and Access to Early Interventions for Pre-School and Primary School Aged Children with Autism Spectrum Disorders (ASD)*. London: National Autistic Society.

Oliver, M. (1990) *The Politics of Disablement*. Basingstoke: Macmillan.

Paul (2011) 'Paul's Film.' In Autism Education Trust, *Autism: Receiving and Understanding a Diagnosis* (DVD). London: Autism Education Trust.

Payne, I. (2012) 'Studying through Diagnosis.' In J. Santomauro (ed.) *Autism All-Stars: How We Use Our Autism and Asperger Traits to Shine in Life*. London: Jessica Kingsley Publishers.

Peters, C. (2011) 'What are the criteria for success in a support group for parents of children on the autism spectrum?' *Good Autism Practice 12*, 2, 19–24.

Pike, R. (2008) *Talking Together about an Autism Diagnosis: A Guide for Parents and Carers of Children with an Autism Spectrum Disorder*. London: National Autistic Society.

Punshon, C., Skirrow, P. and Murphy, G. (2009) 'The "not guilty verdict": Psychological reactions to a diagnosis of Asperger syndrome in adulthood.' *Autism 13*, 3, 265–283.

Sainsbury, C. (2000) *Martian in the Playground: Understanding the Schoolchild with Asperger's Syndrome*. Bristol: Lucky Duck.

Schocker, L. (2013) 'These 8 inspiring people will change the way you think about autism and Asperger's.' *The Huffington Post*, US edition, 12 December. Accessed on 08.08.17 at www.huffingtonpost.com/2013/12/12/autism-celebrities-aspergers_n_4427196.html

Scott, I. (2009) 'Designing learning spaces for children on the autism spectrum.' *Good Autism Practice 10*, 1, 36–51.

Shore, S. (2003) *Beyond the Wall: Personal Experiences with Autism and Asperger Syndrome, 2nd Edition*. Shawnee Mission, KS: Autism Asperger Publishing Company.

Simpson, J. (2007) 'Teachers TV: Secondary SEN – Understanding Autism' (podcast), Birmingham: Television Junction. Accessed on 08.08.17 at www.tes.co.uk/teaching-resource/Teachers-TV-Secondary-SEN-Understanding-Autism-6049006

Sinclair, J (1999) 'Why I dislike "person first" language.' Accessed on 08.08.17 at http://autismmythbusters.com/general-public/autistic-vs-people-with-autism/jim-sinclair-why-i-dislike-person-first-language

Tammet, D. (2007) *Born on a Blue Day*. London: Hodder and Stoughton.

United Nations (1989) *The Convention of the Rights of the Child*. Brussels: United Nations General Assembly.

Vermeulen, P. (2000) *I Am Special: Introducing Children and Young People to Their Autistic Disorder*. London: Jessica Kingsley Publishers.

Vermeulen, P. (2013) *I Am Special, 2nd Edition: A Workbook to Help Children, Teens and Adults with Autism Spectrum Disorders to Understand Their Diagnosis, Gain Confidence and Thrive*. London: Jessica Kingsley Publishers.

Walsh, N. and Hurley, E. (2013) *The Good and Bad Science of Autism*. Birmingham: Autism West Midlands.

Welton, J. (2004a) 'Sharing the diagnosis of Asperger syndrome with our son and his peers.' Unpublished presentation at the Nottingham Regional Society for Children and Adults with Autism Conference, Nottingham, March 2004.

Welton, J. (2004b) *Can I Tell You about Asperger Syndrome? A Guide for Friends and Family*. London: Jessica Kingsley Publishers.

Welton, J. (2014) *Can I Tell You about Autism? A Guide for Friends, Family and Professionals*. London: Jessica Kingsley Publishers.

Whitaker, P. (2001) *Challenging Behaviour and Autism: Making Sense –Making Progress: A Guide to Preventing and Managing Challenging Behaviour for Parents and Children*. London: National Autistic Society.

Whitaker, P. (2006) '"Why's It All So Difficult?" Sharing the Diagnosis with the Young Person.' In D. Murray (ed.) *Coming Out Asperger: Diagnosis, Disclosure and Self-Confidence*. London: Jessica Kingsley Publishers.

Widgit (2016) InPrint 3 (computer program). Leamington Spa: Widgit.

Wing, L. (2002) *The Autistic Spectrum,* new updated edition. London: Constable and Robinson.

Woodgate, L., Ateah, C. and Secco, L. (2008) 'Living in a world of our own: The experience of parents who have a child with autism.' *Qualitative Health Research 18*, 8, 1075–1083.

World Health Organization (1992) *The ICD-10 Classification of Mental and Behavioural Disorders: Clinical Descriptions and Diagnostic Guidelines*. Geneva: WHO.

Yoshida, Y. (2007) *How to Be Yourself in a World That's Different: An Asperger Syndrome Study Guide for Adolescents*. London: Jessica Kingsley Publishers.

Yoshida, Y. (2012) *Raising Children with Asperger's Syndrome and High-Functioning Autism: Championing the Individual*. London: Jessica Kingsley Publishers.

Bibliography for the electronic resources

A. Earlier accounts of how to tell children about their autism diagnosis

Gray, C. (1996) 'Pictures of Me: Introducing Students with Asperger's Syndrome to Their Talents, Personality and Diagnosis.' In *The Morning News*, Fall 1996 edition. Michigan: Jenison Public Schools.

Vermeulen, P. (2000) *I Am Special: Introducing Children and Young People to Their Autistic Disorder*. London: Jessica Kingsley Publishers.

Welton, J. (2004a) 'Sharing the diagnosis of Asperger syndrome with our son and his peers.' Unpublished presentation at the Nottingham Regional Society for Children and Adults with Autism Conference, Nottingham, March 2004.

Welton, J. (2004b) *Can I Tell You about Asperger Syndrome? A Guide for Friends and Family*. London: Jessica Kingsley Publishers.

B. Sources of information related to people who may have been on the autism spectrum

Elder, J. (2006) *Different Like Me: My Book of Autism Heroes*. London: Jessica Kingsley Publishers.

Grandin, T. (1997) *Thinking in Pictures and Other Reports about My Life with Autism*. New York, NY: Vintage Books.

Hoy, R. (2007) *Autism and Me* (DVD). London: Jessica Kingsley Publishers.

Sachs, O. (1995) *An Anthropologist on Mars: Seven Paradoxical Tales*. London: Picador.

Schocker, L. (2013) 'These 8 inspiring people will change the way you think about autism and Asperger's.' *The Huffington Post*, US edition, 12 December. Accessed on 08.08.17 at www.huffingtonpost.com/2013/12/12/autism-celebrities-aspergers_n_4427196.html

Tammet, D. (2007) *Born on a Blue Day*. London: Hodder and Stoughton.

FEB 1 8